The Japan of Pure Invention

The Japan of Pure Invention

Gilbert and Sullivan's
The Mikado

Josephine Lee

University of Minnesota Press
Minneapolis
London

Copyright 2010 by the Regents of the University of Minnesota

All rights reserved. No part of this publication may be reproduced, stored in a retrieval system, or transmitted, in any form or by any means, electronic, mechanical, photocopying, recording, or otherwise, without the prior written permission of the publisher.

Published by the University of Minnesota Press
111 Third Avenue South, Suite 290
Minneapolis, MN 55401-2520
http://www.upress.umn.edu

Library of Congress Cataloging-in-Publication Data

Lee, Josephine D.
    The Japan of pure invention : Gilbert and Sullivan's *The Mikado* / Josephine Lee.
        p.   cm.
    Includes bibliographical references and index.
    ISBN 978-0-8166-6579-2 (hc : alk. paper) — ISBN 978-0-8166-6580-8 (pb : alk. paper)
    1. Sullivan, Arthur, Sir, 1842–1900. Mikado. 2. Japan in opera.
    3. Orientalism.   I. Title.
    ML410.S95L44 2010
    782.1—dc22
2010002945

Printed in the United States of America on acid-free paper

The University of Minnesota is an equal-opportunity educator and employer.

18 17 16 15 14 13 12 11 10   10 9 8 7 6 5 4 3 2 1

Contents

Introduction: Meditations on *The Mikado* ... vii

Part I. 1885

1. My Objects All Sublime:
   Racial Performance and Commodity Culture ... 3
2. "My Artless Japanese Way":
   Japanese Villages and Absent Coolies ... 39
3. Magical Objects and Therapeutic Yellowface ... 65

Part II. 1938–39

4. "And Others of His Race": Blackface and Yellowface ... 83
5. Titipu Comes to America: Hot and Cool *Mikado*s ... 121

Part III. Contemporary *Mikado*s

6. "The Threatened Cloud": Production and Protest ... 141
7. Asian American *Mikado*s ... 169
8. *The Mikado* in Japan ... 187

Acknowledgments ... 219
Notes ... 221
Index ... 247

Figure 1. Caricature of W. S. Gilbert and Arthur Sullivan by E. J. Wheeler in Punch, March 28, 1885.

· Introduction ·

Meditations on *The Mikado*

> *By their strange arts and devices and manner of life, these chosen representatives of a remote race soon attracted all London. Society hastened to be Japanned, just as a few years ago Society had been aestheticised. The Lily, after a brief reign, had been deposed; it was now the turn of the Chrysanthemum to usurp the rightful throne of the English Rose.*
>
> François Cellier and Cunningham Bridgeman,
> *Gilbert and Sullivan and Their Operas*

FRANÇOIS CELLIER, resident conductor of the Gilbert and Sullivan operas at the Opera Comique and then at the Savoy Theatre, gives a triumphant account of how William Schwenck Gilbert and Arthur Seymour Sullivan's *The Mikado, or The Town of Titipu* conquered late Victorian British society. His account of both the opera's origins and his celebration of its success point us toward the peculiar racial history of this opera, a history that is sometimes obscured by its humor. In the second act of the opera, the Mikado declares his intention to find suitably humiliating punishments for social offenders.

> And make each prisoner pent
> Unwillingly represent
> A source of innocent merriment!

His song transforms different wrongdoers, such as "prosy dull society sinners, / Who chatter and bleat and bore," the "amateur tenor, whose vocal villainies / All desire to shirk," "the advertising quack," or "the billiard sharp," into objects of fun and derision.[1] Productions of Gilbert and Sullivan's famous opera, so pleasing to the eye and ear, likewise hide a more serious side.

There have been other scholarly studies of *The Mikado*, many of them devoted to placing the opera within the context of Gilbert and Sullivan's collaboration. My book departs from this critical work in significant ways. My primary interest is in how the long history of *The Mikado* says something about racial perception: how it creates particular fantasies, draws audience members into them, makes them a part of our everyday lives, and weaves them into our unconscious and conscious memories. For countless people who had never been to Japan, never met anyone of Japanese descent, or never seen or heard anything of Japanese culture (as well as for many who had done all of those things), *The Mikado* served as the basis of knowledge of what "Japanese" meant.

In this, *The Mikado* is no different from a host of other operas, plays, or stories that bring to life a vision of the Orient. But it is the manner in which the "oriental" is imagined and performed that seems to distinguish *The Mikado*. The opera brings into being a fantasy of Japan that easily outperforms the real country, linking a fantastical Titipu with Japan as imagined nearly a century later by Roland Barthes in his *Empire of Signs*. Barthes describes Japan as a "fictive nation," the contact with which produces a crisis of meaning that moves him away from any attempts to represent Japan or its people.

> I am not lovingly gazing toward an Oriental essence—to me the Orient is a matter of indifference, merely providing a reserve of features whose manipulation—whose invented interplay—allows me to "entertain" the idea of an unheard-of symbolic system, one altogether detached from our own.[2]

What is striking about Barthes's statement is not only his suppression of any "Oriental essence" in favor of a fiction of Japan, but his stated "indifference," a casting-off of any responsibility in order to encourage a sense of play without anxiety, compunction, or guilt.

Figure 2 captures how both the fantasy and the indifference have become common practice, as has *The Mikado*'s practice of yellowface: the playing of Asian characters by white performers. Two children stand gravely, one wearing a robe vaguely reminiscent of a kimono and carrying a fan, the other with a parasol in a mandarin-collared shirt and coolie hat. Their images, so grave and yet so playful, seem to exemplify how the practices of racial disguise initiated by this opera might seem absolutely innocent. *The Mikado*'s racial mimicry is seemingly without the malice or virulence that so often accompanies other fantasies of the Orient. Clearly the

Figure 2. Middletown, New York, Arthur Fanshon and Edward Phillips Nickinson in a production of The Mikado, *circa 1896. Photograph courtesy of Mary Glen Chitty.*

characterizations of *The Mikado*, at least at first glance, occupy a different place from other instances of racial typecasting: the debased coolie, the threatening gook, the tragic butterfly, or the frightening Fu Manchu.³ The Japan of *The Mikado* seems charmingly exotic, and its inhabitants—Yum-Yum, Nanki-Poo, Pooh-Bah, Ko-Ko, and their compatriots—picturesquely appealing. Even the familiar figure of the despotic Emperor, as channeled through the Mikado, seems whimsically ridiculous rather than evil.

The longstanding popularity of *The Mikado* reflects the endurance of this brand of yellowface performance. Counting the 1871 extravaganza *Thespis*, *The Mikado* was Gilbert and Sullivan's ninth collaboration, the seventh of their collaborations to be produced by Richard D'Oyly Carte at his Savoy Theater. Since initial production of *The Mikado* in London on March 14, 1885, its popularity in Great Britain, the United States, and other countries has been unprecedented. It is still a staple of amateur performances as well as regularly revived on the main stages of professional opera companies. It is performed by children, by high school and college students, by puppets, and in the military.⁴ It merited the first electric recording of a Gilbert and Sullivan opera in 1926, as well as the first LP recording in 1949. Its 1939 film version, directed by Victor Schertzinger, made it the first complete Gilbert and Sullivan opera filmed for the screen. Film and television celebrities have graced its performances; Groucho Marx starred as Ko-Ko in an hour-long version broadcast on the *Bell Telephone Hour* in 1960, and Kukla, Fran, and Ollie sang a discordant "Three Little Maids" on television in the early 1950s, setting the precedent for a myriad of references in popular culture and advertising. Given this popularity, it is perhaps not surprising that a closer examination of the opera's long history is overdue; my particular approach to telling the story of *The Mikado*, however, requires more explanation.

Why *The Mikado*?

One winter day in 2004, on an electronic discussion list for Asian American theater, I came across a brief but intriguing posting that included a link to photos from the 2004 New York Gilbert and Sullivan Players production of *The Mikado*. The photographs showed smiling women in colorful kimonos, their hair piled elaborately on their heads, and a man with a Fu Manchu mustache and impossibly long fingernails, grimacing in ways that made his exaggerated eye makeup seem even more demonic. These white performers in geisha and evil-emperor dress looked like relics from long ago, but they were obviously alive and well.

The posting asked: "is this yellowface production offensive or not? if so, any plans of attack? where are the starving asian actors instead of using yellowface?"[5] I eagerly scanned the postings on the list for some days after, hoping to hear some news of an actual protest (after all, the highly publicized protests against the casting of Jonathan Pryce as a Eurasian character in *Miss Saigon* had not happened *that* long ago).[6] But no record of any protest materialized. I was left pondering the posting's initial question as well as contemplating its consciousness-raising aims. Enticed by the questions raised by the many and various productions that stretched almost continuously from 1885 to the present, I decided that I needed to think more deeply about the complex history of this opera.

Why *The Mikado*? Like Giacomo Puccini's *Madame Butterfly*, this opera regularly graces stages throughout North America and Europe, pleasing audiences with a patently nonsensical vision of Japan. With some notable exceptions, most productions use white performers instead of "starving asian actors," yet these productions arouse little attention or concerted public criticism. What about *The Mikado* allows the opera to maintain such popularity? Is this yellowface production offensive or not? The many fans of the opera might protest that it is not offensive in the least but rather innocent merriment; they claim that the opera pokes fun at Victorian England rather than Meiji Japan or that it is a positive, even admiring, tribute to Japanese culture.

Both these claims of offensiveness and innocence are related to how *The Mikado* presents racial difference. I say "racial" rather than "national" or "ethnic" because the opera's vision of Japan has so much to say about the larger categories and social hierarchies of race, with all its attendant assumptions about biology, bodies, and nature. Productions of the opera draw on what is assumed to be the inherent nature of the Japanese—whether positive (quaint, exotic) or negative (primitive, untrustworthy) or both (undecipherable, foreign)—in images that echo broader ideas of oriental difference. Different productions often reflect the ethnic confusion that is characteristic of broader racial groupings; from the opera's inception, those familiar with Japan noticed that its depictions routinely confused Japanese with other Asian cultures. Its persistent employment of yellowface also marks its involvement with the dynamics of an impersonation that we understand as cross-racial as well as cross-ethnic or cross-cultural.

Thus productions of *The Mikado* afford us ample opportunity to study how race is imagined and performed throughout its long history. This book covers over a century of *Mikado* productions, tracing through them both the changing and often conflicting racial dynamics in England and America and the ways that racial representations persist and mutate over time. I do not pretend to provide a thorough chronological survey of *Mikado* production. In examining these aspects of *The Mikado*'s racial history, I can but touch on a few examples from the long catalogue of productions, most of them from England and the United States, with a later chapter on the opera's production in Japan. These are organized by questions that address both the opera's various depictions of what is Japanese and the nature of racial perception and performance. I hope to use the production history of the opera to describe different racial images, modes of performance, and attitudes.

These do not occur in chronological succession but rather are layered on top of one another, just as productions running concurrently can demonstrate different, even contradictory, racial attitudes. Productions that nostalgically echo the 1885 D'Oyly Carte version might be mounted in the same year as intercultural versions combining kimonos with nineteenth-century Victorian dress, and one might attend a jazzy, multicultural *Hot Mikado* in the same season. *The Mikado* demonstrates a long history of *racial sedimentation*. As Thomas Holt suggests, old and new performances of race do not effectively replace one another, but over time are fused onto one another:

> A new historical construct is never entirely new and the old is never entirely supplanted by the new. Rather the new is grafted onto the old. Thus racism, too, is never entirely new. Shards and fragments of its past incarnations are embedded in the new. Or, if we switch metaphors to an archeological image, the new is sedimented onto the old, which occasionally seeps or bursts through.[7]

Whether an image of a living grafted plant, a now-dead fossil, or a multi-layered rock, these metaphors point to the dynamic negotiation and management of race. They are particularly useful in describing the long history of *The Mikado*, in which racial representations are revealed in a range of forms, types, and practices that arise out of a specific cultural moment but are then relentlessly reactivated in subsequent productions.

The racial meanings of the opera change not only with time but also with location. *The Mikado* was begotten in England but soon made its way to the United States where it took on its own unique life. Throughout the book, some of the most significant examples are of American productions. While *The Mikado* was certainly a sparkling success in England, arguably it became even more of a popular phenomenon in the United States. One reason is simply that there were many more productions in the United States, where companies took great advantage of Gilbert, Sullivan, and D'Oyly Carte's failed attempts to maintain copyright protections over their works. Whereas in the U.K. and many other parts of the world, D'Oyly Carte and his heirs maintained an exclusive control over the production of *The Mikado* until 1962, across the Atlantic many different versions came to life. Though the New York performances were undoubtedly much like those in London (Gilbert, Sullivan, and D'Oyly Carte all traveled to New York for the opera's 1885 premiere in order to impose their stamp on the performance), there were striking variations, some of which eventually made their way, post-1962, back to England.

Inevitably, this proliferation also suggests a sea change in how the opera stages race differently in British and American contexts. Both British and American artists and consumers, like their French counterparts a decade earlier, were captivated in the 1870s and 1880s by Japanese arts and artifacts, and *The Mikado* is formulated, as we shall see, within the context of this more widespread Japan craze. However, the opera's imagining and reimagining of Japan, particularly as suggested in later productions, clearly takes on different shapes in England and the United States. In England, the opera's production and reception were shaped both by specific cultural and political relationships with Japan and by a broader understanding of oriental races underscored by England's role as an empire with colonies in India and the Middle East. The United States, with its mid-nineteenth-century opening and mid-twentieth-century occupation of Japan, clearly imposed on versions of the opera its own understanding of what it meant to play Japanese. It staged *The Mikado* in ways that reflected its own distinctive preoccupations in terms of foreign relations, Asian immigration, and history of slavery, segregation, and racial formation.

Scholarly attention to *The Mikado* has come from multiple perspectives. *The Mikado* is often mentioned in studies of the nineteenth-century Japan craze in Europe and the United States as one of many examples of music, painting, literature, architecture, decorative arts, and design that reflected an interest in Japan. As a work that straddles the porous boundary between art and popular entertainment, *The Mikado* does not usually merit the extended analysis given to more serious influences of Japanese art and culture on the artistic development of Western artists. In discussions of music history, musical theater, and opera, of course, *The Mikado* fares better. Critical studies reflect the continued popularity of the opera. Unlike some of the orientalist musical theater it spawned, such as Reginald De Koven and Harry B. Smith's *The Begum* (1887), J. Cheever Goodwin and Woolson Morse's *Wang* (1891), or Sidney Jones's *The Geisha* (1896), *The Mikado* continues to enjoy popularity among contemporary audiences. A number of operas by Western composers and librettists were specifically set in Japan, including Camille Saint-Saens' *La Princesse Jaune* (1872), Emil Jonas's *Die Japaneserin* (1874), André Messager's *Madame Chrysanthème* (1893), and Pietro Mascagni's *Iris* (1898). These have by and large fallen into critical and artistic obscurity, while *The Mikado* and *Madame Butterfly* have thrived. Of these two, *Madame Butterfly* currently receives more main-stage productions in major opera houses; *The Mikado*, however, outstrips *Butterfly* by far in terms of amateur and semiprofessional reincarnations.

Both the tragic *Madame Butterfly* and *The Mikado* have been identified as orientalist, but these two musical versions of Japan work quite differently. *The Mikado* in particular defies charges that it is a racist work. Though its characterizations, setting, and story clearly misrepresent Japan in ways that can be seen as patronizing and insulting, at the same time it is a comic opera that disclaims the seriousness of these representations. This particular quality—and the longevity of the opera itself—gives us an excellent opportunity to examine complexity, distinctiveness, and mutability of racial construction over time and across space.

Overture

This book is organized into three basic sections. Part I, "1885," centers around the opera's debut in 1885. *The Mikado* can be seen as part of the Japan craze that took hold in Europe and the United States after the opening of Japan to foreign trade in 1853. In chapter 1, "My Objects All Sublime," I show how *The Mikado* is an example of what is often called *japonaiserie*, a term that signals, unlike the alternative term *Japonisme*, a certain irreverence, whimsy, and lack of authenticity. Both japonaiserie and its much more dignified counterpart, Japonisme, are part of the larger infusion of orientalism into Western decorative arts; for instance, chinoiserie, the popular Western taste for Chinese objects and décor, set the precedent for japonaiserie. Born in the middle of this craze, *The Mikado* both articulated and significantly refocused the rage for Japanese objets d'art, costumes, décor, and crafts, staging a world inhabited by fanciful characters whose "Japanese" nature is identified primarily in terms of familiar decorative objects such as fans, swords, vases, screens, and china. It popularized an easy way of playing Japanese, an accessible and to some extent transparent racial impersonation that relied on the display and use of objects, songs, and gestures of the opera.

These initial *Mikado* productions bring into relief the relationship between race and commodity fetishism that Anne McClintock has called "commodity racism." McClintock notes that images in advertising and other media could far surpass scientific discourse in their promotion of racial messages:

> Imperial kitsch as consumer spectacle, by contrast, could package, market and distribute evolutionary racism on a hitherto unimagined scale. No preexisting form of organized racism had ever before been able to reach so large and so differentiated a mass of the populace.[8]

The allure of the commodity racism felt in these first *Mikado*s was potent indeed. The opera is a prime example of how the understanding of racial difference can be shaped by the interaction of consumers and goods rather than by experiences of body contact. *The Mikado*'s extraordinary power to define what was Japanese harnessed the energies of the Japan craze but also changed its dynamics by placing familiar things into an engaging story filled with beautiful music. In a sense, it not only gave these objects new life but also made them sing.

Ultimately, this form of racial performance eroded the responsibility to represent Japanese people or culture in factual ways. The first *Mikado* productions simplified a complicated relationship with the real Japan, turning the Japan craze into a *Mikado* craze. Images and music from *The Mikado* became a ubiquitous part of British and American households, spreading the practice of yellowface from the stage to to the parlor. *The Mikado* popularized a mode of playing in which the pleasure of owning Japanese commodities was magnified by an active engagement in racial impersonation. Not only could one collect beautiful objects of a fantasy Japan, one could even inhabit this world, complete with a story and a musical score. Audiences could escape into an attractive vision of the Orient by viewing the opera and by performing their own versions of the opera through singing songs, taking photographs, or building Mikado rooms. In each instance, each act of racial transformation remained light rather than serious, relying on the possession and display of Japanese objects rather than on a more informed imitation. This even further eroded the sense of *The Mikado* as a mode of racial representation, abandoning any responsibility toward a real people in favor of a world of pure invention.

Yet this fantasy was not impervious. There is a characteristic tension in the history of the opera: at times *The Mikado* makes strategic use of Japanese objects; at other times it denies its own power to represent a real culture and people. Chapter 2, "'My Artless Japanese Way,'" shows how *The Mikado* might be juxtaposed with other accounts of Japan—for instance, in the Japanese Native Villages that appeared in the same year as the opera's debut—to expose inherent anxieties about commodity culture, labor, and bodies. Exhibitions of Japanese artisans at work and other reminders of laboring oriental bodies in these exhibitions made clear the fault lines within commodity racism and revealed precisely what had presumably been erased by the opera's sparkling success. Still, *The Mikado* has maintained its charms to the present day through its consistent ability to present a compelling image of Japan as a place of magical objects and pleasurable, even therapeutic, racial play. Chapter 3, "Magical Objects and Therapeutic Yellowface," examines these legacies of the 1885 *Mikado* in contemporary productions such as Mike Leigh's acclaimed 1999 film *Topsy-Turvy*.

Part II, "1938–39," gives a different perspective on racial masquerade by looking at the intertwined histories of *The Mikado,* blackface minstrelsy, and African American musical theater. Here we consider how race, following Claire Jean Kim's thought-provoking formulation, might be thought of as triangulated rather than as a binary opposition between whiteness and color. For Kim, different racial groups "become racially marginalized in comparison with one another," moreover, "they are differently racialized."[9] *The Mikado* wears this racial triangulation on its sleeve by making overt references to the history of blackface minstrelsy as well as to the practice of yellowface. Song lyrics referring to "the nigger serenader" in *The Mikado* (excised from productions after 1948) are really part of a much broader shared space of multiple racial impersonations.

The very first productions of *The Mikado* in the United States inspired a multitude of blackface minstrel parodies and adaptations. These productions complicate how we understand yellowface performance as the domain of white performers whose racial privilege *as* white was enhanced by their playing of Japanese and other oriental identities. As many *Mikado* productions by African Americans show us, yellowface was not exclusive to white performers. Chapter 4, "Titipu Comes to America," resurrects the particular history of performing Japanese by African Americans in hopes of understanding the complex layering of racial representation buried not just in *The Mikado* but in a much larger history.

Blackface minstrelsy is present even at the very beginning of encounters between modern Japan and the West. Japan's signing of the treaty by Commodore Matthew Perry was prefaced by a gathering on March 27, 1854, at which Perry and his crew entertained Japanese officials with food, drink, and a blackface minstrel show:

> After the banquet, the Japanese were entertained by an exhibition of negro minstrelsy, got up by some of the sailors, who, blacking their faces and dressing themselves in character, enacted their parts with a humor that would have gained them unbounded applause from a New York audience even at Christy's. The gravity of the saturnine Hayashi was not proof against the grotesque exhibition, and even he joined with the rest in the general hilarity provoked by the farcical antics and humorous performances of the mock negroes. It was now sunset, and the Japanese prepared to depart with quite as much wine in them as they could well bear. The jovial Matsusaki threw his arms about the Commodore's neck, crushing, in his tipsy embrace, a pair of new epaulettes, and repeating, in Japanese, with maudlin affection, these words, as interpreted into English: "Nippon and America, all the same heart." He then went toddling into his boat, supported by some of his more steady companions, and soon all the happy party had left the ships and were making rapidly for the shore.[10]

Within this initial encounter, the dynamics of blackface inform the ambiguous racial status of the Japanese. Perry's description suggests multiple interpretations of this encounter. Some assumption of diplomatic equality between the Americans and the Japanese is shared in mutual laughter at the antics of blackface ridicule. Laughing at the "farcical antics and humorous performances of the mock negroes" is a way of establishing common ground or understanding "Nippon and America, all the same heart." At the same time, the description of the drunken Matsusaki suggests another kind of racial spectacle—a Japanese one—that amuses Perry and the other Americans.

This uncertain dynamic of multiple racializations is also at play in the multiple references to blackface minstrelsy and different black productions of *The Mikado*. What happens when a third racial party becomes involved in what is often presumed to be a binary relationship, what Eric Lott has called "a profound white investment in black culture?"[11] Moreover, how is this quintessentially English work, as *The Mikado* is often deemed, connected to the "peculiarly American structure of racial feeling"[12] revealed in blackface? As we have already seen, at times the representation of Japanese echoed the images of primitive energy, sexuality, and debasement so often associated with stereotypes of blackness. Paradoxically, performances of *The Mikado*, as well as other performances of Japanese, have also been used to claim African American advancement and racial uplift. African American performers, such as the minstrel performer Thomas "Japanese Tommy" Dilward, have long used cross-racial acting to gain some measure of freedom. The limited freedoms given to African American performers, however, are closely circumscribed. This comes through in two of the best-known African American versions of the opera, the 1938–39 *Swing Mikado* of the Chicago Federal Theatre Project and its 1939 Broadway competitor the *Hot Mikado*, produced by Michael Todd. These productions were hailed as milestones in the freedom of African Americans to perform a wider range of roles in musical theater, although these productions themselves were rife with stereotypes of minstrelsy and exoticism, sustained by the negrophilia of modernist white America.

The racial history of *The Mikado* shows that we cannot view orientalism solely as an opposition between white and Asian; neither yellowface nor *The Mikado* specifically belongs to white performers. The inclusion of African American performers significantly changed the racial dynamics of the opera. The success of the swinging *Mikado*s shows the intricately linked histories of yellowface and blackface and helps to explain the popularity of a much later version of the *Hot Mikado* to contemporary audiences looking for a more multicultural take on the opera. David Bell and Rob Bowman's *Hot Mikado*, with its jazzed-up score and libretto, has had enormous popularity around the English-speaking world since its 1986 premiere at

Ford's Theatre (Washington, D.C.), with runs in London's West End and other prominent commercial theaters as well as a host of amateur venues; it currently rivals the original version in popularity. Productions of the 1986 *Hot Mikado* claim their roots in the 1939 Michael Todd version and prominently bill themselves as celebrating the triumph of African American performers, even though most of the performers remain white. In this "cool" version and others, Gilbert and Sullivan's imagined locale changes from a fantasy Japan to a multicultural America. Through this geographical and musical relocation, *Hot Mikado*'s racial politics becomes redefined around the jubilant inclusion of African Americans in the American racial landscape, which is projected onto a Japanese setting.

These new *Hot Mikado*s are not the first vision of *The Mikado*'s Titipu as a multiracial paradise nor the only versions that update the stodgy, Victorian old-world music and language for the liberated rhythms of the new world. Chapter 5, "Titipu Comes to America," takes a look not only at the newer *Hot Mikado*s but also a now-obscure 1963 film *The Cool Mikado*, which features a vision of Japan transformed by U.S. occupation and modernization. Though it is jet-age Tokyo that we see on the screen, *The Cool Mikado* still presents a fantasy of Titipu as an exotic playground in which the newly cosmopolitan and urbane protagonists, both British and American, might freely wander. This film has been deemed "dreadful," "terrible," and "bad" even by Gilbert and Sullivan fans;[13] yet though artistically embarrassing, it presents a fascinating reminder of how the opera accommodates a changing image of Japan.

Part III, "Contemporary *Mikados*," concentrates on contemporary productions of the opera, all of which confirm that in the present there are many kinds of racial imaginings. What reanimates these contemporary productions of *The Mikado* is not simply habit or nostalgia (though both undoubtedly play a role in production) but rather an ongoing fascination with staging versions of the Japanese fantasy at the heart of the opera. Some contemporary productions still echo D'Oyly Carte's Japanese style in costume, setting, gesture, and delivery, using this look to present a nostalgic vision of Victorian England. Others seem to move radically away from the traditional Savoy style, updating these queer and quaint characterizations into images and references that frame Asians as yellow peril, whether as immigrant worker or corporate threat. Both the retro and racist *Mikado*s can show us much about how new cultural productions continue to harbor old racisms. At the same time, this seemingly deathless opera has had a new life that defies the more predictable forms of racial formation. Recent productions and adaptations of the opera performed and directed by Asian American artists suggest alternative directions and new ways of thinking about an opera that continues to attract willing and eager performers. Finally, this book concludes with an examination of the opera's productions in Japan, which provides perhaps the most robust examples of its complicated racial history.

As I mentioned earlier, it would be impossible to catalog all the types of *Mikado* productions. Nor is my aim primarily to point out artistic excellence or failure. This little list includes *Mikado*s good and bad, famous and forgotten, critically acclaimed and despised, all singled out primarily as they articulate different contexts for and ways of performing race. Organizing a project of this scope is always a challenge: while it makes sense to focus on key productions that are undoubtedly characteristic of their times—1885, 1938–39, the 1980s and after—the larger racial histories behind this opera move much less linearly and much more erratically. Though the book presents a series of chronologies, its many examples belie this organization. As we shall see, surveying the history of this opera means a constant movement backward and forward in time, as well as the examination of moments in which time seems to stop completely.

A final note before proceeding. Although it tries to get at the heart of what makes *The Mikado* so popular, this book does not attempt to analyze the enthusiasm of fans for *The Mikado* and other Gilbert and Sullivan operas. The contemporary aspect of this fandom has been thoroughly documented by Ian Bradley, who writes of "that company of enthusiasts who border on the obsessive, collect G&S memorabilia, write books on the subject, know every nuance of every recording, and sit in theatres waiting for a wrong word in a patter song or a move which deviates from the D'Oyly Carte norm."[14] Although it is by now obvious that I do not write from their perspective, my scholarship is nonetheless now indebted to those fans and their obsessive habits of collecting. Much of the material for this book was available only because they so enthusiastically shared their fascinating documents, facts, and details. In gratitude, I would like to express a hope that my work, despite its rather sober approach, might in fact bridge a certain divide between the fans who continue to produce and attend *The Mikado* with unabashed enthusiasm and those who protest its production as patently racist. The latter group decries the performances of *The Mikado* for embodying the living spirit of colonialism and white privilege; the former pooh-poohs these charges of racism ("Can't they see that *The Mikado* is really about England, not Japan?"), furiously defending their enjoyment of the work against what they see as the overbearing oppression of political correctness against free artistic expression or old-fashioned fun. I have been asked many times whether my real objective is to prevent the opera from ever having another production. I would say without any false humility that I can't imagine this book to have that kind of power. Perhaps its best hope is to accompany and enliven future productions of *The Mikado* with some reminders of its thorny racial history.

Ian Bradley describes the lasting appeal of Gilbert and Sullivan for fans as not only an expression of "nostalgia and patriotism," but also, and even more significantly, because of its comfort factor:

> What I have already called its quality of "divine emollient" could from a less enthusiastic perspective be dismissed as the musical equivalent of comfort food. It is relatively undemanding and serves as an instant pick-me-up, particularly in our disordered and angst-ridden age. Its characters exist in a self-contained, make-believe world where, on the whole, order prevails and virtue is, indeed, triumphant.[15]

Comfort can be derived both from enjoying and reviling Gilbert and Sullivan's most popular work. However, working through the complexities of *The Mikado*'s racial history—digging through the multiple layers of its racial sedimentation in order to unearth something of new interest—is a reward and a triumph of a different kind. According to the Web site of Minneapolis's Gilbert and Sullivan Very Light Opera Company, in 1985 then-mayor Donald M. Fraser declared Minneapolis and the fictitious town of Titipu to be "sister cities."[16] From the sister city then, let us proceed.

Synopsis of *The Mikado*

The opera opens in the courtyard of Ko-Ko's palace in Titipu, where a chorus of Japanese nobles is "standing and sitting in attitudes suggested by native drawings" ("If You Want to Know Who We Are"). Nanki-poo enters with "a native guitar on his back and a bundle of ballads in his obi." He identifies himself through his opening song ("A Wandering

Minstrel"). He seeks his love, Yum-Yum, having heard that her guardian Ko-Ko, to whom she is betrothed, has been condemned to death for flirting. He learns from Pish-Tush, a noble lord, that Ko-Ko has escaped beheading and been made Lord High Executioner. Pish-Tush relates ("Our Great Mikado, Virtuous Man") how this was done in order to circumvent the Mikado's decree that flirting is punishable by death. Ko-Ko was next in line to be executed, but by promoting him from lowly tailor to the exalted rank of Lord High Executioner, no one else can be put to death until Ko-Ko decapitates himself. Pooh-Bah appears and introduces himself as a nobleman of great family pride who has taken on the multiple duties (and salaries) of all the officers of state who resigned when Ko-Ko was put in charge. For a bribe, he reveals to Nanki-Poo that Yum-Yum will be wed to Ko-ko that afternoon ("Young Man, Despair" and "And Have I Journeyed for a Month"). The chorus of nobles herald the appearance of Ko-Ko ("Behold the Lord High Executioner") who sings of his rise to power and promises to carry out his duties as executioner with appropriate victims ("As Someday It May Happen," popularly called the "Little List" song). He negotiates plans for his forthcoming wedding with Pooh-Bah in his various capacities.

A chorus of schoolgirls arrives ("Comes a Train of Little Ladies"), followed by Yum-Yum and her sisters Pitti-Sing and Peep-Bo ("Three Little Maids"). Yum-Yum greets Ko-Ko reluctantly but gives a warm welcome to Nanki-Poo, who confesses his love and then is taken away. Ko-Ko asks Pooh-Bah to greet the girls appropriately, but he finds this duty painful for a man of his position. The girls respond with laughter and teasing ("So Please You, Sir, We Much Regret"). All exit except for Yum-Yum. She is joined by Nanki-Poo, who tells her of his true identity: he is really the son of the Mikado. He had the misfortune to inadvertently captivate Katisha, an elderly and ugly lady of the court. He was ordered to marry Katisha or face execution for flirting and subsequently fled the court, disguised as a second trombonist. Nanki-Poo and Yum-Yum bemoan the laws against flirting and contemplate—through an enactment of kissing and embracing—what they could do romantically if it were not forbidden ("Were You Not to Ko-Ko Plighted").

Ko-Ko receives a letter from the Mikado that threatens to abolish the position of Lord High Executioner and demote the city of Titipu to the rank of a village unless someone is executed within a month. Ko-Ko, Pooh-Bah, and Pish-Tush consider who might best fit the bill ("I Am So

Proud"), and Pooh-Bah points out that Ko-Ko is already next in line. Ko-Ko tries to bemoan his predicament in a soliloquy but is interrupted by the entrance of Nanki-Poo, who is preparing to hang himself out of romantic despair. Nanki-Poo agrees to let Ko-Ko execute him in a month's time if he can marry Yum-Yum the next day. In the finale of the first act ("With Aspect Stern"), Ko-Ko introduces Nanki-Poo as his volunteer. Congratulations and songs ensue ("The Threatened Cloud Has Passed Away") until Katisha arrives on the scene ("Your Revels Cease!"). Pitti-Sing taunts her ("Away, nor Prosecute Your Quest," also known as "For He's Going to Marry Yum-Yum"). She threatens to reveal Nanki-Poo's true identity but is drowned out by the crowd, who sings "O ni! Bikkuri shakkuri to!" She leaves, vowing revenge.

Act 2 opens in Ko-Ko's garden, where Yum-Yum, her sisters, and the ladies' chorus prepare for her wedding ("Braid the Raven Hair"). She celebrates her own beauty with a solo ("The Sun, Whose Rays," popularly known as "The Moon and I"), and all seems joyous until she is reminded of Nanki-Poo's sentence of execution. Nanki-poo enters and tries to cheer everyone up ("Brightly Dawns Our Wedding Day"). Ko-Ko enters and informs them of an overlooked aspect of their plan: under the Mikado's law, when a married man is beheaded, his wife has to be buried alive. Nanki-Poo and Yum-Yum are dismayed ("Here's a How-de-do!"). Nanki-Poo declares his intent to kill himself immediately instead, and Ko-Ko is suddenly left again with the prospect of having to behead himself, even as the Mikado and his entourage are approaching the city. Even when Nanki-Poo offers himself up for immediate execution, Ko-Ko finds that he cannot carry out his official duties. He decides that perhaps he doesn't really need to kill Nanki-poo after all and that simply producing an affidavit stating that the execution has happened will do. Nanki-Poo agrees provided that he is allowed to marry Yum-Yum anyway, and Pooh-Bah is persuaded by "ready money" to act as the multiple witnesses. Nanki-Poo and Yum-Yum leave to be married immediately by Pooh-Bah the Archbishop.

The choruses enter singing ("Miya sama") and then the Mikado himself, followed by Katisha ("From Every Kind of Man"). The Mikado relates his ideas of governance, which entail finding appropriate punishments for different offenses ("A More Humane Mikado"). He is told of the execution and asks for the delightful details, which Ko-Ko, Pitti-Sing, and Pooh-Bah relate with dramatic intensity ("The Criminal Cried"). The Mikado tells them that he has come to Titipu not to affirm the execution, but in search of his son Nanki-Poo. After Katisha discovers that the executed man on the affidavit is the heir apparent, the Mikado calmly and routinely schedules the punishment ("something humorous but lingering, with either boiling oil or melted lead") of Ko-Ko, Pitti-Sing, and Pooh-Bah for after lunch. The unfortunate trio bemoan their impending doom ("See How the Fates Their Gifts Allot") and, after the Mikado and Katisha depart, frantically conclude that they must produce Nanki-Poo in order to save themselves. Nanki-Poo and Yum-Yum appear, but Nanki-Poo tells them that since he has just married Yum-Yum, he cannot reveal himself to his father for fear of risking execution for himself and live burial for Yum-Yum. He proposes that Ko-Ko persuade Katisha to marry him in order to mitigate this risk. Ko-Ko reluctantly agrees ("The Flowers that Bloom in the Spring").

The mourning Katisha sings of the loss of Nanki-Poo ("Alone, and Yet Alive!"). Ko-Ko woos her at first without avail but then captures her heart with the touching ballad of a lovelorn bird who commits suicide ("On a Tree by a River," popularly known as the "Titwillow" song). Together they celebrate the union of beauty and horror ("There Is Beauty in the Bellow of the Blast"), and when the Mikado returns from lunch, Katisha asks him for mercy for all three culprits. Nanki-Poo and Yum-Yum present themselves, and Ko-Ko explains the deception in ways that satisfy the Mikado. All join in a final song and dance ("For He's Gone and Married Yum-Yum" reprise).

1885

Chapter 1

My Objects All Sublime:
Racial Performance and Commodity Culture

Columbus discovered a new world. Mr. W. S. Gilbert has created one. He has evolved from his inner consciousness, as the German did the camel, a Japan of his own, and has placed a territorial fragment thereof upon the stage of the Savoy Theatre, labeling it The Mikado; or, the Town of Titipu.

"Our Captious Critic: Gilbert and Sullivan's New Opera,"
Illustrated Sporting and Dramatic News, March 28, 1885

Heavens! why, I know her already! Long before setting foot in Japan, I had met her, on every fan, on every teacup with her silly air, her puffy little face, her tiny eyes, mere gimlet-holes above those expanses of impossible pink and white cheeks.

Pierre Loti, *Madame Chrysanthème*

IN 1885, when *The Mikado* first appeared on the stage, it gave new life to an already existing European and American interest in things Japanese. Even during Japan's period of isolation, large quantities of Japanese ceramics were shipped to Europe during the seventeenth and eighteenth centuries and enjoyed great popularity among aristocrats.[1] But a full-fledged Japan craze, prompting a considerable market for Japanese arts and crafts such as prints, pottery, bronzes, china, fans, silks, swords, and kimonos, was set into full motion by Japan's opening to the West in 1853 and subsequent exhibitions of Japanese arts in Paris, London, and Philadelphia. By the time of *The Mikado,* this phenomenon was no longer the province of artists, connoisseurs, and wealthy patrons. *The Mikado* fueled the japonaiserie that infected both Europe and the United States.

Those involved in the first production of March 14, 1885, whether as producers or consumers, recognized and acknowledged the extent to which *The Mikado* was fixated on the spectacular display of objects. Savoy music director François Cellier commented that the inspiration for the opera did not come from direct observation of Japanese people. Cellier writes:

> It must not be supposed that Gilbert discovered the originals of any of his *dramatis personae* in the chronicles of the times of Jimmu Tenno, first Emperor of Japan, or his descendants. "Pooh Bah"—that worthy who comprehended within his own person a complete cabinet of ministers, together with other important offices—Pooh Bah, it will be remembered, traced his ancestry back to a "protoplasmal primordial atomic globule"; consequently, no Japanese gentleman of rank, however sensitive, could imagine himself or his progenitors to have been made the subject of the English author's satire. Likewise neither Koko, the Lord High Executioner, nor Nanki-Poo disguised as a second trombone, could possibly be identified with persons associated with Old Japan. Figuratively, all these notabilities may have been portrayed on lacquer-trays, screens, plates, or vases, but none of them had ever lived in the flesh before they came to life at the Savoy Theatre.[2]

The likeness of *Mikado* characters to images found on Japanese imports resonates with Gilbert's own accounts of being inspired by a Japanese sword:

> In May 1884, it became necessary to decide upon a subject for the next Savoy opera. A Japanese executioner's sword hanging on the wall of my library—the very sword carried by Mr. Grossmith [Ko-Ko] at his entrance in the first act—suggested the broad idea upon which the libretto is based. A Japanese piece would afford opportunities for picturesque scenery and costumes, and moreover, nothing of the kind had ever been attempted in England.[3]

Gilbert is inspired more generally by the opportunities for depicting a spectacular fantasy world through "picturesque scenery and costumes" but suggests a particular fixation with the sword. In another account of the genesis of the opera, it is again the sword (which he presumably hefts at the interview) that becomes the focus of his inspiration:

It is very difficult to tell how you begin. I cannot give you a good reason for our forthcoming piece being laid in Japan. It has seemed to us that to lay the scene in Japan afforded scope for picturesque treatment, scenery, and costume, and I think that the idea of a chief magistrate, who is king, judge and actual executioner in one, and yet would not hurt a worm, may perhaps please the public. This is the sword of a Japanese executioner! You will observe that it is a double-handed sword, with a grip admitting of two distinct applications of strength.[4]

Attractions to the Japanese object were amply demonstrated through the course of the first production of the opera, where swords, kimonos, parasols, the "Japanese guitar" (samisen), fans, and other props, costumes, and scenery drew much praise. Reviews of the first production noted the pleasing effect of fans in songs such as "Three Little Maids":

> The girls came on with short, shuffling steps and fluttered their fans with a precision that would have delighted a regimental sergeant-major. The magazine *Moonshine* commented in its review of the first night: "Society will discover a new source of entertainment after witnessing the fan operations. There will be 'fan drill' at boarding schools. Present fans! unfurl fans! flutter fans! recover fans!"[5]

The weight of objects in the first production draws our attention to a certain consistent attraction of *The Mikado*: how playing Japanese is performed through the display and use of iconic Japanese imports. *Mikado* characters do not only inhabit a world filled with these imported goods: their very being is understood as inseparable from these objects, as indicated in the opening lyrics for the men's chorus of "Japanese nobles discovered standing and sitting in attitudes suggested by native drawings":

> If you want to know who we are,
>   We are gentlemen of Japan;
> On many a vase and jar—
>   On many a screen and fan,
>   We figure in lively paint:
>   Our attitude's queer and quaint—
>   You're wrong if you think it ain't, oh!

This connection of playing Japanese to consumption of Japanese crafts allowed for the immediate recognition of these characters by already seasoned consumers of fans, lacquerware, porcelain, and screens. Characters in *The Mikado* were described in the same terms; as Anna Jackson has outlined, adjectives such as "quaint" and "curious" informed many critical assessments of Japanese arts and crafts.[6] Yum-Yum's descriptions of herself as a "child of Nature" echoes the assumptions of art critics that Japanese artisans had an innate feeling for nature.[7]

The connection between characters in *The Mikado* and Japanese imports also makes a deeper statement about what it means to play Japanese. These performers in yellowface did not simply act as referents for an imagined Japan; they demonstrated their own intimate relationship with very tangible commodities. For instance, Ko-Ko's successful pretense of love to Katisha is made through his "Titwillow" song ("On a Tree by a River"), the music and refrain of which, as multiple scholars note, may well have been influenced by the verses of Nicholas Rowe, the "Willow" song of Shakespeare's *Othello*, and other literary sources.[8] However, one of Gilbert's inspirations was more domestic than literary, for the song's elements—a bird, a river, thwarted love, suicide—also echo a story first circulated in the Victorian magazine the *Family Friend* in 1849. This story was used to sell the popular Willow pattern china, first developed by Josiah Spode in 1795 and manufactured in Staffordshire, England, but associated with both China and Japan.[9] This romantic legend connected the china's blue-and-white figures with a story of forbidden love (a wealthy merchant's daughter who elopes with her father's clerk), death (the father's pursuit), and birds (the sympathetic gods transform the lovers into a pair of turtledoves). In *The Mikado*, Ko-Ko makes his pretense of love for Katisha more convincing by adopting a similarly sentimental romance ("It's an affecting tale, and quite true. I knew the bird intimately"), and the love-starved Katisha consumes his story wholeheartedly.

Other characters have similar connections to commodities. The romantic figure of Nanki-poo as the wandering minstrel evokes not only the romantic troubadour but also T. J. Jackson Lears's description of the "mythic peddler" in antebellum America. For Lears, the peddler "brought spectacles of Oriental splendor to provincial audiences," becoming "an emissary of the marvelous, promising his audience magical transformations not through religious conversion, but through the purchase of a bit of silk, a pair of earrings, or a mysterious elixir."[10] Nanki-Poo's playing

Japanese equates his musical repertoire and other romantic appeals with a certain adaptability to the many needs of the consumer. His opening song, "A Wandering Minstrel," emphasizes his desire to please, as he is able to suit all moods with musical selections from sentimental songs, patriotic ballads, and sea shanties.

> My catalogue is long,
>   Through every passion ranging,
>   And to your humours changing
>   I tune my supple song!

Robert Lee begins his illuminating study of oriental stereotypes by quoting a student who makes the memorable distinction that "Orientals are rugs, not people."[11] Yet in *The Mikado* Japanese things and people have become inextricable from one another. As one reviewer of the first production remarked:

> From the moment the curtain goes up upon the glittering spectacle of *The Mikado* until it finally drops, the whole scene is drolly familiar.
>   It is the very world of the "willow pattern" china, and these are our old friends of the dinner service, the tureens and dishes and plates and vases, who are forever crossing impossible bridges, and sitting under ridiculous trees, and standing in unprecedented postures, and looking with queer slits for eyes set in chubby pink knobs for faces.[12]

The Mikado not only enters into a familiar world of Japanese things, but makes this intimate relation between character and object an indispensable aspect of its yellowface. Not only does the opera stage desire for popular items of japonaiserie—vases, screens, fans, swords, china, kimonos, and parasols—it also stages the inseparability of Japanese characterization from these imports.

Thus one important aspect of *The Mikado*'s appeal is how it sets forth a tantalizing vision of a wholly spectacular Japan that has no obligation to represent Japan except through its playful display of objects. The opera effectively channels the desire for things into a distinctive form of performance in which white actors *become* Japanese not only through convincing costume and makeup, but perhaps even more strikingly through their intimacy with and inhabitation of objects. We can see this at play in the cover art of the proliferation of sheet music published in the United States at the time of *The Mikado* premiere. Particular covers place characters from the opera in relation to objects that visually command equal authority with human figures: a fan, a plate, a vase. Published by I. L. A. Brodersen, L. von der Mehden's arrangement of "The Mikado Lancers" depicts Louise Paullin as Yum-Yum playing a stringed instrument; her image is superimposed on a decorated plate and captioned "Designed by the Artist of Ichiban." The cover of W. F. Shaw's arrangement of "As Some Day It May Happen" features the image of the Three Little Maids positioned on a fan. In making this link between *The Mikado* and the Japanese exports these covers are appreciably different from most other sheet music covers of Gilbert and Sullivan arrangements; few images accompany any of Sullivan's music. These oversized objects on the covers of musical arrangements from the opera also seem quite different from earlier instances of "oriental" sheet music that features Japanese or Chinese figures or scenes where landscapes and objects are generally in proportion to human figures.[13]

These moments in *The Mikado*—where Japanese characterization is determined by established relationships to domestic commodities—marks two concurrent shifts. First, the fascination with understanding Japanese culture becomes replaced by a need to see more typecast, familiar representations of an exotic Japan. As Toshio Yokoyama suggests, the 1880s marks a shift in attitudes toward Japan whereby "from about 1880, the image of an unreal Japan became firmly established in Britain and began to exert a broader influence."[14] Second, the late nineteenth-century shift into mass consumer culture increasingly makes commodity fetishism a part of everyday life. *The Mikado* exists where fantasies of race and commodities meet. The conditions by which Japan was rendered as an "elf-land"[15] were the same by which the specific institutions and mechanisms of Victorian commodity fetishism took on their specific form. Bill Brown describes the developing institution of the late nineteenth-century department store as the inculcation of a particular mode of desire for objects. In this "newly theatricalized world of goods," both the relationship between maker and object and the connection between seller and potential buyer are erased: "By establishing fixed prices, the department store eliminated the human interaction of bargaining, and restricted the act of consumption to a

Figure 3. Sheet music cover, "The Lancers," from The Mikado, *I. L. A. Brodersen and Company, 1885. Library of Congress, Music Division.*

Figure 4. Sheet music cover, "I've Got Him on the List," from The Mikado, W. F. Shaw, *1885. Library of Congress, Music Division.*

relation between the consumer and the merchandise." Furthermore, as Brown describes, such settings made the goods themselves seem like living things: "In such theaters, objects assumed lives of their own, magically made animate not because of their status as autonomous and abstract values, but because of their sensuous appeal."[16]

Domestic Deviance and the Japanese Object

The "senuous appeal" of Japanese imports reflected contradictions in the ways that the Japanese were considered a race. As Rotem Kowner describes, the racial identification of Japanese people by Europeans and Americans varied greatly over the period from the 1860s until the Second World War. Different visitors to Japan, including "specialists" (ethnographers, physicians, and archaeologists, who came to Japan mainly for research and provided most of the primary data on its people), "impressionists" (short-term visitors, non-"specialist" residents, as well as popular and travel writers) and "raciologists" (prominent scholars of race and anthropology, who has no close contact with Japan) gave differing, even contradictory accounts of how the Japanese might be categorized, often making such claims based on perceptions of Japan's relationship to modernization and its power on the world stage.[17] Most influential to Gilbert's libretto and the first productions of *The Mikado* were those accounts that defined Japan's contributions to art. These accounts defined a contradiction between the evident refinement of certain Japanese crafts and the perceived barbarity of the Japanese culture and people.

Anna Jackson notes that while Japanese art received high praise from Western critics for its beauty, it was also seen as "decorative" rather than "high art," appealing to the senses rather than the intellect.[18] The Japanese were seen as being in only the "first stage of progress"[19] in the arts that would define their civilization. As testimony, critics pointed to their "seeming disregard for the human form" that "most seriously damned them as artistic barbarians."[20] Rutherford Alcock's influential *Art and Art Industries of Japan* reminds readers of "the influence which Art and Art culture have exercised in developing national character and civilization in all ages of the world." The Japanese, however, are "dead to any sense of beauty in the human figure," and this "one fact seems to have determined the direction of their Art culture, and its degeneration into grotesque conceptions of humanity."[21]

Not only was Japanese art considered to be devoid of appreciation for the human form; the Japanese people themselves were, in accounts such as Sir Rutherford Alcock's *Capital of the Tycoon*, depicted as practicing bodily arts that rendered their own figures grotesque. Alcock comments on skin disease among working-class men, perhaps due to a perceived lack of hygiene in laundry and public baths: "The truth is, they wash their bodies often enough, but much less frequently their clothes, and there is a vast deal too much of promiscuous herding and slopping together at the baths of all the lower orders for much purity to come out of them, moral or physical."[22] Describing the penchant for tattooing among Japanese men, Alcock marvels,

> to see them in their habitual costume (*videlicit*, a girdle of the narrowest possible kind), the greater part of the body and limbs scrolled over with bright blue dragons, and lions, and tigers, and figures of men and women, tattooed into their skins with the most artistic and elaborate ornamentation—"scantily dressed but decently painted," as has been said of our own ancestors when Julius Caesar first discovered them—it is impossible to deny that they look remarkably like a race of savages, if not savages, in their war paint.[23]

Of Japanese women, Alcock remarks that many of them "might make some considerable pretensions to beauty" ("I have seen many as fair as my own countrywomen, and with healthy blood mantling in their cheeks") and their elaborate hair "displays a marvelous amount of feminine ingenuity."[24] However, their practice of whitening their faces, blackening their teeth, and plucking their eyebrows renders them hideous:

> When they have renewed the black varnish to the teeth, plucked out the last hair from their eyebrows, the Japanese matrons may certainly claim unrivaled pre-eminence in artificial ugliness over all their sex. Their mouths thus disfigured are like open sepulchers, and whether given to "flatter with their tongues" I can not undertake in this my novitiate to say, but they must have sirens' tongues or a fifty-horse power of flattery to make those red-varnished lips utter any thing which could compensate man or child for so much artificial ugliness![25]

The Mikado seems to present a much more palatable vision of Japanese people, even while referencing such details of bodily hygiene and adornment in descriptions of Nanki-Poo as "a thing of shreds and patches" and a "very imperfect ablutioner," or in the adornment of Yum-Yum ("Braid the raven hair" and "dye the coral lip") for her wedding. Katisha's appalling appearance is much more evocative of such descriptions, combining the "artificial ugliness" of the hideously made-up Japanese woman with the grande dame of English pantomime. Yet *The Mikado* does highlight a deeper fascination with the perceived barbarity of the Japanese, a difference that attracts as well as repels.

In his account of the opera's genesis, Gilbert comments that "our scenery is quite Japanese, and our costumes have been imported.... I am anxious about the clothes being properly worn ... and have my doubts about the flat black hair."[26] Cellier is more direct in his statements that impersonating the Japanese would have been perceived as ugly rather than admirable:

> To begin with, one of the most essential qualifications of Savoy actors and actresses was that of physical grace; the poise of each limb, the elegant sway and easy motion of the figure, the noble dignity of action which distinguishes the English stage. All this had to be undone again, only more so than had been necessary in the case of Bunthorne, Grosvenor, and their followers in the play of "Patience." Every proud, upright, and lithesome Savoyard would have to be transformed into the semblance of a Jap who, to our Western eyes, was not the ideal of perfect grace and loveliness.
>
> But Gilbert soon found a way out of that difficulty. Here were living models, real Japanese ready to hand. They should teach the ladies and gentlemen of the Savoy how to walk and dance, how to sit down, and how to express their every emotion by the evolutions of the fan. Confident, then in his ability to overcome all obstacles, our author applied his mind to the subject of Japan, read up the ancient history of the nation and, finding therein much from which to extract humour, soon conceived a plot and story.[27]

These accounts suggest that *The Mikado*'s fantasy of Japan is attractive because it is at least in part pointedly counter to "the noble dignity" of the English stage. The fascination with the racial grotesque, "the semblance of a Jap," is integral to the opera. Such an idea is also alluded to by the reviewer who complimented Durward Lely, the tenor who played Nanki-Poo in the first production, on "his heroism in sacrificing some of his personal attractiveness to the exigencies of a Japanese make-up in the matter of hair and eyebrows."[28]

The opera works within an existing contradiction. Opinions about Japan varied; its crafts were at once testimony to the height of its civilization, but at the same time it was considered a heathen and barbaric country. Thus what is "Japanese" brings together two opposing sets of qualities: the one primitive and uncivilized, and the other overly civilized and repressed. In the opera both the patrician and the primitive versions of the orient collide. Japan becomes a place where strict class hierarchies and rigid laws seem implacable, making cruel and unusual punishments—decapitation and death by boiling oil—inevitable. And yet these laws only give way to multiple acts of transgressing these roles. The love duet between Nanki-Poo and Yum-Yum ("Were You Not to Ko-Ko Plighted") emphasizes how the formal prohibition of flirting ("You must never do") makes its enactment all the more deliciously arousing ("I would kiss you fondly thus"). Human impulse is under such restraint that any act of flirting, real or imagined, is punishable by execution.

The imagined Japan of the opera clearly satirizes aspects of Victorian society and fits a standard romantic formula in which young love triumphs over repressive law. However, the depiction of Titipu is more than a thinly disguised England. The racial image of the Japanese as a contradictory mix of civilization and barbarity allow for the censure of Japan as a country with aspirations toward modernization. Thus the opera comments on the display of cruel and strange customs by a people who are nonetheless convinced of their own civilization. Such pretenses are projected onto the character of the Mikado, who claims to be "humane" yet demonstrates a degree of bloodlust well befitting the oriental despot, albeit one made humorous. The opera's Japan is defined by its strange and cruel customs, such as burying new widows alive, boiling prisoners in oil, and committing "The Happy Despatch." This was not lost on William Beatty-Kingston, one of the opera's early reviewers, for whom the characters

> are carefully shown to be unsusceptible of a single kindly feeling or wholesome impulse; were they not manifestly maniacal they would be demoniacal. This view of them is rendered imperative by the

circumstance that their dearest personal interests are, throughout the plot, made dependent upon the infliction of a violent death upon one or the other of them. Decapitation, disembowelment, immersion in boiling oil or molten lead are the eventualities upon which their attention (and that of the audience) is kept fixed with gruesome persistence; what wonder that their brains should be unsettled by such appalling prospects, or that their hearts should be turned to stone by the petrifying instinct of self-preservation? . . . Having resolved to deal with the grimmest subject ever yet selected for treatment from the comic point of view by any dramatic author, and to exhibit his fellow-men to their contemporaries in the most disadvantageous light imaginable, Mr Gilbert has done his self-appointed work with surpassing ability and inimitable *verve*.[29]

Sexual fantasies in particular run rampant in this world where punishment and desire go hand in hand. These erotic fantasies were openly racialized. From the "supple song" of Nanki-Poo to the Three Little Maids "who all unwary / come from the ladies seminary," the erotic attractions of *The Mikado* are enhanced by its Japanese connections. The Japan craze included the import of relatively chaste items, but also objects accompanied by stories of geishas, customs such as the nude bathing of men and women, and *shunga* (Japanese erotic art, an explicitly sexual type of *ukiyo-e*) that created impressions of Japan as a place of sexual license, pleasure, and deviance. While many American and European artists painted respectable, upper-class women in kimonos as a sign of their fashion and good breeding, others such as van Gogh, Tissot, and Monet posed their figures in kimonos as courtesans or low-life entertainers.[30] Monet's *La Japonaise*, for instance, is a portrait of Monet's wife Camille in a pose reminiscent of Japanese woodblock prints of courtesans.[31] The more openly transgressive Aubrey Beardsley freely borrowed from Japanese woodblock prints to create his own distinctive and sexually explicit style.[32] Such eroticized images set the stage for later moments of interest in *The Mikado*.

As Sally Ledger suggests, late nineteenth-century caricatures of the New Woman as unwomanly and masculine were often accompanied by figures of effeminate men.[33] In *The Mikado*, it is Katisha who is the figure of voracious and deviant female sexuality. Paired with the ineffectual executioner Ko-Ko, who never "even killed a bluebottle," she finds "beauty even in bloodthirstiness"; their duet celebrates the morbid taste for violence and danger ("There is beauty in the bellow of the blast, / There is grandeur in the growling of the gale) as well as in the presumably unnatural enjoyment of elderly sexuality of which Ko-Ko sings:

> There is beauty in extreme old age—
>   Do you fancy you are elderly enough?
>   Information I'm requesting
>   On a subject interesting:
> Is a maiden all the better when she's tough?

Of course the "fascination frantic / In a ruin that's romantic" is not just Ko-Ko's predilection. Aspects of the Japan craze became more generally suggestive of excessive luxury and a decadent attachment to oriental commodities. Collectors such as Edmond de Goncourt encouraged this association by their particular expressions of consumerist fantasy. Goncourt wrote of his mad passion for things Japanese; he vividly describes a particularly memorable spending spree:

> We went to inspect the arrival of two shipments from Japan. We spent hours in the midst of those forms, those colours, those objects in bronze, porcelain, pottery, jade, ivory, wood and paper—all that intoxicating and haunting assemblage of art. We were there for hours, so many hours that it was four o'clock when I had lunch. After these debauches of art—the one this morning cost me more than 500 Francs—I am left worn out and shaking as after a night of gambling. I came away with a dryness in the mouth which only the sea water from a dozen oysters could refresh. I bought some ancient albums, a bronze... and the gown of a Japanese tragedian on whose black velvet there are gold dragons with enamel eyes clawing at each other in a field of pink peonies.[34]

Notorious aesthetes such as Whistler, Wilde, and Beardsley were likewise flagrant in their praise of Japanese objects and styles, thus marking this taste as deviant, as satirized by George du Maurier's drawing "The Six-Mark Teapot" in *Punch*, where a newly married couple resolve to live up to their teapot (based on Wilde's own famous quip, "I find it harder and harder every day to life up to my blue china").[35] As the aesthetic bridegroom and intense bride initiate married life, their ritual of consummation takes place through worship of things Japanese, evidenced by the vase and screen as well as the china teapot. The oriental object becomes a model for human perfection, an icon on which is placed both sexual desire and religious fervor. In du Maurier's drawing, the "intense bride" touches the teapot; moreover, her rounded sleeves and the floral and avian patterning of her dress suggest that she has indeed become one with the object.

Figure 5. George du Maurier, "The Six-Mark Tea-Pot," Punch, October 30, 1880.

THE SIX-MARK TEA-POT.

Æsthetic Bridegroom. " It is quite consummate, is it not ! "
Intense Bride. " It is, indeed ! Oh, Algernon, let us live up to it ! "

The revenge of the ordinary on the decadent, Japan-smitten aesthete is the subject of Gilbert and Sullivan's earlier *Patience,* where the self-serving Reginald Bunthorne pretends to be a poet in order to win attention and admiration from Jane and the other "twenty lovesick maidens." The women in turn despise their suitors, the Dragoon Guards, for being "fleshly men." They urge the guards, whom they once favored ("since then our tastes have been etherealized, our perceptions exalted"), to change their red and yellow uniforms to "a cobwebby grey velvet, with a tender bloom like cold gravy, which, made Florentine fourteenth-century, trimmed with Venetian leather and Spanish altar lace, and surmounted with something Japanese—it matters not what!" The exaggerated romantic devotion of the lovesick maidens also satirizes a feminized and orientalized consumer capitalism. The maidens of *Patience* treat the men as objects to be consumed, and in so doing, rob them of their manly demeanor and dignity. Pretending to love "something Japanese," such as the aesthete Bunthorne, is a sign of submission to a world of commodities with its fickle, feminine tastes:

> Then a sentimental passion of a vegetable fashion must excite your languid spleen,
> An attachment *à la* Plato for a bashful young potato, or a not-too-French French bean!
> Though the Philistines may jostle, you will rank as an apostle in the high aesthetic band,
> If you walk down Piccadilly with a poppy or a lily in your mediaeval hand.
> And every one will say,
> As you walk your flowery way,
> "If he's content with a vegetable love which would certainly not suit *me,*
> Why, what a most particularly pure young man this pure young man must be!"

Though a more general satire on the aesthetic movement, with figures like John James McNeil Whistler, Algernon Swinburne, and Gabriel Dante Rossetti, the "Japanese young man" of *Patience* was of course most linked with Oscar Wilde, whose 1882 American tour was financed by D'Oyly Carte. Wilde was carefully scheduled to appear in U.S. cities with the opening of the opera, acting, as Max Beerbohm suggested, as "a sandwich board for *Patience*."[36]

Ultimately Bunthorne confesses his pretense ("I do *not* long for all one sees / That's Japanese") and in pursuit of the milkmaid Patience's affections, turns himself into an "ordinary young man." The dragoons finally appear dressed as aesthetes, posing laboriously in attitudes, whereupon the maidens pronounce them satisfactory: "perceptively intense and consummately utter." This final posturing of *Patience* prefigures the opening men's chorus in *The Mikado*; both sets of men pose as objects, either aesthetic or Japanese. But unlike the dragoons of *Patience*, who have difficulty "attitudinizing," the "gentlemen of Japan" fully inhabit their difficult and "unnatural" postures, opening the opera with a racial display that again evokes strange, deviant, and grotesque bodies:

> If you think we are worked by strings,
>   Like a Japanese marionette,
> You don't understand these things:
>   It is simply Court etiquette.
>   Perhaps you suppose this throng
>   Can't keep it up all day long?
>   If that's your idea, you're wrong, oh!

The Mikado's invitation to perform Japanese extended the consumer's pleasure in the Japanese commodity, the thing that might add a frisson of the novel, the exotic, and even the transgressive to the British and American home. Mari Yoshihara describes how the consumption of Asian art and domestic goods transformed ideas about Asia "from what had been a highly specialized, esoteric knowledge of select male intellectuals to a popular commodity purchased and used not only in upper- but also middle-class American households, particularly by women." It is the "material culture of Orientalism" that "packaged the mixed interests Americans had about Asia—Asia as seductive, aesthetic, refined culture, and Asia as foreign, premodern, Other—and made them into unthreatening objects for collection and consumption."[37] In making its characters resemble the docile objects of the parlor and dining room, their deviance was turned into quaintness. *The Mikado*, like the everyday world of the china teacup and the decorative screen it emulated, naturalized orientalism, making the "foreign" a standard aspect of the domestic sphere.

Playing Japanese in *The Mikado*

This tension between playing Japan as both refined and primitive was rigorously regulated in the acting style of the opera's Savoy productions. This was in keeping with the rigid control the D'Oyly Carte Opera Company generally had over performances of Gilbert and Sullivan operas until the expiration of copyright at the end of 1961. No other professional productions were allowed, and all amateur productions had to pay royalties and base their productions on D'Oyly Carte orchestrations and promptbooks. But it was more than legal control that lent the company its authority. All improvisation was carefully controlled; later versions of the standard company contract included a clause to the effect that "the artist shall not introduce into his performance any material not previously approved by Bridget D'Oyly Carte (granddaughter of Richard and later head of the company) and shall not without such consent alter the music, words, or business of the part which he is playing."[38] Savoy productions of *The Mikado* remained remarkably consistent with Gilbert's 1885 vision, with its most drastic innovations an overhaul of scenery and costume, redesigned by Charles Ricketts, in 1926.[39] Gilbert's direction was notoriously rigid; in one instance he complained to Carte:

> I hear great complaints of [Rutland] Barrington's gagging. . . . The piece is, I think, quite good enough without the extraneous embellishments suggested by Mr. Barrington's brief fancy. Anyway it must be played *exactly as I wrote it*. I wont have an outside word introduced by anybody. If once a license in this direction is accorded it opens the door to any amount of tomfoolery.[40]

Some of this movement and gesture was developed by copying the dances and gestures of Japanese men and women employed at the Japanese Native Village that had opened in the suburb of Knightsbridge a few months before the opening of the opera. Cellier describes how both "a Japanese male dancer and a Japanese tea-girl" were employed to coach the Savoy players, and it was to

> their invaluable aid in coaching the company it was mainly due that our actors and actresses became, after a few rehearsals, so very Japanny. . . . It was extremely amusing and interesting to witness the stage rehearsals, to note the gradual conversion of the English

to the Japanese. One was sometimes inclined to wonder if the Savoyards would retain sufficient native instinct adequately to study the English music.[41]

What dance steps or movements of the fan were borrowed cannot be precisely determined, but any imitation of Japanese movement and posture was most likely translated into something more palatable. This movement was then codified into the disciplined and precise performance style that was characteristic of D'Oyly Carte's company. This careful orchestration can be noted in promptbook notations such as those for Nanki-Poo's entrance song, where the chorus is directed to "strike attitude" when Nanki-Poo addresses them as "Gentlemen"; "fan slowly in time" through the first four lines, put their fans away at the ninth line; and when Nanki-Poo asks, "Are you in sentimental mood?" "all assent / all sympathize." The chorus clasps their hands at "lover's fears," touches their eyes at "sympathetic tears," drops their heads at "Oh, sorrow, sorrow!," assents to "patriotic sentiment," and expresses delight with Nanki-Poo's song of the sea, performing "rowing action four times / twice *on* stage and twice *off* / hauling eight beats / then smack & hitch."[42]

The version of Japanese behavior produced for the first *Mikado* was carefully monitored in nearly every detail. But despite the strict control over the performers, some elements of improvisation inevitably crept in, and fans delighted in these familiar instances of clowning. Comic gags abounded in the history of the Savoy production, to Gilbert's great consternation. *Punch* describes an incident in which George Grossmith, playing Ko-Ko, showed his legs, clad in white stockings, under his Japanese dress.

> Forthwith the house felt a strong sense of relief. It had got what it wanted, it had found out accidentally what it had really missed, and at the first glimpse of George Grossmith's legs there arose a shout of long-pent-up laughter. George took the hint; he too had found out where the fault lay, and now he was so pleased at the discovery that he couldn't give them too much of a good thing.... From that time to the end of the piece there wasn't a dull minute.[43]

In her autobiography, Savoy performer Jessie Bond confessed that when she played Pitti-Sing,

There was nothing much to single me out from the Three Little Maids from School, so I persuaded the wardrobe mistress to give me a big obi, twice as big as any of the others.... She did—I wonder she dared, or that the eagle eyes of the Triumvirate passed it—and I made the most of my big, big bow, turning my back to the audience whenever I got a chance, and waggling it. The gallery was delighted, but *I* nearly got the sack for that prank! However, I did get noticed, which was what I wanted.[44]

Thus *The Mikado* became a place where audiences could see a Japan of extreme contradictions, which demonstrated both the measured dignity expected of "civilized behavior" but also allowed the most blatant displays of erotic and corporeal humor. Such contradictions were absorbed into the overall fantasy of Titipu and would become central, as we shall see, to later productions of the opera such as the *Swing Mikado* and the *Hot Mikado*.

Mikado Rooms and Object Fantasies

The craze for Japanese things, and its important part in what historians have described as the culture of consumption that arose in both England and the United States in the later part of the nineteenth century, definitely set the stage for *The Mikado*'s success.[45] But the opera initiated its own distinctive brand of yellowface performance that defined for many what it meant to play Japanese. To see this we have only to look at the descriptions of the Mikado rooms that became popular in the wake of the New York opening of *The Mikado*, as the *New York World* described:

> Instead of putting fugitive Japanese ornaments miscellaneously about a house, stuck here and there like plums in a pudding, among all sorts of incongruous things, the latest is to set apart one room to be devoted to Japanese art and to call it the "Mikado room."[46]

These rooms were "a revival, in one sense, of the former taste for Japanese art in decoration" but also a direct "result of the popularity of Gilbert & Sullivan's opera." "Mikado rooms" ranged wildly in expense. At the high end were the opulent room at H. G. Marquant's Madison Avenue home, costing at least $150,000; the Japanese collections of Mrs. Morgan valued at $300,000; and the Mikado room of Mr. W. T. Walters of Baltimore, with a collection of swords "which are alone worth about $100,000." But these rooms were also available at much more affordable prices, such as "a small room in an ordinary flat" for $25. The *World* finds, "That is the great beauty of Japanese wares. You can find the greatest diversity in values and all of artistic worth."[47]

A similar story in the *Chicago Tribune* concludes, "Our best people have always had a sneaking regard for Japanese fiance [pottery] and curios," with such "connoisseurs as Marshall Field, George L. Duniap, L. Z. Leiter and his nephew Barton Leiter, Mr. and Mrs. Bross, and dozens of others" who "have collected some of the finest specimens of Japanese art manufactures and feel a just pride in the possession of their beautiful curios." Yet there is also a more egalitarian spirit in the Mikado rooms of Chicago:

> The Mikado craze is tending to popularize Japanese art, and you will find in a very short time the inevitable fan, ranging in price from two cents to $20, will be as common in the homes of our people [of] all classes as was formerly the much-abused *chromolithograph*.[48]

In purchasing essential decorations such as fans, the *Tribune* assures readers,

> There is no limit in the fanciful and beautiful specimens which a person of ordinary taste can secure at a comparatively trifling expense.... The beauty of it all is that it is inexpensive as compared with any other style of decoration. While the well-to-do mechanic can make a house, or at least one room, beautiful by a minimum of outlay, the wealthy merchant can furnish such a room at 100 times the cost, and each will be in its own style consistently and artistically attractive.[49]

Such sentiments are echoed in the pamphlet *The Mikado Room and How to Furnish It*, where Estelle Stoughton Smith discusses how "lots of interest in things Japanese has been stimulated by the production of Gilbert and Sullivan's *Mikado*" and describes "a freak which the new opera has sprung upon us ... 'The Mikado Room,' with 'its odd-finical beauty and stiffness.'" In her self-published pamphlet she counsels readers on how to buy the proper outfitting for such a room, with crepe-paper pictures, hanging scrolls, a hanging cabinet for the display of old bronzes and "cloisome

[sic]," porcelain vases, cups, teapots, rattan chairs, black wood tables, chintz draperies, umbrellas, and lanterns. She also assures readers that such a room "is inexpensive as compared with any other style of decoration."[50]

The descriptions of these rooms with their particular attention to cost mark a transition from a more limited idea of oriental luxury, affordable only by the elite, to one configured for a variety of consumers. In *New York before Chinatown*, John Kuo Wei Tchen distinguishes between patrician and commercial forms of orientalism. In the United States, the associations of the Orient with luxury, wealth, and aristocracy originated in the taste of the landed gentry for Chinese porcelain and other fine goods, as epitomized by such prominent figures as George Washington, who cultivated a taste for fancy china. This patrician orientalism contrasted with the commercial orientalism that emerged later in the nineteenth century, as displays of oriental curiosities and monstrosities, such as Chinese and Japanese acrobats or the Siamese twins Chang and Eng Bunker, became part of the broader demand for new forms of entertainment.[51] Marketed to the middle class, this more commercial orientalism revolved around the consumption of Asian objects and people:

> Much in the way aristocrats and patricians engaged in travel writing, the urban middle classes could now consume a visual array of commercial "edifying curiosities" to discover their own personal relationship to other cultures, peoples, and parts of the world. To survey a panorama of China, a miniature of a primitive village, or a living animal or exoticized human on display or to witness an "oriental conjuror" all evoked a sense of wonderment and situated one's place in the world.[52]

The Mikado had both its commercial appeal and its patrician elements; most important, it reconfigured the patrician orientalism associated with the connoisseurship of Japanese arts and crafts into a broadly popular phenomenon. In doing so, it fed the desire to see oneself as part of an elite even while catering to the casually curious spectator. Buying things Japanese retained some measure of patrician authority even while available to those of much more modest means. Thus tensions around class might be alleviated through the rhetoric of mass availability, and a supporting fantasy of democracy through consumerism—the idea that all can purchase equally—could be focused on the Japanese object. Importantly, the description of the Mikado room suggests that differences in wealth matter little in this new decorative scheme. The patrician tastes of the wealthy might still be accessible, as "you may spend any fortune you may happen to have, but many pretty things are really cheap."[53]

By 1885, many Japanese goods were readily available to middle-class consumers in Europe and the United States. The shift to the mass consumption of oriental items led to the disdain of some connoisseurs such as Edmond de Goncourt, who declared, "The taste for things Chinese and Japanese! We were among the first to have this taste. It is now spreading to everything and everyone, even to idiots and middle-class women. Who has cultivated it, felt it, preached it, and converted others to it more than we; who was excited by the first volumes and had the courage to buy them?[54] But *The Mikado* simply capitalized on this liberalization of orientalism. The opera was a boon to importers, for it made Japanese goods intelligible to a range of new consumers, prompting the ongoing purchase and collection of these objects. The description of how a Mikado room might work suggests multiple activities of acquisition and exchange that were colored by the opera; part of the "amusement," according to the article in the *World,* is that "young ladies levy contributions on their friends, those with whom they are sufficiently intimate, to add to the attractions of their 'Mikado rooms' and it is not at all the proper thing to take a young lady to see the opera without sending her some Japanese curio as a souvenir of the evening and to be placed in her 'Mikado room.'" Even after the opera was over, it invited further participation through acts of buying and exchanging souvenirs. These souvenirs then became indelibly marked as artifacts of *The Mikado* as well as imports from Japan. Their presence in the home, moreover, might give rise to future home performances that would recall the opera, whether through music, gesture, language, or most important, buying things.

The allure of the first productions of *The Mikado* was clearly tied to a familiarity with imported Japanese goods. But the popularity of the opera itself in turn generated a whole set of orientalized commodities, many of which were substantively different from those things imported directly from Japan. The seemingly limitless reproduction of *Mikado*s and related items, especially in the United States where copyright law did not hold, gave images from the opera a reach on the imagination far beyond the stage. Unauthorized versions, both faithful and blatantly illegitimate, abounded. Sheet music made musical performances ubiquitous. The characterizations, dialogue, and movements of *The Mikado* were used to advertise everything from corsets to soap to thread.

In this proliferation of *Mikado*s a distinctive tension between authenticity and fantasy emerges. These productions exhibited a marked casualness about their representational power, emphasizing yellowface as a kind of transparent disguise in which racial impersonation is performed simply by picking up the right objects. At the same time, a certain realism was put at a premium, suggesting a certain anxiety about the "authentic" that could not be so easily put off. This was particularly true in the hard-fought battle over copyright and ownership of *Mikado* productions in the United States.

American Knockoffs and Racial Imitations

In England, the presentation of *The Mikado*, like other Gilbert and Sullivan operas, was strictly controlled by Richard D'Oyly Carte and his Savoy company. In the United States, however, productions of *The Mikado* took on a life of their own, as H. L. Mencken described in 1910:

> The people of the United States were "Mikado" crazy for a year or more, as they had been "Pinafore" crazy some time before. Things Japanese acquired an absurd vogue. Women carried Japanese fans and wore Japanese kimonos and dressed their hair in some approach to the Japanese manner. The mincing step of Yum-Yum appeared in the land; chopsuey, mistaken for a Japanese dish, became a naturalized victual; the Mikado's yearning to make the punishment fit the crime gave the common speech a new phrase; parlor wits repeated, with never-failing success, the lordly Pooh-Bah's remark about the "corroborative detail designed to lend verisimilitude to an otherwise bald and unconvincing narrative"; his other remark, about the ultimate globule of primordial protoplasm, engendered a public interest in biology and sent the common people to the pages of Darwin, then a mere heretic and the favorite butt of windy homiletes.[55]

After his experiences with the many unauthorized versions of U.S. productions of *Pinafore* and *Pirates of Penzance*, D'Oyly Carte took great care to try to forestall similar imitations of *The Mikado*. But he did not, as he had with *Iolanthe* in 1882, plan simultaneous premieres in London and New York. *The Mikado* had its London debut on March 14, 1885, whereas its New York production was first anticipated for October. D'Oyly Carte had initially negotiated with two American managers, John Stetson and James C. Duff, for rights to the New York premiere. He eventually settled with Stetson, while Duff returned to the United States, intent on staging a production nonetheless. In the months following, D'Oyly Carte and Stetson made a series of moves to try to foil Duff's plans. When Duff sent an agent to London for Japanese costumes, D'Oyly Carte bought up every Japanese costume available through major importers in London and Paris. Duff sent detectives to spy on Stetson and his theater, the Fifth Avenue; D'Oyly Carte advised Stetson to do the same to Duff and his Standard Theater. When Duff announced that his *Mikado* would debut on August 24, D'Oyly Carte quickly arranged for a company of Savoy players to travel to New York. The performers left under conditions of great secrecy, traveling under pseudonyms, to escape public announcement. They arrived on August 17, and Stetson announced that his New York production would take place on August 20. Duff countered by moving his premiere date to August 19, and Stetson declared that his opening would also be on the 19th. Duff relented, and moved his first night to August 24.

Stetson and D'Oyly Carte's production was a great success, while Duff's proved a critical failure. Duff's performance did not use Sullivan's orchestration but rather relied on imitations specifically designed to circumvent copyright. His costumes and scenery could not match the lavish treatment of the Savoy company, and his performers were criticized for their lack of acting skills. Ironically, however, when there was a hiatus in Stetson's lease for January and February 1886, he, with D'Oyly Carte's knowledge, paid Duff to move his production to Chicago as a licensed production so that the Savoy Company could use Duff's theater space. The Stetson/D'Oyly production eventually moved back to the Fifth Avenue Theatre and ended its run on April 17, 1885, after 250 performances.

The earlier American productions of *The Mikado* were neither D'Oyly Carte's touring production at the Fifth Avenue Theatre nor the rival production produced by James Duff. They began with a much more modest affair at a small theater, the Chicago Museum, in which a version of the opera performed by the Bijou Opera company competed for attention with other curiosities. Joseph Herbert, who played Ko-Ko, reported, "There were three attractions all at the Museum at the same time—Lucia Zarete, the Mexican Dwarf, 21 inches in height, a double-headed cow, and 'The Mikado.'" Herbert later recalled, "The manager of the double-headed cow became upset with the amount of business being done by 'The Mikado'... and tried to claim a breach of contract. He used to take the cow to the door of the theatre, and then claimed that it was the cow and not 'The Mikado' which drew the crowds into the Auditorium. Finally, there had to be a compromise with the cow manager."[56] The *New York Times* later commented on this production, noting its "singers and actors, all of whom are unknown to fame in the East" and speculating on the terms of its piracy:

> Undoubtedly the persons responsible for this unauthorized performance obtained a pianoforte score of the piece, such as may now be bought in the music stores, and had an orchestral arrangement hastily made. They did not have exact reproductions of the original scenes and dress, and probably supplied antics of their own in place of Mr. Gilbert's carefully prepared "business." As we have intimated, the Chicago Museum is not a fashionable theatre. The modest sum of 10 cents was asked as an admission fee for this performance, which may become historical, and the unanimous opinion of the intelligent persons in the audience was that the people on the stage could neither sing nor act, but it was a production of "The Mikado" all the same.[57]

The second American *Mikado* also took place in Chicago. Theater manager Sydney Rosenfeld brought *The Mikado* to the Grand Opera House on July 6, 1885, to great profit. When he announced his intention to produce the opera in New York at the Union Square Theatre on July 20, Gilbert, Sullivan, D'Oyly Carte, and Stetson appealed to the law. A temporary injunction was issued to prevent *The Mikado* from being performed until a trial occurred to determine American performing rights. Nonetheless, Rosenfeld arranged for the theater to be sublet to a friend, Edward J. Abrahams, and *The Mikado* had another production on July 20. The following day, warrants were issued for the arrest of Rosenfeld and Abrahams, who promptly fled to New Jersey and Chicago. Rosenfeld was eventually released after being fined $750. On August 10, Harry Miner also produced a version at the Harry Miner People's Theatre, using a cast almost identical to Rosenfeld's. Another judge refused to grant an injunction against Miner's version, although he required him to enter into a bond. But D'Oyly Carte could not get an injunction against James Duff. A test case was heard by Justice Divver, of New York City, who issued the ruling: "Copyright or no copyright, commercial honesty or commercial buccaneering, no Englishman possesses any rights which a true born American is bound to respect."[58] The law ultimately supported the ruling that in light of the absence of international copyright law, theater managers in the United States could produce Gilbert and Sullivan's work without permission or royalties. In the following year, the Berne Copyright Convention of 1886 brought together convention countries that reciprocally agreed to protect published works; the United States was not a participating country.

Eventually, Congress did pass the International Copyright Act in 1891; however, this was much too late to curb the spread of *Mikado*s of all kinds. Hundreds of versions were performed in the few years following, with many variations, including children's companies; a German version at the Thalia Theatre in New York that included characters such as Puh-Bah, Pisch-Tusch, and Pup-Bah; and a mostly female cast at Tony Pastor's Theatre with a male Katisha.[59] There were also, as we shall discuss later, numerous blackface minstrel versions. These often played concurrently; for instance, advertisements in the *Chicago Daily Tribune* for October 25, 1885, included several *Mikado*s: one by Sydney Rosenfeld's company ("The First Perfect Production yet given in Chicago of this Most Famous Opera"), the final performances of the Goodwin Opera Company at the Chicago Museum ("As the Company leaves by special train after the evening performance for Minneapolis"), and a burlesque by Haverly's Home Minstrels, the "High-Card-O!" complete with "New and Gorgeous Costumes!" and "Characteristic Paraphernalia!" as well as characters such as "Yankee-Pooh," "Ko-Ko Nuts," "Poor-Boy," "Sing-Sing" and "Peek-a-Boo."[60]

The competition between these early versions brings out some of the tensions inherent in the transition from the patrician orientalism that connected *The Mikado* to the world of luxury commodities and legitimate theater on the one hand, and the commercial orientalism of theaters that were not fashionable on the other. Told of Sydney Rosenfeld's version, John Duff declared that he was not worried about this first *Mikado* trumping his own unauthorized premiere: "It will be a Japanese burlesque and that is all."[61]

Interestingly enough, Duff's comment reveals how producers of these first U.S. *Mikado*s were eager to claim a certain degree of verisimilitude in order to establish their versions as the most definitive. D'Oyly Carte's version established a reputation for authenticity through its use of Japanese costumes as well as authorship. "Only Mikado" reads advertisements for the Carte/Stetson production: "Only Mr. R. D'Oyly Carte's Company have the Composer's Original Orchestration, the Author's Original Stage Business and the Real Antique Japanese Costumes. All Other Versions are Unauthorized Imitations."[62] Arthur Sullivan commented on the Chicago version that "it is extremely annoying to have it put on the way it must be here by this fellow Rosenfeld, who got all he knows about Japanese customs, and everything else he knows about the opera, from a dollar score book. Why, do [you] know in London the rehearsals lasted for eight weeks? We went to the Japanese village in London and brought the people to the theatre, so that the production was true down almost to the inimitable Japanese gestures."[63] This dedication to making costuming, scenery, and acting more "Japanese" gave the Savoy productions more weight than the "Japanese burlesque" of their competitors. Comparing the D'Oyly Carte/Stetson version with the Duff one, a reviewer for the *Boston Globe* noted, "There is a distinct Japanese color to one representation, which, being absent in the other, is replaced by an individuality that belongs to the actors."[64] With the seal of approval of such Japanese specialists as Algernon Mitford and Sir Rutherford Alcock,[65] *The Mikado* of the D'Oyly Carte versions successfully held on to a certain kind of authority as an "authentic Japanese" opera.

Claims to authenticity notwithstanding, most of what D'Oyly Carte was promoting in terms of its fidelity as a representation of Japanese people was not much different from its competitors. Real Japanese kimonos could be used and the scenery made as convincing as possible; heavy eye makeup and elaborate wigs could be carefully applied; the performers could be coached in mincing steps, fluttering fans, and exaggerated bowing. Nonetheless, at the core of all of these productions was a racial performance that appealed precisely because it was not wholly convincing as a representation. The formal stylization of movement and the care in costuming was undercut by multiple moments in which the characters themselves called attention to the ruse. "Sometimes I sit and wonder, in my artless Japanese way," Yum-Yum muses, "why it is that I am so much more attractive than anybody else in the whole world." The chorus hails Nanki-Poo's volunteerism with "the Japanese equivalent for hear, hear, hear!" Ko-Ko tells the Mikado that Nanki-Poo's name "might have been on his pocket-handkerchief, but Japanese don't use pocket-handkerchiefs! Ha! ha! ha!" These jokes directly undercut racial impersonation with a certain insouciance, and *The Mikado* thus disavows any serious intention to represent Japan faithfully. Though Japan always served as the putative point of inspiration for yellowface practice, the opera could absolve the player from any errors of fact by claiming itself as a nonsensically humorous fiction.

The proliferation of American *Mikado*s was enabled and encouraged by a certain style of playing intrinsic to the opera in which authenticity becomes a moot point. This is consistent with the opera's commodity racism, whereby playing Japanese becomes a matter of associating oneself with objects that can be quickly disposed of. The *Mikado*'s yellowface supported playing Japanese as a style that performers might take on and off at will. Yellowface is thus performed as a flirtation rather than as a more lasting bodily transformation. Performers easily transform themselves into Japanese through formulaic racial gestures and iconic objects and just as easily retreat from these racial incarnations. The stories told of Grossmith and Bond's clowning might well substantiate this; what audiences came to see was not real Japanese performing but their favorite Savoy performers pretending to be Japanese and at the same time still operating in the familiar comic modes that identified them.

This lightness became the quality by which these representations became known and famous in the following decades. This style of yellowface had many advantages. It was affordable and accessible. It could be practiced with very little expertise on the part of the performer with a few strategically placed objects and with minimal translation. These practices of yellowface could also employ all the modern technological means of reproduction: photography, printing, recording, and, eventually, film, to allow its actors to capture and inhabit the spaces of this fantasy Japan. Cards, buttons, and fabric displayed images from the opera, and scenes from *The Mikado* appeared on scrapbooks, crazy quilts, hand-painted china, and pottery. Children could play with Mikado dolls and toy theaters. Kimonos, swords, and fans became common elements of masquerades for private photography sessions and parties. All of these became alternative venues for *Mikado* performance; the opera initiated what became a widespread practice of racial cross-dressing. It was these fantasies of cross-racial impersonation, rather than simply an idea of Japan per se, that caught the fancy of many who sought to have themselves captured à la *Mikado*. As Yuko Matsukawa has noted, yellowface practices were spread by advertising as well as by performances of the opera. Many of these images were copied directly from cabinet photographs of the U.S. *Mikado* production as well as other popular works of art, such as Monet's *La Japonaise*. These images consistently featured the transparency of this racial cross-dressing in which, as Matsukawa writes, white women playing Japanese "disseminated and naturalized the idea that the loose kimono, the oversized fan and *Caucasian* features were the hallmarks of Japanese womanhood."[66]

Scholars have documented the importance of Japan as a site of aesthetic, literary, intellectual, and spiritual inspiration for Westerners. As T. J. Jackson Lears, Christopher Benfrey, and others have documented, a host of intellectuals, artists, and statesmen made Japan the locus of serious study and travel.[67] However, the mass of *Mikado* audiences had neither the privilege nor the inclination to be this serious. Thus *The Mikado*

Figure 6. Cabinet photograph, "Three Little Maids." D'Oyly Carte New York production, 1885.

Figure 7. Tintype photograph, unidentified photographer, circa 1885. William B. Becker Collection / American Museum of Photography.

marks a radical realignment of the Japan craze, a "lite" version of orientalism that, as suggested by Jeff Nunokawa, has an "ostentatiously theatrical character [that] relies upon and reproduces Japan's reputation as pure artifice."[68] *The Mikado* did not demand an understanding of or even curiosity about actual Japanese culture. No expert opinion or Japan specialist was needed to certify the value of the Mikado screen or crazy quilt as racial representation.

Eventually, this imagined Japan even became the frame for the real one. A short film of the "Sarashe Sisters" performing an "Imperial Japanese dance," produced by W. K. L. Dickson, was made by Edison's Black Maria studio in 1894; although the women performing a traditional Japanese dance look nothing like Gilbert and Sullivan's Three Little Maids,

Figure 8. Advertisement for Thomson's corsets, circa 1886.

the Edison film catalog advertises that the film contains "a charming representation of *The Mikado* dance by three beautiful Japanese ladies in full costume. Very effective when colored."⁶⁹ Even informed travelogues such as G. Waldo Browne's encyclopedic *The New America and the Far East* (1907), otherwise replete with a wealth of seemingly authoritative information about Japan, cannot resist titling a picture of three Japanese women "Three Little Maids."⁷⁰

In a milieu wherein Japanese objects had already become a familiar and ubiquitous part of everyday decor, *The Mikado* suggested that Japan could be known solely through the life of these things. *The Mikado* could safely banish anything that was ugly, sloppy, or inconvenient about actual encounters with Japanese people and instead substitute its own charming version of Japan; moreover, this conveniently packaged and easily digested version of cultural contact could be distributed to places where real Japanese never set foot. *The Mikado* offered a mode of musical performance that accentuated these attractions: the living, breathing, and

Figure 9. "*Three Little Maids*," in G. Waldo Browne, The New America and the Far East *(1907).*

singing inhabitants of Titipu, spectacular and harmonious, defined what was Japanese in ways that mere mortals could not.

If the commodity fetishism inherent in japonaiserie fosters fantasies of objects animated as if they were living and breathing, *The Mikado* imagines a reversal of this relationship, with characters imagined as real and living primarily through their proximity to and connection with these objects. Such a precedent invites Oscar Wilde's famous remarks in "The Decay of Lying" (1891):

> Now do you really imagine that the Japanese people, as they are presented to us in art, have any existence? If you do, you have never understood Japanese art at all. The Japanese people are the deliberate self-conscious creation of certain individual artists. If you set a picture by Hokusai or Hokkei, or any of the great native painters, beside a real Japanese gentleman or lady, you will see that there is not the slightest resemblance between them. The actual people who live in Japan are not unlike the general run of English people; that is to say, they are extremely commonplace, and have nothing curious or extraordinary about them. In fact, the whole of Japan is a pure invention. There is no such country, there are no such people. One of our most charming painters went recently to the Land of the Chrysanthemum in the foolish hope of seeing the Japanese. All he saw, all he had the chance of painting, were a few lanterns and some fans. He was quite unable to discover the inhabitants, as his delightful exhibition at Messrs. Dowdeswell's Gallery showed only too well. He did not know that the Japanese people are, as I have said, simply a mode of style, an exquisite fancy of art. And so, if you desire to see a Japanese effect, you will not behave like a tourist and go to Tokio. On the contrary, you will stay at home and steep yourself in the work of certain Japanese artists and then, when you have absorbed the spirit of their style, and caught their imaginative manner of vision, you will go some afternoon and sit in the Park or stroll down Piccadilly, and if you cannot see an absolutely Japanese effect there, you will not see it anywhere.[71]

Within five years, Japan had finally become a "pure invention" of the artistic mind, an invention that seems to operate best without interruption from any real Japanese whose bodies do not conform to their artistic representations. In Wilde's framing, as urged on by *The Mikado,* Japanese things magically appear without the human hands that make them and take on a life of their own. This, of course, is a defining property of commodity fetishism. For Marx, even the "ordinary, sensuous" table turned into a commodity "changes into a thing which transcends sensuousness . . . It not only stands with its feet on the ground, but, in relation to all other commodities, it stands on its head, and evolves out of its wooden brain grotesque ideas, far more wonderful than if it were to begin dancing of its own free will."[72] The human hands that make the table are all but forgotten.

The Mikado populates its fantasy of Japan with familiar objects that sing and dance and in doing so seem to leave behind any sense of their Japanese origins. One particularly effective demonstration of this power comes in yet another set of instructions on how to decorate a Mikado room, as Estelle Stoughton Smith, the author of the self-published pamphlet *The Mikado Room and How to Furnish It,* elaborates on how to use the Japanese fan to enhance feminine attraction and to aid in courtship: "Soft whispers breathed from behind a pretty Fan," she describes, "will only reach the ear for which they are intended. Hence the potency of the Fan in those delicious little episodes which lead to orange blossoms, the shower of rice and of slippers, and the honeymoon." Smith also suggests how fans serve to keep records of these intimate encounters; the "society belle" uses the fan "to keep count of her conquests; of the compliments a single evening has brought from bearded lips" or as an autograph album, in which case "the latter days of that Fan are passed in ease and solitude. Its burden of pencil marks and the associations these have in the mind of its fair owner, render it too precious for continuous use. It is laid away among love letters and lavender." Smith's homage to the fan is clearly inspired by *The Mikado:* "Arthur Sullivan has shed a new luster upon the Fan; has added to its glories and increased its stock of laurels . . . His charming opera will come to mind wherever the Fan *à la Japonois* is fluttered, and wherever feminine beauty is enhanced by the rich colors and crown like head-gear of *Yum-Yum* or *Pitti-Sing.*" In her lavish descriptions, the object rules triumphant:

> It is evident to all who keep their eyes open, and whose faculties are unclouded, that this is the Fan Age as much as it is the Iron Age. Be that as it may—to everyone this has been especially apparent,

since Gilbert and Sullivan launched their tuneful "Mikado,"—that the Fan has become all-powerful in the realm of Society, in Music and the Drama.[73]

The Mikado's style of playing Japanese through the object models itself on how commodity fetishism erases human relations in favor of objects. This erasure is double: in the absence of the Japanese labor that makes these objects and in the Japanese people that the objects might represent. The banishment of any real Japanese means that neither the reminder of work nor the grossness of actual bodies intrudes into this new intimacy with things. *The Mikado*, then, allows a particular desire—not just for possession but for inhabitation—to realize itself on a broad scale. What might easily step into the places of these absent Japanese are the white performers of yellowface, who are imagined as both the possessors of objects and as inhabitants of the fantasy world they represent. This confident act of racial performance has tremendous power. And yet, as we shall see in the next chapter, it is not quite all-encompassing.

· Chapter 2 ·

"My Artless Japanese Way": Japanese Villages and Absent Coolies

> As we toiled slowly up, leading our horses, we heard some very sweet notes of the unguissu, not unlike the notes of a nightingale, and I think nearly the only bird in Japan that sings. It had one or two very sweet notes. They say the Japanese teach them to sing beautifully, which is the more extraordinary, if true, as they certainly do not teach themselves; and, if I had not lived among the Chinese, I should have said they had the least conception of either harmony or melody of any race yet discovered.
>
> Sir Rutherford Alcock, *Capital of the Tycoon*, vol. 2 (1863)

THE PARADOX OF *The Mikado* lies not in pure fantasy, but in its artful embellishment of fiction with corroborative detail; for instance, the Savoy's 1885 production in New York relied on a certain authenticity to elevate itself above its commercial rivals. In London too, a certain amount of verifiably Japanese detail was necessary to give the production value. Patrician orientalism relies on the assurance of authenticity to sustain the value of imported objects for collectors and connoisseurs. In many ways, the opera borrowed a number of identifiably Japanese details, but it did so with great care.

This strategic use of realistic detail becomes clear in the music of the opera, which, as some have remarked, is replete with resolutely English musical forms. Ian Bradley notes that "the music for *The Mikado* could hardly have been more English," with its employment of "the English folk-song tradition" in the variations of ballad, military march, and sea shanty in "A Wandering Minstrel," the madrigal "Brightly Dawns Our Wedding Day," and the series of duets "The Flowers That Bloom in the Spring." "Even the entrance of the Lord High Executioner is set to a tune remarkably similar to the traditional air 'A Fine Old English Gentleman.'"[1] The opera does employ one real Japanese song, "Miya sama," a march

· 39 ·

composed in 1868 by Japanese military commanders Masujirō Ōmura and Yajirō Shinagawa,[2] which it features prominently in the overture and echoes musically through multiple parts of the opera. The overture highlights the more Japanese aspects of the tunes, including the use of "Miya sama"; the melodies of the opening chorus ("If you want to know who we are") not only echo the pentatonic scale used in "Miya sama," first heard in the overture, but actually replays its framing patterns in reverse. Musically, as Raymond Knapp and Michael Beckerman have highlighted, the opera uses variations on this song to present its Japanese subjects as alternately strange and familiar.[3] In any case, the uses of "Miya sama" and other Japanese musical elements seems more to underscore exotic difference than to expose audiences to Japanese music, which was described in travel accounts, such as Sir Rutherford Alcock's *Capital of the Tycoon*, as being the very antithesis of Western music. If the idea of the wandering minstrel from accounts such as Alcock's might have been captivating, the actual music of Japan apparently was not.[4] Alcock complained of the Japanese:

> The discord they both make when they set themselves to produce what they call music, is something that baffles all description. Marrow-bones and cleavers are melodious in comparison, and the notes they bring out of a sort of lute and guitar is something too excruciating for endurance. And yet they make it a study, and there are professional singers and teachers who as sedulously cultivate their art as any in Europe. The professors are often blind; to judge by their performance, I should have guessed them to be deaf also—certainly the audience should be.[5]

In many ways, *The Mikado*'s fantasy is as brittle as it is beautiful, and in constant danger of interruption from the "authentic" sources it draws on. Confirmation of its power to represent Japan faithfully was frequently sought from Japanese living in the United States, such as S. Takeda, whose thoughts on the opera were printed by the *Chicago Daily Tribune*. Takeda gives a systematic accounting:

> Having been asked the question many times, "How do you like 'The Mikado'?" I as a Japanese would like to express my opinion on the subject as it strikes me. I might say, on the whole I am very much pleased with it, and also might add that the production by the Duff opera company is the best I have yet seen, and I might

Figure 10. "*Japanese Wandering Minstrels,*" *in Sir Rutherford Alcock,* Capital of the Tycoon *(1863).*

further say that I have seen every company of importance that has yet played it. To me of course it appears very amusing. Twenty years ago the Mikado of Japan was unapproachable, even to his subjects, and was never seen by the outside world.

The costumes strike me as being beautiful, especially that of the Mikado himself. The embroidery was very fine. The Kimonos and dresses of the three sisters—Yum-Yum, Pitti-Sing, and Peep-Bo—are worn correctly, and the obis are in their proper position, and in their dancing, bowing, etc., they would hardly be distinguishable from the ladies of my own country. Ko-Ko, or as we in Japan would call him, the Shogun Tokugowa Easyassu [sic], struck me as being especially amusing. The dressing of this company is proper, the armor, arms, etc. being of the old Japanese pattern, and are worn correctly.

Everything is in accordance, with the exception of the names, which are purely mythical, and to look as [sic] them as they are printed one would take them more for Chinese than Japanese, with which nation we do not wish to be confounded (the Chinese), as their manners and customs are entirely different from ours. Also I might add that the flowers, although beautiful, did not especially represent a Japanese garden scene. In my country the prevailing flower, and the one, I might add, which we especially admire, is the eakra [sic], or cherry-tree, the blossom of which is cultivated by the acre for the fragrance alone.

The houses are a correct representation: and on the whole I was very much pleased with the representation by this company, which is the best that I have yet seen.[6]

Such observations point out nuances in how the opera might indeed reference Japanese culture, dress, history, and people; notably the misspelling of Takeda's reference to Ko-Ko as Tokugawa Leyasu (the first Tokugawa shogunate) or to the sakura blossom. As seen by the misspellings, such nuances were lost to most American readers of the time. And yet Takeda's assertions, even if solicited as a statement from a native informant, are significant because they mark a point of curiosity and vulnerability that remain part of the opera's legacy.

Discussions of *The Mikado* often fixate on attempts to authenticate or dismiss the opera's putative Japaneseness, asserting that the opera is or isn't really Japanese. Those who seek to authenticate the opera's depictions note that Gilbert may have brought in real Japanese to coach Savoy performers on their gestures and mannerisms, or that the productions used costumes imported from Japan, or that Sullivan incorporated a number of Japanese music motifs into his score. Those who claim that there is nothing Japanese about *The Mikado* point to its patently un-Japanese setting, names, and satiric lyrics. Both sets of arguments, however, miss some of the opera's complex relationship to the racial representation of Japan.

The Mikado was a boon to importers and purveyors of Japan goods. But it did more than sustain interest in Japanese products; it incorporated desires for those objects into its productions, and it promoted a fantasy of a Japan that was fully accessible through familiar, domesticated objects. Thus *The Mikado* marks a particular strain of the Japanese epidemic in which things are willfully confused with people. Its insouciant brand of yellowface, in which decorative beings named Yum-Yum, Nanki-Poo, and Pooh-Bah cavort with fans and swords, thrives only in the absence of all but the most carefully managed encounters with Japanese people. The world of Titipu was not only devoid of actual Japanese, but also banished references to the bodily labor, Japanese or otherwise, necessary to produce, import, and sell these familiar commodities. This fantasy of racial consumption was inevitably interrupted when such concerns intruded.

The fantasy of *The Mikado* encountered such interruptions at the Japanese Native Villages, built first in Knightsbridge, a suburb of London, shortly before the opening of *The Mikado,* and then in several major U.S. cities following the success of the opera. Within these exhibits, spectators saw Japanese artisans at work on those beautiful objects that they so admired. How their craft was presented is consistent with seeing the "primitive" arts of Japan as an alternative to the alienating and capitalist values of modern society; in many accounts a romanticized image of the Japanese artisan prevailed. However idealized, the accounts also included reminders that were far removed from the fantasies of *The Mikado.*

Descriptions of these villages provide important clues as to how these Japanese at work disrupted the fantasies of commodity racism, which inevitably prefers the valuable object to the unruly hand that makes it. Descriptions of these villages and their inhabitants resonated with the discrepancy between the world of *The Mikado* and the presence of foreign workers. Ultimately, examining these Japanese Native Villages against the terms set by *The Mikado* allows us to reflect further on the tensions of commodity orientalism more generally, comparing japonaiserie with its decorative predecessor, chinoiserie. *The Mikado*'s success comes at a time when the Japan craze came upon the heels of chinoiserie's decline in fashion, a decline in which the patrician value of formerly coveted Chinese objects was diminished by China's loss of international stature and, in the United States at least, by association with the despised bodies of Chinese immigrant labor. *The Mikado* in a sense avoids this fate through its pointed exclusion of the coolie laborer, whose conspicuous absence from the opera nonetheless leaves us wondering.

Veritable Japanese Villages

On January 10, 1885, several months before the opening of *The Mikado,* a Japanese Native Village managed by Tannaker Buhicrosan opened in the suburb of Knightsbridge outside of London. Over a hundred Japanese, twenty-six of them women and children, inhabited the interior of Humphrey's Hall, which was fully rebuilt to imitate a Japanese street full of shops. One commentator notes that these buildings were "not mere painted fronts but well-built apartments of varied appearance, each with its own characteristic ornamentation of parti-coloured bamboo, on solid panels, with shingled or thatched roof, and with sliding trellis-shutters and translucent paper screen to serve as a substitute for glass in cold weather." These structures were decorated with "effective landscapes, in which the world-known Fusi-yama appears now and again, . . . painted by native artists, whose clever manipulation of two brushes, one in each hand, will be seen with astonishment by many."[7] Visitors could see Japanese artisans at work making fans, pottery, baskets, barrels, lanterns, trays, cabinets, pipes, and umbrellas; weaving and embroidering silk, satin, and crepe; carving wood; and painting screens and scrolls. They could drink tea at a tea shop staffed by Japanese women as well as walk through a Japanese garden and view a Buddhist temple, "a place of worship . . . something like a temple, or at all events an inclosure devoted to a hideous idol, before which two lanterns burn continually."[8] At the temple, they could witness two Japanese priests "perform their devotions at suitable hours"; however, the *London Times* reports that "it is satisfactory to know that there is no intention of making a show of their religious ceremonies."[9] They could hear Japanese music, watch stick fighting and wrestling, and conclude these entertainments by viewing "a dance, or rather the fantastic posturing of three girls in slow measured time to a thrumming accompaniment kept up by some of the women on small stringed instruments played with a broad pecten, two of the number chanting in a high key."[10]

The Mikado playfully references the Japanese Native Village, as a desperate Ko-Ko explains to the Mikado that his son has gone "abroad [to] Knightsbridge"! Many have commented that the initial success of *The Mikado* might have been enhanced by the Japanese Native Village opening earlier that year, and that some of the inhabitants, perhaps these three dancers, served as models for Savoy performers. Yet the relationship of the Japanese villagers to their yellowface counterparts in *The Mikado* is more complicated than either advertising or inspiration suggests. These villagers presented a dilemma of how to reconcile the real bodies of Japanese people with the fantasy of *The Mikado*. Although their presence tends to be absorbed into the general history of the opera as proof of the opera's Japanese authenticity, they in fact disrupt the fantasy of the easy consumption and inhabitation of Japanese things and people.

Newspaper accounts of the Japanese Village registered curiosity about the Japanese, as well as predictable accounts of their racial difference. But unlike *The Mikado,* these seemed based at least on a desire for firsthand observation. The village itself was constructed to convey the sense that one had indeed traveled to Japan. The *Illustrated London News* reports,

> The experiment of transporting a complete village with its shops, tea-house, theatre, and place of worship, as well as their inhabitants, from warm, sunny Japan to murky London, during the coldest and dullest months of the year, has been a very bold, but an entirely successful one. The almond-eyed artisans are encamped in Humphrey's Hall, Knightsbridge, and look most wonderfully at home there. The planks for their shops, the platforms on which they sit, or rather squat, and the low desks, or tables, at which they work, have all been brought over bodily; and if only the sunshine, the blue sky, and the tropical foliage could have been added, the picture of Japanese life would have been perfect. As it is, the men and women evidently enjoy the joke immensely, glance up at their visitors with quick bright eyes, make remarks about them to one another in their strange, but not unmusical tongue, and go on with their work in the unhasting yet unresting manner which so eminently distinguishes the oriental from the western races.[11]

And yet the sensation of travel is mediated by the awareness that this is England, not Japan. If the observer notes that "the Japs tuck their feet up under them in the most comfortable fashion" and hears "a sound of barbaric, but not discordant, music [that] comes in single notes from the annex, where a vocal and instrumental performance is going on," at the same time he sees not only Japanese, such as "a remarkably pretty woman, with a complexion of roses and lilies and a sweet happy expression of face," who "flits about from stall to stall, inquiring how her compatriots fare in their new quarters." The observer also sees English people, describing "a couple of tiny children, with an unmistakably English nurse," who "toddle about in their warm long-sleeved blue frocks.[12]

The stated purpose of the exhibition was charitable rather than commercial. The *London Times* reported that the profits would be given to Mrs. O. Buhicrosan, "a Japanese who had embraced Christianity, and who, having been 20 years absent from her country, was anxious to return and to organize a mission there with the special object of improving the social position of women in that country."[13] Her book *Japan: Past and Present; The Manners and Customs of the Japanese* was made available to visitors for one shilling. The book gives a detailed description of Japanese history, geography and climate, customs, and culture of Japan, with an eye toward educating the reader about Japanese progress toward modernization. Mrs. Buhicrosan expresses her hope that the recognition and respect of Japan as a nation might indeed emerge with admiration of its craft:

> My readers will, perhaps, kindly bear in mind that a quarter of a century ago Japan was known to exist as it were only on a map; the Japanese were thought of (if indeed they were thought of at all) as being a semi-barbaric race, and it was only through an established intercourse with civilized and powerful nations that they became known, and that their Art Manufactures and products were introduced to, and admitted to be worthy of notice by, the representatives of Western Powers. At the same time I feel assured that many may be interested to glean some information concerning a people, who have during the last few years made progressive strides towards civilization and, by untiring energy and enterprise, have succeeded in raising themselves from comparative obscurity to a position of eminence in the eyes of Europe.[14]

The book reminds its Western readers that Japanese people were indeed worthy of being considered equals: "I have endeavoured to write impartially concerning my country, and to prove that the Japanese are worthy in many respects of being classed in the same category with great Western powers."[15] Mrs. Buhicrosan makes a special case for missionary work in Japan with regard to bringing about reforms for women. Her discussion of the problems of marriage is particularly impassioned:

> From the moment a Japanese maiden becomes a wife her troubles commence.... Hence, after bringing children into the world, it becomes her duty to attend and wait upon them as a menial, she being always a slave to her husband and her mother-in-law; her own parents she must scarcely think of. Should her husband ill-treat her or be guilty of infidelity she must not complain, but still toil unceasingly on; and should he even tire of his patient, suffering wife, and live in a state of concubinage, she can only humbly submit to the will and caprice of her lord and master.

Her book is geared to raise awareness of the need for reform, proposing that "marriage should no longer be looked upon in Japan as a civil obligation, but should be regarded in the light of a solemn religious ceremony placing both the husband and wife on an equal footing, and celebrated according to the rites and ceremonies of the Christian faith." Until marriage laws can be reformed, she insists, "civilized Europe will still look coldly upon Japan."[16]

Ironically, although the aim of the Knightsbridge Japanese Village was ostensibly to support the improvement of the status of Japanese women, Japanese visitors to the Knightsbridge exhibition such as Yano Fumio deplored how the Japanese were exhibited on a par with "Hottentots, or inhabitants of Madagascar or Sudan" and objected in particular to the display of women, music, and dance in the village. Sensitivity to these concerns by Japanese government officials, as Ayako Kano notes, made it increasingly difficult for Japanese performers to obtain visas for travel in the years following the exhibition.[17]

Thus the Knightsbridge Japanese Village had its foundations in nationalistic promotion, education, and cultural exchange; its connections to promoting the commodity fetishism of Japanese goods were more indirect. Newspaper accounts as well as the book insisted on the noncommercial function of the exhibition. One reviewer wrote, "Disappointment will assuredly be felt by some of the lady visitors when they see the quaint and fanciful productions of the hairpin makers and other artificers of pretty trifles, by the determination of the management not to permit anything to be sold, at all events until near the time for closing the exhibition. It has been thought best, however, not to make the affair a bazaar."[18] Although the framing of the exhibition reflected a desire to see the enterprise as in the service of cultural exchange rather than of profit, there was nonetheless inevitably a strong interest on the part of attendees in Japan arts and crafts. Though "the single-stick and theatrical performances attract large numbers of spectators . . . the most abiding interest seems to be that taken in the shops and artisans."[19] Mrs. Buhicrosan's book finishes with sections on each of the crafts demonstrated, with technical descriptions borrowed from Christopher Dresser's *Japan: Its Architecture, Art, and Art Industries* and Sir Rutherford Alcock's *Art and Industries of Japan*.

Japanese commodities did in fact carry weight in demonstrating, if not the advanced civilization, then at least the potential for civilization of Japan. Alcock, a former British consul-general to Japan and a noted expert on Japanese crafts, paid such a tribute in the inauguration ceremony:

The admiration and popular demand for every kind of Japanese work—fans, baskets, lacquer, bronzes—all were there, unrivalled in beauty and cheapness.... [He thought] the surpassing superiority of the work... was principally due to the painstaking character of the workmen. Their love of the work itself and constant desire to make each article the best of its kind and the excellence which resulted mutually aided each successive effort in their daily avocation, and left them with little desire of other greater enjoyment. There might be, no doubt, workmen in Japan, as elsewhere, who scamped their work and did not care how imperfect or fraudulent it was, but all he could say was that the conclusion he arrived at after living several years among them was that such cases were rare, for the main characteristic of all Japanese work was its conscientious perfection of detail in every particular, in that which was hidden as well as in that which was exposed to the eye, and this might be seen in the cheapest and most trifling toys almost as well as in the costly lacquered cabinet or the enameled *cloisonné*.[20]

The appeal of the Knightsbridge Japanese Village was in its display of the production of crafts and of the ever-diligent and dedicated workers. Unlike previous exhibitions, such as that of Japanese crafts at the 1862 World's Fair, and unlike the Japanese acrobats popular in the following decades, the emphasis was not just on the display of objects or on spectacular, exceptional bodies, but on the performance of work. This seems akin to what Bill Brown has described of anthropological displays, those museum and exhibition tableaux that became popular in the late nineteenth century. Such displays arranged figures in "occupational groups" that "constellated person, place, and thing into an absorbing drama, supposedly bringing a local culture to life."[21]

> These were the exhibits that wrested anthropology away from natural history and insisted that the meaning of things is disclosed by their function within a specific environment, not by their place within a history of technology.... Together the sketches and the exhibits help disclose the logic—or the synecdochal magic—whereby an object emanates an aura of culture, whereby an everyday object becomes a cultural thing. The tableau is an especially simple and thus powerful mode for producing such magic,

and it shows how much the cultural thing depends on our willingness to accede to what political economy would call the labor theory of value—to believe that what is "cultural" about a human artifact is what it tells us about the history of human work.[22]

Despite the overwhelming emphasis on labor and work, newspaper accounts of the Knightsbridge exhibition also expressed some concern about the inhabitants, calling them "guests." A correspondent reporting on the construction of the village in December 1884 finds, "The whole of the village will be under cover, and the weather will not, therefore, interfere with the pursuits and entertainments of its inhabitants, who are unacclimatized to London fog and humid cold."[23] Newspaper articles on the Knightsbridge exhibition stressed that the treatment of the workers was humane and imagined that the workers might be there for the purposes of cultural exchange and perhaps even mutual benefit. The *Illustrated London News* expressed a desire for "kindness" that goes beyond the terms of "business" when describing the

> Japanese men, women, and children—one hundred, we believe, in number who are now amusing the public at Knightsbridge, [who] display, although in a foreign land, the cheerfulness characteristic of the race. If they feel their temporary exile, they show no signs of homesickness, and seem as much amused as the spectators with their work and entertainments. The pleasure they are giving so many visitors daily makes one wish it were possible to give them some real pleasure in return before they leave the country. How this might best be done is a matter for discussion and arrangement. We do not know what would give the Japanese the greatest enjoyment and leave the most lasting impression on their minds; but this can be readily ascertained. And one would like them to see that even in this business-loving country there is a disposition to show a little kindness that is not business-like to strangers from the Far East. It may be remembered, by the way, that Mr. Buhicrosan's Japanese village is not a commercial speculation, but has been promoted with a charitable object.[24]

Despite these concerns, the Japanese Village became the site for tragedy in May 1885 when it caught fire. One Japanese man, "a young Japanese woodcarver named Ennemi,"[25] died in the blaze, which spread to the surrounding buildings. The artisans were temporarily relocated to Berlin, where the response was on the whole negative, especially regarding the "ugliness of the women."[26] The Knightsbridge exhibit reopened December 2, 1885, in a space that was "twice as large," and the improved village was reported to be "very much larger and more attractive than the one which met with such an untimely end."[27] The village ultimately closed in 1887, and the members dispersed.[28]

The Knightsbridge Japanese Native Village and its emphasis on working conditions presents a contrast with *The Mikado*, which highlights the magical qualities of the Japanese commodity without the more sordid aspects of the human work that produced it. Notably, in the opera itself there is a marked absence or devaluation of labor. Ko-Ko is both a tailor and an executioner, but never actually carries out either of those duties; in fact, his job as Lord High Executioner is imperiled when he is actually confronted with his duties as such. Nanki-Poo disguises himself as a second trombone, but declares himself no musician, a fact that Yum-Yum herself suspects "directly I heard you play!" Pooh-Bah has a multitude of official duties, but his quick assumption of each in fact renders these offices, from Lord High Exchequer to Groom of the Back Stairs, ridiculous. This undermining of work is consistent with imagining Japan as more aesthetic than material.

The Japanese Native Village in Knightsbridge and its American counterparts, which opened that following winter and spring, staged Japanese arts and crafts as the products of very human hands rather than as magical objects ready for consumption. Interestingly enough, the influence of *The Mikado* was felt on how these Japanese exhibitions were received in the United States. The Japanese Native Villages in New York, Boston, and Philadelphia were financed by the San Francisco–based Deakin brothers rather than being a presumably charitable enterprise. These backers had experience with both the import business and the stage. Walter and Frederic Deakin were the first to import Japanese goods to San Francisco in 1871; Frederic Deakin subsequently went to Japan, and the firm opened a manufacturing branch and emporium in Yokohama that exported and sold the products of three hundred workmen. Joined by their brother Harry Deakin, a theatrical manager who formerly ran Deakin's Academy of Music in Milwaukee and Deakin's Liliputian Opera Company, the brothers opened different versions of "A Veritable Japanese Village" on December 4, 1885, in New York's Madison Square Garden and subsequently in 1886 in

Horticultural Hall in Boston and in Philadelphia.[29] Not surprisingly, these exhibitions were unabashed in their commercialism. The *New York Times* reports of the Madison Square Garden exhibition, "The exhibition is unique and interesting, and it is likely to attract much attention in the city, to be a source of amusement and instruction for the people, and of profit for the managers."[30]

The Mikado plays an important role in making the American versions of the Japanese Native Villages intelligible. As the *New York Times* notes:

> The first sensation experienced upon entering the gaily-decked inclosure, with its two long rows of booths, is one of surprise that the busy artisans in their loose-fitting attire seem so familiar to us. We have all had the Japanese craze lately. We have been reading up on Japan, buying more or less authentic Japanese curios, and seeing "The Mikado"; so the obliging Kakemono painter, the newly married tailor working away at a blue crape kimono for his pretty bride, the industrious coppersmith, and the patriarchal silk weaver seem almost like old friends.[31]

A lengthy book by Mrs. Buhicrosan was the offered accompaniment to trips to the Knightsbridge Village; in contrast, those viewing the American versions were guided by short pamphlets with an eye toward increasing the consumer's appreciation of each exhibit. References to *The Mikado* abounded throughout these guides. The tea house, in particular, and the serving women within, were described:

> Very Japanese indeed, from the picturesque point of view, is the bamboo house with its thick, soft matting, and pot of tea boiling cheerfully in its box of coals. As the visitor advances, he is met by the pretty little woman with her shining hair and sweet smile, and offered a tiny cup of the Oriental beverage. All the romance of this domestic drama centers on this bamboo bower. Here are the representatives of the "Three little maids from school," and the chorus, who, doubtless, have many a little comedy of their own.

These "ladies of the Tea-House" were described as "very pretty, even to our ideas"; and directly compared with Yum-Yum, Pitti-Sing, and Peep-Bo: "As a race, they are naturally inclined to pose, and here are to be found the most picturesque attitudes, which, if they could be introduced into the opera of 'The Mikado,' would make it of intrinsic value from a realistic point of view."³² In the description of the tailor's shop, "the comic opera of 'The Mikado'" is credited for the "sudden discovery that the Japanese costume is capable of great beauty as a matter of adornment."³³

At the same time, the presumed familiarity with *The Mikado* presented its own problems. At least for some observers there was a tension between the relentless commercialism of the village and the fantasy world of the opera. One notes that the presence of the "three little maids ... tend[ed] to heighten the quaintness and romance of the scene—an effect that lasts until you see the best looking of the three draw from some mysterious spot in the folds of her gown a dirty white bag into which she drops the coin that that you give."³⁴ Another visitor to Boston's Japanese Village openly resented the commercialism, noting the "small, ridiculous trade in tiny teapots, painted paper and rice-flour carrots" as well as the "strong flavor of advertisement of a certain firm in Yokohama, Japan."³⁵

In both England and the United States, Japanese Native Villages were sites of management, negotiating the discrepancy between the admiration of beautiful objects and the work needed to produce them. While Alcock's lauding the Japanese craftsman's "painstaking character" suggests superior diligence and skill, the descriptions of the Japanese craftspeople in the United States highlight their "primitive" or exotic methods of production. The pamphlet noted that "there are some queer things connected with Japanese sewing" insofar that the tailor "with his lap full of crape, sits and slides his needle through, much as we put in a drawing string ... In a straight seam he wastes no time drawing the needle out at arm's length, but keeps it sliding through the cloth with considerable dexterity, meanwhile making use of his feet to hold the cloth in place."³⁶ Another description rendered the work of the cabinetmaker equally strange:

> Now he must use his saw. Is he going to put his work on a saw horse, or carpenter bench? Nay, this is not Oriental. He lays the board upon the floor, a little raised on his block, holds it firm in place with his left foot, and bending his head down to the floor, and making a singular loop of his entire body, he saws away free and unconstrained in this peculiar attitude.³⁷

These workers, while not pictured as completely brutish and uneducated, were described nonetheless as far from equally civilized. Their practices were seen to demonstrate Japanese racial inferiority, such as the descriptions of the "old weaver and his wife, a quaint looking pair... For weeks they labor setting these silken threads in the loom; one by one, in the most primitive fashion, regardless of time, have they been placed and stretched across the bamboo poles."[38] Their "primitive methods" are depicted as "fascinating" in showing "the processes of mind by which man came up from his childhood in the ages long ago. To be without steam power seems to us to-day as the distinguishing mark of a race still in its childhood."[39] Such descriptions of the exhibits simultaneously present the Japanese craftspeople as geniuses at their craft and as part of a simple and primitive race. The terms of *The Mikado* are ultimately reflected back onto the "queer and quaint" workers of the Japanese Villages.

Little was made of actual working conditions or the relationship between the Japanese inhabitants and their American viewers; rather, accounts emphasized how different crafts were magically produced by enigmatic people with remarkable Japanese powers. The guide relates, for instance, how the visitor might enter the "mysterious realm of the potter, with his fascinating wheel and obedient mass of clay, responding to his faintest wish, and rising before him into mystic shapes at will."[40] The description marvels, "What a world of patience must exist in an Oriental nature when he can devote himself to these details of ornamentation."[41] The same holds true for the glorious embroidery or decorative design rendered by the Japanese embroiderer or the Shippo designer. The former is praised for the choice of colors ("this race excels in the blending of hues, having an Oriental eye for gorgeous color effects");[42] the latter is described as "an artist of skill and genius" for his drawing on the copper vase "the thousand and one teeming fancies of his brain—the delicate and multitudinous tracery of a Japanese imagination."[43] The idealization of what is Japanese as being decorative rather than useful is clearly at play.

Thus Japanese workers were framed both as romanticized artisans and representatives of a primitive culture that magically produced rare and beautiful objects. Any glimpse into other dimensions of their working lives were momentary interruptions to the buzz of commerce that surrounded them. And yet one comment from the Boston edition of the guide does suggest that some anxieties might have intruded:

> The finest skilled labor in Japan has been specially gathered—doors, mats, samples, wares and tools, of a thousand descriptions—amounting in all to fifty tons, the whole being transported and produced in its present condition, at enormous expense direct from Japan.

> Not the least of the difficulties connected with this enterprise has been the human side of the question—the management of the little brown people so busy at work. That they may be contented, their wives, and, in several cases, their children, have been brought along, and when any of them becomes homesick, he is immediately returned to his native land, and another sent to take his place.[44]

The "human side of the question" is addressed, only to be quickly appeased. American viewers might well be contented with the assurance that these workers were humanely treated, much more humanely, in fact, than other oriental laborers whose skills were not so refined. In closing, the same pamphlet also comments on the courteous behavior of the workers.

> "As polite as a Japanese," is an expression already being formulated among us, and falling from lips daily, as a result of coming in contact with the courteous artists and artisans of this little village. Perhaps it might not be so flattering to know what they think of us. Indeed, it would not be strange if the potter at his wheel should have some very queer ideas of the greedy little hands held out and waved under his very eyes for "just another vase."[45]

Because the Japanese people are treated as exotic mysteries, the possibility that these workers might have "some very queer ideas" of their American spectators is voiced, only to be left unanswered. Ultimately, these Japanese workers are framed as "courteous artists and artisans" who never can speak directly to their working conditions or treatment. However, their very unintelligibility or silence keeps doubts alive. Unlike *The Mikado,* Japanese Native Villages provided a space of actual contact between white viewers and Japanese performers, exposing the inherent tensions within commodity racism's fantasies.

Oriental Exhibitions and the Absent Coolie

If even the carefully managed display of artisans in the Japanese Native Village could unsettle some of *The Mikado*'s fantasies, then more gritty depictions of labor presented an even deeper challenge to its "queer and quaint" Titipu. Interestingly enough, in Gilbert's original conception for the opera, he set the initial scene in "a Japanese market place" with a chorus of both "Japanese noblemen and market people (men and women) discovered."

This idea was subsequently altered, "for scenic reasons," to a palace courtyard. But though the new setting erased any direct allusion to commerce, Gilbert did make another intriguing revision in changing the chorus of characters from "market people,"[46] to "School-girls, Nobles, Guards, and Coolies." While the other roles have stated functions in the libretto, the "Coolies" are the only group who seem to have no discernible role. That Gilbert specifically listed coolies in the cast offers some speculation; *The Mikado*'s list of characters departs from other Gilbert and Sullivan operas, whose choruses may include more humble members such as "villagers," "citizens," and "pages," but nothing that specifically refers to the equivalent of the coolie. Perhaps the coolie signals only the rigid yet picturesque social hierarchy imagined in Japan; travel accounts often included references to and drawings of farm laborers or rickshaw operators. Yet the opera's plot offers no significant enactment of menial labor (though many productions fill out their casts with dancers or other performers transporting Katisha and the Mikado onto the stage) and only light-hearted references to work of any kind. The Japan of the opera is a fantasy not only of culture but also of magical work, a setting animated by characters whose connections to their occupations are arbitrary at best; thus a "cheap tailor" might be elevated to the Lord High Executioner, Pooh-Bah might serve in every other official capacity, and the Mikado's son might become a second trombonist (who, moreover, wanders with ballads and "native guitar" in hand) without any demonstrable musical ability.

This reference to coolies serves no crucial purpose for the opera's plot or characterization; such a dismissal acts as a reminder that those who do the lowest forms of work are conspicuously unimportant in the opera. In this the coolie differs from the craftspeople who inhabited the Japanese Villages and who were dignified, at least, by the public's appreciation of their craft. A coolie is not one of the picturesque "market people" first envisioned by Gilbert, but rather seems understood in the context of servant or laborer. Such servitude, as Vijay Prashad has pointed out, is commonly associated with field labor on the plantations of early capitalism. After the end of chattel slavery in Australia, South Africa, and the Caribbean, as well as South America, planters tried to hire convicts and freed slaves and then finally turned to thousands of British Indians and Chinese emigrants: "The word *coolie* entered the European lexicon in the context of imperialism to index a person of inferior status who simply labors for hire."[47] The term reminds us, Prashad suggests, of the most basic and degraded form of human labor:

Coolie is a word that produces, among Indian and Chinese people, the same gut response as does *nigger* among blacks. It has no established etymology; some place it from the Tamil *kuli* ("hire"), others find it in the use in sixteenth-century Portugal as *Koli*, after the name of a Gujarati community, still others notice that it sounds like the Chinese *ku-li* ("bitter labor") or like the Fijian *kuli* meaning "dog." One way or the other to be called a coolie is to be denigrated, and to be considered at best as a laborer with no other social markers or desires. The word *coolie* operates, then, like the nineteenth-century English word for factory worker, *hand* (where the entire ensemble of human flesh and consciousness is reduced to the one thing that is needed to run the mills of industrial capitalism).[48]

Including coolies in the list of characters in *The Mikado* seems strangely inconsistent with the opera's overall fantasy of Japan, evoking, as it does, the discrepancy between beautiful objects and menial labor. Even in the carefully managed space of the opera's fantasy, coolies are present but not accounted for.

We might contrast the decorative characterizations of *The Mikado* with a very different image of the Japanese as coolie labor and a racial threat, which came to a head in the United States with successive laws that limited and then barred Japanese immigration: the 1907 Gentlemen's Agreement with Japan, the 1917 Immigration Act that created the Asiatic Barred Zone, and the 1924 Johnson-Reed Act. But it would be a stretch to say that the association of Japanese immigrants with despised and feared coolies had any impact on early productions of *The Mikado*, even in the United States where anti-Asian sentiment was high. By the time Japanese immigrants arrived in large enough numbers to be deemed an economic and political threat to white interests, the opera was well established in its success. Yet we might dwell just a bit further on the relationship between how *The Mikado* stages the desire for Japanese objects and how it disavows the figure of the coolie, the lowest class in the imagined race to which these objects are intimately connected.

We begin by using this mention of coolies in *The Mikado* to shed some light on the relationship between japonaiserie and its predecessor chinoiserie. Though it is hard to find direct contrasts between the playful fantasies of *The Mikado* and depictions of Japanese immigration, there is a much more immediate parallel in the stark contrast between two comparable racial images: the equally popular and quaint objects of chinoiserie and racial stereotypes of the Chinese coolie that helped mobilize strong anti-Chinese sentiment, particularly in the United States.

Chinoiserie provided a space for japonaiserie and in turn for *The Mikado*. In Europe and the United States, interest in Chinese products created a lasting market for oriental objects in both the public square and the domestic space of the home. As David Porter has noted, the fantasies of chinoiserie drew from a "hedonistic conception of a mythical Cathy detached from time or place and given over to an anarchic abundance of disjointed images and delightfully meaningless signs" and played into "an aesthetic of the ineluctably foreign, a glamorization of the unknown and unknowable for its own sake."[49] The inaccessibility of China, commercially and politically, increased the perception of these objects' rarity, novelty, and value. Chinoiserie set a precedent for collecting Japanese objects and associating them with mystery, exoticism, and sensuality; it also gave them value as signs of luxury and wealth. Thus it is not surprising that elements of traditional Chinese style and décor inevitably make their way into productions of *The Mikado*. This confusion does not so much comment on the considerable influence of Chinese culture on Meiji Japan as it is about the larger racial categories into which both Chinese and Japanese are placed, categories created through the meaning and value placed on objects as well as on people.

From the history of chinoiserie we learn not only about its affinities with japonaiserie but also about the conditions under which one became less valuable and the other more so. Chinoiserie was on the wane by the time a more popular interest in Japanese objects began to rise. Dawn Jacobson suggests that chinoiserie's fall from favor had to do not only with a fashionable weariness but also with the interruption of the fantastical Cathay by a real China where familiarity bred contempt. In the mid-nineteenth century, China suffered great political losses to the British in the Opium Wars. China was defeated at Nanking in 1842, followed by the Treaty of Nanking by which Hong Kong was ceded to the British and four ports, including Shanghai, were opened to foreigners; Jacobson notes that "China was widely seen throughout Europe as a country of liars and fools, whose defences were pitifully weak and whose emperor's claims to universal sway were absurd and meaningless."[50] Chinoiserie also came to be associated with middle-class mass markets, losing something of its patrician value. In 1842, a London exhibit of Chinese art, financed by a rich American China-trade merchant, Nathan Dunn, "removed the last remnant of China's mystery":

> A specially built hall erected at Hyde Park Corner housed an immense array of the arts of the newly vanquished nation. Sections of temple, houses, rooms and shops were on display, fully furnished and available for further inspection. There were models of Chinese figures from all walks of life, together with the tools of their trades. There were hundreds of Chinese paintings and a number of architectural models. Anyone could walk in and see the real China; over 100,000 catalogues were sold at the door.[51]

Chinoiserie could no longer claim prestige through association with a powerful, inaccessible empire, nor, as this cheapened display suggests, could it claim to be the purview of the wealthy and cultural elite.

Japan's opening to the West provided a valuable decorative surrogate. In his writings on Japan, Sir Rutherford Alcock remarked on the "dead level mediocrity and immobility of the Chinese mind" and that Japan, like China, was "profoundly stirred up in its depths by the sudden contact of Europe" but might respond differently, since it was "not so steadily bent on a collective mediocrity."[52] Such a sentiment seems borne out by responses to both Japanese and Chinese exhibitions at late nineteenth-century world expositions. The Japanese exhibit at both the 1876 Philadelphia Centennial and at the 1893 Chicago World's Columbian Exposition helped popularize Japanese crafts in the United States. In 1876 Japan had a large and expensive exhibit at the Philadelphia Centennial, with 17,831 square feet in the main building, 284 separate exhibitors, and one of the nine foreign government buildings.[53] Observer James McCabe notes of the Philadelphia Japanese exhibit, "It is about three times as large as the Egyptian space, and is filled in every part with a rich and valuable display, the variety and beauty of which are one of the great surprises of the Exhibition."[54] McCabe describes many features of the Japanese exhibit with admiration, including "a number of bronze vases... which are the wonder and admiration of all visitors," and finds that "the work is unique and cannot be reproduced by the most skilful artificer in either Europe or America." The porcelains too draw superlatives: "The display of porcelains in this single department surpasses in beauty of forms and ornamentation the combined exhibit of every other nation in the building. One must see the collection here to realize this, but few will doubt the statement, having once made the comparison for themselves." McCabe ultimately concludes:

> The visitor who makes even a hasty inspection of the display of which we have given but a mere outline, must amend his ideas of Japan. We have been accustomed to regard that country as uncivilized, or half-civilized at the best, but we find here abundant evidences that it outshines the most cultivated nation of Europe in arts which are their pride and glory, and which are regarded as among the proudest tokens of their high civilization.

The smaller Chinese exhibit, on the other hand, does not draw the same praise. McCabe notes, "[It] is enclosed by a pavilion, the entrance to which is a copy of the portal of a celestial pagoda, gaudily painted and ornamented with hideous curled-up dragons, which, though ugly, are well carved." For McCabe, "Every part of the enclosure is of the gaudiest character, and here and there rise tall pagodas and towers, ornamented with the most brilliant colors. All the show-cases are in the Chinese style of architecture, and are as gay and odd-looking as the pavilion itself." He describes the lacquerware as "also very beautiful, but not equal to those in the Japanese collection." McCabe describes other Chinese objects with more enthusiasm; the silks are of the "finest quality" and the display of inlaid tables and stands and other articles of household use is found to be "as handsome and as well executed as anything of the kind in the Japanese section, which is saying a great deal."[55]

The rise of interest in Japan "at a time of Chinese decline was, perhaps, not accidental," as Rotem Kowner states:

> The opening of Japan facilitated its role to replace China and to be favourably perceived by the West: a charming, exotic, and relatively developed country. Japan, at least, seemed less stagnant than China, and its willingness to emulate the West was gratifying. Moreover, it was reputed to be a land of great beauty, and was much admired for its aesthetic style in certain artistic circles in the West. . . . Harold Isaac's chronology of Western attitudes toward the Chinese suggests that whenever China was despised, Japan was

in favor, and vice versa, and that this pattern was to repeat itself even after the Second World War.[56]

However, relating this pattern to the relative valuation of Chinese and Japanese objects by the West is not so simple. China's prominence may have suffered decline, but in the second half of the nineteenth century Japan also was under Western domination, rising slowly into political and military strength only in the new century.

We might explore another dimension of the decline of chinoiserie and rise of japonaiserie. One significant difference, at least around the time of *The Mikado*'s opening, was in the visible and politically sensitive presence of Chinese immigrant labor and the relative absence of Japanese coolies. In the United States in particular, the interest in chinoiserie as a signal of privilege and luxury collided violently with the actual presence of Chinese immigrant labor. By the time of *The Mikado*'s premiere in 1885, the large-scale immigration of Chinese had already begun to inspire the anti-Chinese sentiment that so easily extended to anti-Japanese feeling later in the twentieth century. As Robert Lee states, Chinese immigrant labor was designated "coolie labor" in order to alleviate the tensions felt after wage labor declined in value after the 1870s:

> The myth of the Chinese coolie laborer allowed white American workers, both native-born and immigrant, to racialize a stratum of wage work equated with wage slavery while reserving for whites a semi-artisan status within the wage labor system.... The construction of coolieism was an attempt to insulate the white working-class family from the worst consequences of proletarianization by defining the lowest stratum of menial work as fit only for the coolie or the nigger, and preserving the ideal of artisan labor, with its hope for upward mobility, for the white working man and his family.[57]

Such a myth would prove formative in the legislation against Chinese immigrants that barred both their entry and their ability to settle as landowners, husbands, and citizens. The anti-Chinese movement framed the immigrant as posing a threat not only to white working-class labor interests (a main force behind the eventual success of anti-Chinese legislation in the U.S. Chinese Exclusion Act of 1882) but also to the domestic space of the home.

The degraded racial status of the Chinese coolie could not be reconciled with the more patrician forms of orientalism. This is illustrated clearly within the lyrics of Septimus "Sep" Winner's "The Coolie Chinee" (1871), a comic song that clearly references the familiar stereotypes of the anti-Chinese movement. The song portrays a "Coolie Chinee" with "skin... the color of coffee and milk," and a "queu... that reaches way down to his knee." Using a chorus of gibberish "Hong Kong, Oolong; Hari Kari, ding-a-dong" in "a nasal tone," the song details the oddities of the "elegant," and yet "terrible," "troublesome," and "cunning" figure who is employed as a cheaper option for domestic work than the Irish immigrant or African American servant ("We sent off our Biddy and also our cook / Because that their wages were high"). He serves his employers "our little pet cat" and a "cussed old rat" for meals, accompanied by "a cup of steaming hot tea"; likewise, when the family buys him "a silk hat and a duster so neat / To keep off the sun and the dirt," he confuses these items: "But the hat for a basket to market he took, / And the duster he wore for a shirt." Ironically, some of the greatest faults of the "Coolie Chinee" are that he misuses his Chinese counterparts, the imports that also might trace their origins back to China. Ultimately, the final words of the song urge the listener against the hiring of the "Coolie Chinee":

> Oh never be foolish, dear people, I pray,
> Oh never be silly like me,
> And if you need help, in the future, I pray,
> Engage not a COOLIE CHINEE.[58]

The allure of Chinese objects contrasts with anti-Chinese sentiment, and the figure of the Chinese American immigrant laborer is associated with cheap labor, unintelligible manners, and the disruption of the easy consumption of Chinese imports.

During his 1882 D'Oyly Carte–funded tour of the United States, Oscar Wilde commented on the incongruity of the juxtaposition of beautiful china with a brutish Chinese worker:

> If everything is dainty and delicate, gentleness and refinement of manner are unconsciously acquired. When I was in San Francisco I used to visit the Chinese Quarter frequently. There I used to watch a great hulking Chinese workman at his task of digging, and used to see him every day drink his tea from a little cup as delicate in

texture as the petal of a flower, whereas in all the grand hotels of the land, where thousands of dollars have been lavished on great gilt mirrors and gaudy columns, I have been given my coffee or my chocolate in cups an inch and a quarter thick. I think I have deserved something nicer."[59]

Even though Wilde suggests a degree of refinement for the "great hulking Chinese workman," he clearly was not above declaring him worthy of exclusion. During his lecture at San Francisco's Platt's Hall, he is reported to have quipped to a receptive audience, when praising the beauty of Whistler's Peacock Room, "But don't borrow any Chinese art, for you have no need of it any more than you have need of Chinese labor"—a piece of advice that was hailed by the anti-coolie esthetes near the door with loud applause."[60]

Christopher Bush noted that the Chinese laborer was associated with "the dehumanizing effects of industrial labor," representing "the horrors of modernity by embodying both its abstractness (as faceless working mass) and the unfortunate realities of the actual conditions of 'free' labor." The Japanese worker, in contrast, was "imagined to be a kind of atavistic remainder of something very much like the noble Anglo-Saxon medieval handwork whose final traces were being lost to industrial modernity," suggesting the lure of what is figured as "premodern, a utopian modernity of consumption, one in which beautiful things are cheaply available to all, with no alienated labor at the base of the economic pyramid."[61] In the Japanese Native Villages or other exhibitions, Japanese workers could still be seen as the ideal of artisan labor rather than as the "hulking" worker representing wage slavery. McCabe's description of the Chinese exhibit at the Philadelphia Exhibition of 1876 assumes familiarity, even homeliness: "Two elaborate bedsteads are exhibited, which are very handsome, and show that John Chinaman has an eye to solid comforts in the midst of all his love of gaudy colors and gingerbread ornaments"; it also smacks of real encounters with a not-so-dignified clientele: "a number of almond-eyes, pigtailed celestials, in their native costumes, are scattered through the enclosure, and you may for a moment imagine that you have put the sea between you and the Exhibition and have suddenly landed in some large Chinese bazaar."[62] In his description of the Japanese exhibit, however, McCabe describes only an imagined gentry: "The Japanese gentleman takes great pride in his collection of screens, which embody the best pictorial art of his country, and regards them as the European or American does his gallery of paintings."[63]

Other spectators at the Philadelphia exhibition also did not hesitate to compare the Japanese positively in comparison to both the Chinese exhibits and the Chinese bodies they supposedly represented. Marietta Holley's fictional and folksy commentator Samantha concludes that "China and Japan are both queer, but Japan's queerness has an imaginative artistic quirl to it that China's queerness don't have."[64] Edward Bruce comments that if Japan was China's student, "the pupil has surpassed the teacher."[65] One might attribute the negative light that China was cast in to the relative inferiority of the exhibits, the novelty and quality of Japanese craftsmanship, and a perceived deterioration in Chinese imports; the Chinese exhibit simply may not have been as remarkable as the Japanese exhibit was clearly felt to be. But in these and other responses, there is clearly something more than an artistic judgment at play. One newspaper account concludes, "We relegate the Chinese to the half-civilized class without hesitation, or without feeling that any indignity has been offered, and this fact shows what an important difference there is between Japanese and Chinese civilization."[66] Notably, observers of the exhibits at the Chicago exhibition also reiterated this difference. Julian Hawthorne (Nathaniel Hawthorne's son) found Japanese art humorous and lively, but Chinese humor reminded him of a "weird grimace," and he assumed the Chinese were "without souls" in their "worship of antiquity and their earthly everlastingness."[67] For Mrs. D. C. Taylor, China was a "strange, cold, homeless, heartless, heathen land" filled with "down-trodden women, priests, and tyrant-ridden men," and a "strange depression of mind and sickness of heart" came over her when she thought of the Celestial Kingdom. Japan, however, was quite different for her, and the "suave, smiling" Japanese just the opposite of the "pigtailed, avaricious Chinese."[68] Finally, H. G. Cutler reflects, "The Japanese have not the staid, placid dispositions of the Chinese. They are more light-hearted, and even at table often enliven the simple courses with music upon the guitar."[69] The musical turn of this attribution contrasts with the *New York Times* description of the Japanese workers building the official pavilion for the Philadelphia Centennial decades earlier: "Contrary to what has been observed of the Chinese in California and the mining regions, the children of the Flowery Land do not burst into song when plying the implements of carpentry, but work away in absolute silence."[70]

In the United States at least, the intense admiration of the beauty and exoticism of the oriental object was clearly at odds with the revulsion and fear of oriental bodies that prompted exclusion laws and violence. If the Chinese immigrant body detracted from chinoiserie's value, perhaps the relative invisibility of the Japanese immigrant worked to favor japonaiserie as a satisfactory replacement of oriental décor. The popularity of Japanese things was related not only to Japan's aura of novelty and mystery and the high quality of its products, but also to the conspicuous absence of its people. At the time of *The Mikado*'s U.S. premiere in 1885, the wave of Japanese immigrant labor had yet to arrive, with only 2,039 Japanese on the U.S. mainland in 1890. Within two decades, the Japanese would surpass the Chinese in number, 72,257 to 71,531; after twenty more years had passed, with Chinese exclusion firmly in place, the Chinese population had remained virtually constant, while the Japanese had nearly doubled to 138,834.[71] Japonaiserie's value for at least several decades would be secure from contamination by the actual presence of laborers whose bodies could not be easily aestheticized. *The Mikado* could breathe easy in a space only casually interrupted by the presence of the artisan and relatively free from the threat of the hulking laborer and the servile coolie.

· Chapter 3 ·

Magical Objects and Therapeutic Yellowface

AT THE HEIGHT of *The Mikado*'s first wave of popularity, Chicago's leading society matron Mrs. Marshall Field gave a Mikado Ball in honor of her son and daughter. The *Chicago Tribune* reported that the Field residence was "transformed into a Japanese Palace" complete with screens, silk and satin hangings, gigantic parasols, bronze statues, porcelain vases, and party favors designed by James Whistler. About four hundred friends of seventeen-year-old Marshall Field Jr. and twelve-year-old Miss Ethel attended, with

> every one of them . . . in full Japanese costume from wig down to sandals. Roguish cheeks and lips had been made redder by the vermilion of the Jap, and many of them showed that they had practiced effectually at the mincing walk of the various comic-opera Japs.[1]

On September 1, 2007, a similar set of attractions inspired the Mikado Ball organized by PEERS (Period Events and Entertainments Recreation) at the Masonic Lodge of San Mateo, California.[2] Though presumably less lavish than Mrs. Marshall Field's event, it similarly involved dancing to the tunes of Sir Arthur Sullivan and dressing up either in "evening dress of the late 19th century" or in "costumes inspired by the operas of Gilbert and Sullivan, including 'The Mikado,'" "from the most refined Lord High Executioner to the most deliciously evil Bad Baronet; from the most demure Japanese maiden to the most dashing Daughter or Pirate of Penzance."

We have described how a distinctive commodity racism defined the first yellowface productions of *The Mikado*, setting the terms of subsequent *Mikado* productions. The opera turns the commodity fetishism of japonaiserie into a popular, accessible mode of performance. Its display of fans, spectacular costumes, clever lyrics and dialogue, and catchy tunes proved a winning combination, as shown in its rampant reproduction. As *Mikado* productions and variations filled the spaces of public and private performance, the lure of this fantasy of Titipu became almost irresistible—particularly because it could claim both the pleasure of playing Japanese and the freedom of pure invention.

The allure of playing Japanese through evoking the fantasies of Gilbert and Sullivan's opera can be as attractive today as in 1885. How is this possible? For the most part, playing *The Mikado* does not seem to strike either performers or audiences as cross-racial pretense, even though there are both momentary and more sustained instances of protest (such as the Asian American drama listerv suggests). The opera by no means prompts the outrage that blackface still does, even though rooted in similar comic and musical traditions. One possible reason has to do with proximity: the racial fantasies of *The Mikado* have all to do with distance, both figurative and actual. Where blackface minstrelsy suggests a similar mode of typecasting through impersonation, it also plays off an assumed familiarity; the impulses of "love and theft," as Eric Lott has suggested, are inspired by a sense of intimacy. The libidinal desires inherent in *The Mikado*'s brand of yellowface emphasize Japaneseness as deeply foreign and its attractions as those of the alien: novelty, mystery, strangeness, and difference. Engagement with this fantasy of Japan promises excitement, escape, and even liberation from one's own identity.

This lightness gives *The Mikado* a certain adaptability and buoyancy in the present that, when coupled with Sullivan's memorable score, has carried many a production to success. The widespread popularity of the opera, however, does not mean that all is right in Titipu. *The Mikado* may not allow its coolies center stage, but at the same time the queer and quaint images of Japan that it offers may not be as impervious as they seem. We have examined, for instance, how the display of Japanese workers in the Native Villages interrupts as well as supports the commodity racism of *The Mikado* and japonaiserie. As we shall see, subsequent productions and responses to the opera pose other challenges by responding to the place of Japan on the world stage, different attitudes toward Japan, and the interruptions to privilege of the white performance of yellowface by other racial actors, including some "yellows" themselves. As the preceding chapter suggested and later chapters will confirm, the history of the opera demonstrates multiple anxieties around racial representation, anxieties that grow in complexity as multiple racial formations interact and accrue over time. However, in this last chapter of Part I, let us for a moment contemplate how the particular pleasures of the opera so prevalent in 1885 still draw audiences in the present. Two contemporary views of the opera—one for the stage and one cinematic—reflect back on the opera's original productions and the initial moments of *Mikado* madness.

The first example, productions in the 1980s and 1990s directed by Christopher Renshaw and designed by Tim Goodchild, specifically highlights *The Mikado*'s fascination with commodities. The second, Mike Leigh's award-winning 2000 film *Topsy-Turvy*, provides a much heavier critical understanding of the opera that nonetheless falls under the spell of another familiar fantasy of Japan as a source of creative and spiritual rejuvenation for the modern Western artist. Though radically different in conception and effect, both help us think about the legacies of 1885: the lasting appeal of the opera's spectacular commodity racism and the deeper satisfactions of playing Japanese.

Christopher Renshaw's Magical Objects

Until its final demise from lack of funding in 1982, the D'Oyly Carte Opera Company set the standard for performing Gilbert and Sullivan. Painstakingly repetitive and carefully controlled staging, gesture, delivery, design, and orchestration bred both familiarity and contempt, seen by diehard fans as having "simple charm"[3] and by others as petrification. For the performers, adherence to the style was serious business. Kenneth Sandford, the company's principal baritone from 1957 until 1982 (Pooh-bah in the 1966 videorecording), found "a kind of upper class gentility pervading the principal's dressing rooms—a sort of public school ambience—and the cloister-like quiet backstage, as if the company was taking part in some time-honoured ritual far too serious to warrant any light-hearted banter."[4]

For nearly one hundred years of performing *The Mikado*, the D'Oyly Carte style defined an authoritative Japaneseness whose appearance was defined by elaborate latex headpieces and wigs, heavy eye makeup, and spectacular costumes, and whose gestural vocabulary included mincing steps, fluttering fans, and exaggerated bowing. This definitive style of playing can be seen in the 1939 Schertzinger film and the 1966 videorecording of the D'Oyly Carte Company with the City of Birmingham Symphony, directed by Anthony Besch. Different performance choices became trademarks of the opera, as fixed as elements of the libretto or score. In an interview, longtime Savoy member Donald Adams recalled that when he took over the role of the Mikado from Darrell Fancourt, he wanted to change, among other things, Fancourt's characteristic laugh: "I went to Bridgit D'Oyly Carte and told her I didn't want to become a carbon copy. I wanted to try out some things of my own." Bridgit D'Oyly Carte "understood, told me to go ahead and said she would inform me when I had stepped over the mark." Having received permission, Adams did not change the laugh, but rather developed a variation that "begins much like Fancourt's, but I wanted to top his, so the second time, mine is more extended."[5] This tradition was to some extent aided by the law because, with the significant exception of the United States, the legal hold that D'Oyly Carte exerted over Gilbert and Sullivan productions prevented any experimentation until 1962.

In many ways, the productions directed by Christopher Renshaw in England, Australia, and the United States from 1983 to 2004 depart consciously from this tradition. These productions originated in 1983 at London's Sadler's Wells Opera, then moved to the Sydney Opera House to celebrate the centennial for the opera house. With striking sets and costumes designed by Tim Goodchild, Renshaw also staged similar productions at England's Opera North, the Opera Pacific in Orange County, and the State Opera of South Australia. A videorecording of the Opera Australia production, released in 1990, suggests Renshaw's playful and engaging style. He has described his overt departure from D'Oyly Carte tradition and his desire to "kick" the more traditional style of Gilbert and Sullivan opera "in the nether regions": We have a wonderful word in England called 'twee,' which is untranslatable.... The style [of Gilbert and Sullivan opera] was very twee—very unisexual, unforward, very nice, like taking tea. [My staging] is raucous and sexy and very popularistic in its approach."[6] This departure from D'Oyly Carte tradition is signaled openly when, in the first act finale of the Opera Australia version, Pish-Tush (John Germain) is chided by Pooh-Bah (Gregory Yurisich) for his overly exuberant cymbal-playing; he retorts "Well, that's the way we did it at the D'Oyly Carte, I tell yeh!" Audience members familiar with D'Oyly Carte have the pleasure of recognizing these innovations, and for those who are not familiar, allusions such as this hammer the difference home.

Yet the D'Oyly Carte traditions are by no means dispensed with. Of a 1983 performance, reviewer Noel Goodwin noted, "Instead of profiting from lapsed copyright to revivify a fossilized tradition," the New Sadler's Wells version "seemed concerned to put back by the D'Oyly Carte-load the fidgety choruses, hops and skips, madly twirling parasols and other meaningless gestures."[7] Certain characteristic elements are retained, such as the mincing steps of the chorus of the "gentlemen of Japan," Ko-Ko's (Graeme Ewer) clowning with his ax, and Yum-Yum's (Anne-Maree McDonald) graceful posing in "The Sun Whose Rays." The Mikado (Robert Eddie) ends "My Object All Sublime" in a characteristic pose with upturned hand and fan. At the same time, performers are kept busy embellishing these traditional movements. At the end of "Three Little Maids" Yum-Yum uses a drill-sergeant whistle to direct the others to unfurl their fans in unison. The mincing and bowing of the Gentlemen of Japan becomes a set of stylized movements mimicking London businessmen on trains and subways. Nanki-Poo (Peter Cousens) is transformed into a seductive and rebellious roué who rides a bicycle during "A Wandering Minstrel, I"; however, the movement of the chorus accompanying him still echo the gestures established in Gilbert's promptbooks. The ladies' chorus poses elegantly in D'Oyly Carte fashion for "Braid the Raven Hair," but they also blow bubbles. The Mikado's characteristic laugh dissolves into a snicker that sounds more like Bert Lahr's Cowardly Lion in *The Wizard of Oz* (or, for more contemporary viewers, the cartoon canine Scooby-Doo).

D'Oyly Carte's "Japanese" gestures are juxtaposed with styles of Hollywood film, British comedy, and music hall to produce the effect of dissonance between what is British and Japanese, modern and traditional, familiar and foreign. Costumes, a crazy quilt of Japanese, Victorian, and contemporary styles—kimonos combined with schoolgirl collars and knickers, or with bowler hats, kid gloves, carnations, trousers, and spats—enhance this effect. Most memorable are these productions' use of stage objects and design. In the Opera Australia version, the opening curtain is embellished with a host of Victorian advertisements, including a reproduction of the familiar 1885 Savoy playbill as well as ads for Beecham's Pills, Liberty's Art Fabrics, Cycles Clément, Beecham's Music Portfolio featuring "Banjo Praises," and Katisha's Corsets. Prominently placed at the center of the curtain is an image of a "geisha" Queen Victoria positioned on a fan. The Gentlemen of Japan carry briefcases and umbrellas as well as fans that read "The Times." Nanki-Poo enters riding a bicycle, and the "train of little ladies" rides a railcar made of parcels. The ladies' chorus carries not only fans and parasols but also butterfly nets, lollipops, tennis rackets, field hockey sticks, balloons, and a soccer ball. The Mikado and Katisha become figurines on a mantelpiece, seated next to a stack of gigantic Gilbert and Sullivan librettos.

Renshaw consciously foregrounds the opera's connections to japonaiserie, which he described as "just a fashion statement of that age, which was restlessly looking for things that were new."[8] But rather than providing a more pointed commentary on nineteenth-century British culture's commodity racism, these productions play up the pleasurable dimension of this fashion so that its racial dimensions are notably muted. They do so by framing the craze for Japanese objects as part of a larger world of antique Victorian clutter, repositioning the opera as an amiable celebration of commodity fetishism rather than as a more troubling representation of a fictive Japan. The opera thus subsumes the Victorian obsession with collecting Japanese things into a contemporary fascination with Victoriana, the current interest in the nineteenth century that Cora Kaplan describes as "a complementary miscellany of evocations and recyclings . . . a constellation of images which became markers for particular moments of contemporary style and culture."[9]

In the patrician setting of the Sydney Opera House, at least, the considerable musical and dramatic talents of the performers are emphasized over any racial mimicry. Yet these productions still remind us how difficult it is to leave behind the oversized and overdetermined icons of Japaneseness with its equally weighty reminders of Victorian racialization. The blended look of Japanese and Victorian English costume is by no means a seamless hybrid, but is yoked together in ways that seem cumbersome and even, in the case of the heavily made-up and awkwardly garbed figures of the Mikado and Katisha, even monstrous. The juxtaposition of what is familiar and what is figured as Japanese and foreign still generates much of the spectacular effect as well as the humor of these productions. In the videotaped Opera Australia version, audience laughter is heard not only at various modernizations, such as the topical references to particular politicians in office and national scandals and the pointed use of Australian slang, but also at the racialized humor of Ko-Ko's improvisational clowning, complete with karate chops and aggressive cries of "Daihatsu," "Honda," and finally, "Kiri Te Kanawa!" After Ko-Ko and Katisha's duet, "There Is Beauty in the Bellow of the Blast," a backdrop descends with a picture of a Victorian valentine inscribed "Love is a virtue that Endures For Ever"—and in smaller letters, "Made in Japan." Such moments comment on the continued space the opera provides for commentary on contemporary fantasies of Japan as a source of foreign imports.

This implicit commentary, however, remains overshadowed by full-scale enjoyment of the spectacular nature of the objects themselves. In the Renshaw productions, the pleasure of *The Mikado* is not only that of a nostalgic look at Victorian commodities but also the sheer magic of their modern staging. Familiar Japanese things take on a new life, as characters pop in and out of giant porcelain vases, stand on huge Willow pattern plates, emerge from lacquered chests, or pose in front of massive fans. Pitti-Sing struggles to pour tea from an oversized teapot. Katisha (Heather Begg) drives a chariot made from a gigantic vase. Yum-Yum bathes for her wedding in a huge porcelain jar, pulling out a series of rubber ducks for comic effect. In the final scene, Pish-Tush feeds the Mikado his lunch with enormous chopsticks. Renshaw's production recalls the spectacular display of japonaiserie in the 1885 *Mikado,* yet the objects on Renshaw's stages no longer serve to draw the audience into a representation of Japanese life. The production invents new uses for these objects: parasols become shields or turn into displays of fireworks; fans serve as screens, swords, or executioner's blocks. As these Japanese things become grossly enlarged or are put to new and ingenious uses, they recall the obsession with things Japanese at the heart of the opera's first productions.

The japonaiserie of 1885 promoted a fiction of Japan, the knowledge of which was gained not through direct contact with people but by the possession of exotic objects. In turn, these items were not valued for their usefulness but rather for their ability to transform the domestic space with a touch of magic. This magic rubbed onto yellowface performance, whereby racial transformation promised immediate pleasure as well as more profound salutary effects.

Beginning with the 1885 *Mikado*s, objects came to stand in for what is Japanese, robbing people of the power to signify themselves. Within this dynamic, it no longer mattered whether these objects had any actual connection to Japan (after all, the Willow pattern china was manufactured in England); the world of Titipu became known not as a flawed copy of Japan but as its own reality. The Renshaw productions build on this dynamic, whereby magical things define performances and give the stage its true vitality. That this production concept has traveled so well from London to Orange County, California, and to Sydney, Australia, testifies to how it is concept driven rather than performer driven. Any racial commentary necessarily becomes subsumed within these spectacular effects. Thus *The Mikado* becomes "lite" once more, buoyed by a blithe eclecticism that seems to wipe the opera free of racial intent.

Mike Leigh's *Topsy-Turvy*

In contrast to the Renshaw version, Mike Leigh's much-acclaimed 1999 film *Topsy-Turvy*[10] brings our attention back to the racial significance of yellowface. By creating a behind-the-scenes film about the opera's 1885 premiere, Leigh presents an engaging and moving portrait of his characters. The understandings of *The Mikado* presented in these two versions seem radically different. Renshaw's productions highlight the particular power of objects, featuring displays of japonaiserie and Victoriana that carry the show, regardless of its particular casting. *Topsy-Turvy*, in contrast, emphasizes characterization and the work of individual performers. Renshaw's productions create a postmodern pastiche of dazzling effects that erases distinctions between past and present delights; Leigh, on the other hand, deliberately chooses to undercut what he calls a "chocolate box" approach to period drama.[11]

> But I certainly thought it would be a good idea and somehow [a] healthy and necessary thing to cut through the layers and layers of encrustations and rusty barnacles of bad performances, all those fat middle-aged people pretending to be young in croaky voices—the arch conceit of it all. That's not what it's about. It's much healthier than that, and much more organic and lively. And I just wanted to kind of get back to the essence of the thing, for what it's worth."[12]

But within this gritty realism, the film also does its share of racial imagining whereby performing *The Mikado* offers the promise of authentic cultural contact and Titipu becomes a space to play out a restorative fantasy of Japan. The film helps us understand *The Mikado* in terms of a more serious side of the Japan craze. T. J. Jackson Lears and Mari Yoshihara have suggested that a therapeutic or liberatory sensibility might be inherent in the Victorian penchant for Japanese art. Lears suggests that for those seeking to escape the neuroses of modern industrialized life, "premodern art promised spiritual comfort and therapeutic restoration."[13] In other words, *The Mikado* offers a way of *inhabiting* the beautiful world of Japanese things, a mode of performance that served to alleviate anxieties about the ills of modern life and to offer alternative ways of being. As a variety of scholars have documented, many artists, writers, intellectuals, politicians, travelers, and collectors from the later nineteenth into the twentieth century sought to satisfy multiple kinds of desire—aesthetic, spiritual, personal—through engagement with Japan.[14] In comparison with these endeavors, *The Mikado* seems a quick fix, hardly to be taken seriously. But Leigh's film does its best to stage the story of the opera in these terms.

The film details the tumultuous partnership of Gilbert, Sullivan, and Carte leading up to the premiere of *The Mikado*. In the early part of the film, Sullivan (Allan Corduner) and Gilbert (Jim Broadbent) have reached impasses in their creative life. Reviewers accuse Gilbert's *Princess Ida* of exhibiting "symptoms of fatigue," and Sullivan frets that "my orchestrations are becoming repetitious." He expresses serious reservations about continuing to work with Gilbert's "artificial and implausible situations." Their collaboration is in danger of ending, with Sullivan threatening to break his contract with D'Oyly Carte in order to concentrate on grand opera rather than "trivial soufflés," and Gilbert complaining of his inability to write a story that might suit his musical partner. This impasse affects more than just the reputations of Gilbert and Sullivan. One early scene depicts a dialogue between performers after a particularly difficult performance of *Princess Ida,* which has been made more trying by the effects of a heat wave. Savoy performer Richard Templeton (Timothy Spall) worries about the strain on his voice and playing before half-empty and inattentive houses: "One's knocking one's pipes out in a vain attempt to elicit a response from three colonial bishops, two elderly ladies, and an intoxicated costermonger. They're all roasting in their own lard like the Christmas goose." Templeton's real concern, however, is about the future of the Gilbert and Sullivan operas, on which his own career depends; he tells tenor Durward Lely (Kevin McKidd), "I fear that dear Mr. Gilbert has run out of ideas."

Ironically, it is *The Mikado* that helps resurrect some kind of authenticity and profound artistic commitment from the light "topsy-turvydom" of Gilbert and Sullivan's earlier work. In a pivotal sequence, Gilbert's creative block is removed when his long-suffering wife Lucy (or "Kitty," played by Lesley Manville) asks him to accompany her to the Knightsbridge Japanese Native Village. There he is deeply affected by the swordplay, dance, and music of Japanese performers; the film shows the apocryphal moment when a decorative Japanese sword, presumably from the exhibition, falls off his wall. He picks up the sword and engages in a moment of mock fighting, grimacing and uttering unintelligible imitations of the Japanese performers he has seen. Finally, a broad smile appears on his face as he has a sudden moment of inspiration. The next scene shows the chorus singing

"Behold the Lord High Executioner," followed by Grossmith's entrance as Ko-Ko. In the following scene, Gilbert presents his new libretto to a now-laughing Sullivan.

In the making of the film, Leigh paid excessive attention to re-creating historical detail, such as period objects, even going so far as to using specially made lightbulbs and interior wallpaper that would be faithful to the 1885 setting.[15] Despite careful attempts at historical fidelity in other aspects of the film, Leigh rearranged one important aspect of the opera's genesis: the timing of the opening of the Japanese Native Village in Knightsbridge. In the film, the resolution of Gilbert's creative crisis is prompted by his trip to the Japanese Native Village. But in reality, by the time the Japanese Village had opened, Gilbert and Sullivan were already deeply involved in the composition of the opera. On May 20, 1884, Gilbert had already sent to Sullivan the sketch of his plot for *The Mikado*, of which Sullivan wrote, "I think the subject excellent—funny."[16] Many of the numbers, including "Three Little Maids," had already been conceived by the time the Japanese exhibition opened on January 10, 1885.[17] Leigh has openly acknowledged that he changes this time frame: "There are one or two actual, factual deviations from the truth, the most basic of which is that Gilbert thought of *The Mikado* before the Japanese exhibition opened in London in 1884," because in his words, "It was actually more dramatically interesting for him to get the idea by going there."[18]

What is "dramatically interesting" is how, through this and other seemingly minor alterations, Gilbert is portrayed as having been inspired by a deep moment of cultural contact rather than by a more superficial exposure to japonaiserie. This is in keeping with the larger premise of the film in which communion with real Japanese people—rather than objects—becomes a necessary part of the larger revitalization of Gilbert and his company.

In another key scene, Gilbert brings in three Japanese women from Knightsbridge, accompanied by a Japanese man, to teach his Three Maids—Leonora Braham as Yum-Yum (Shirley Henderson), Sybil Gray as Peep-Bo (Cathy Sarah), and Jessie Bond as Pitti-Sing (Dorothy Atkinson)—how to use their fans and walk properly. This scene rings true with Leigh's historical sources, such as François Cellier's account of how Japanese inhabitants of the Knightsbridge Village attended rehearsals for the first *Mikado* and helped develop some of the choreography for the production:

As usual, the ladies proved more apt pupils than the men. Most apt of all, perhaps, were the "Three little Maids from School," who fell into their stride (if such a term can be applied to the mincing step of the East) with remarkable readiness, footing their measures as though to the manner born.[19]

Yet *Topsy-Turvy* again changes subtle details in its rendition of this history. Cellier's account suggests that at least one of the Japanese brought into the rehearsal understood enough English to make himself a valuable contributor to the coaching:

> The Japanese dancer was a fairly accomplished linguist. The little gentleman artist was far too polite and refined to need any of the rude and hasty vernacular common to the impatient British stage-manager of the old school. For polished adjectives or suitable pronouns he would turn to the author, or, it might be, to Mr. John D'Auban, who was, as usual, engaged to arrange the incidental dances.[20]

In Leigh's film the Japanese man, though dressed in Western clothing, is unable to understand any of Gilbert's directions; neither he nor his bewildered female counterparts have much to do with the actual direction of the scene. These Japanese characters, though Cellier and others identified them as dancers, do not contribute any artistic skills to the *Mikado* cast; their presence is valuable only insofar as they "naturally" model the presumably typical Japanese gait and manner. Leigh's scene highlights again how *The Mikado*'s success came from a creative genius that places value on Japanese authenticity. The scene emphasizes cultural insensitivity—Gilbert only shouts louder at the Japanese villagers when it becomes clear that they don't understand English—but it also lauds Gilbert's departure from the stock racial caricature. Gilbert's desire for his performers to move in new and exciting ways "in the Japanese manner," is contrasted to the predictably comic music hall movements previously taught to them by choreographer John D'Auban (Andy Serkis). The success of Gilbert's inspiration is confirmed in the scene immediately following: the singing of "Three Little Maids," in which the quick movements of the fan and the women's walking is shown to be a theatrical revelation.

This fantasy of therapeutic cultural contact is sustained even as the film does not make claims for the believability of *The Mikado*'s yellowface. The Savoy players are portrayed as deliberately unconvincing racial impersonators; their believability as Japanese characters is compromised by close-ups of exaggerated stage makeup, obvious wig lines, and exaggerated posing. Even though Gilbert tells his players that "this is an entirely original Japanese opera," he is also well aware that he is fabricating yet another topsy-turvy scenario. In a rehearsal scene, Gilbert instructs Barrington, Grossmith, and Bond to hold their fans in an exaggerated manner, as if they were using them to thumb their noses, and utters, "Thus! The traditional Japanese posture as adopted by well-meaning but misguided underlings upon the departure of their august superiors." Grossmith inquires, "Would that be a recognized Japanese attitude, Sir?" to which Gilbert replies, "Not as yet, Grossmith, but I have every confidence that it will become one." Leigh himself is drawn by the irony of the first Savoy production, with "all the stuff about striving for authentic Japanese detail . . . in the context of a piece of work that is about as Japanese as fish and chips or steak and kidney pudding—it's fascinating."[21] He cites a scene in which Gilbert objects to George Grossmith's (Martin Savage) affectation of a cockney accent for his character of Ko-Ko:

> He says, "I'm a cheap tailor, I thought it would be . . ." and Gilbert says, "Nonsense! We're in Japan, not [London]. Do it properly! [Laughs.] Of course, that is such nonsense anyway, because they're interpreting Japanese in English terms. Grossmith is probably right, really.[22]

Yet the film still sustains the romance of characters artistically transformed by their contact with the natives. The film may gently mock the racial mimicry of the opera, but it also preserves a vision of an enigmatic and mystical authentic Japan as a curative to Western ills. Leigh's film sets the drabness of Victorian England in stark contrast to the vivid settings and costuming of Titipu. Scenes from *The Mikado*, brightly lit and spectacularly staged, become the visual and sonic relief to the ugly realism of Victorian London. If earlier productions of Gilbert and Sullivan's *Princess Ida* and *The Sorcerer* encase the performers in heavy velvet and fur, force them into armor, or transform them into spirits and ghouls, *The Mikado* seems substantively different, a transformational moment in which troubled Victorian lives may be forgotten by playing Japanese.

In the film, wearing Japanese costumes is an extension of this imagined therapeutic encounter. The Savoy actors are transformed by their Japanese costumes as well as by their contact with the Japanese people. While their racial impersonation is not convincing, their playing Japanese does allow them to reach new heights of inspiration and performance. In two parallel scenes, the film depicts the radical responses of the men and women to their authentic Japanese dress, either careful reconstructions of Japanese clothing sized for his British actors or actual kimonos "imported from Japan via Liberty," as Cellier also describes:

> Most of the ladies' dresses came from the ateliers of Messrs. Liberty & Co., and were, of course, of pure Japanese fabric. The gentlemen's dresses were designed by Mr. C. Wilhelm from Japanese authorities. But some of the dresses worn by the principals were genuine and original Japanese ones of ancient date; that in which Miss Rosina Brandram appeared as "Katisha" was about two hundred years old. The magnificent gold-embroidered robe and petticoat of the Mikado was a faithful replica of the ancient official costume of the Japanese monarch; the strange-looking curled bag at the top of his head was intended to enclose the pig-tail. His face, too, was fashioned after the manner of the former Mikados, the natural eyebrows being shaved off and huge false ones painted on his forehead.
> The hideous masks worn by the Banner-bearers were also precise copies of those which [were] used to adorn the Mikado's Body-guard. They were intended to frighten the foe. Some antique armour had been purchased and brought from Japan, but it was found impossible to use it, as it was too small for any man above four feet five inches, yet, strange to say, it was so heavy that the strongest and most muscular man amongst the Savoyards would have found it difficult to pace across the stage with it on.[23]

The evident pride of costume designer Wilhelm (Jonathan Aris) and dresser Madame Leon (Alison Steadman) in the authenticity of the Japanese costumes is contrasted with the reactions of the different singers. In one scene, the Three Little Maids try out their kimonos in their dressing room and luxuriate in the sensual qualities of the silk that they are asked to wear. Leonora Braham thrills to the thought that there might be something indiscreet in her kimono, whereas Jessie Bond is more concerned that she will not be wearing a corset. Her fears of impropriety are echoed in a later scene in which Durward Lely is similarly worried about his having to perform in a scandalously short tunic and without his customary corset. In the next sequence we see Lely as Nanki-poo singing "A Wandering Minstrel, I" and displaying plenty of leg. Again, the film takes some liberties with history in imagining Gilbert's performers as so offended; there is plenty of photographic evidence that Lely and male Savoy singers performed other roles that prominently displayed their legs. From her own accounts of waggling her extra-large obi, Jessie Bond was evidently not worried about drawing attention to key features of her Japanese costume. But the film insists on showing how the experience of wearing these Japanese costumes deeply affect how the Savoy actors displayed their bodies. Again, the radically transformative effects of these Japanese costumes, like the contact with Japanese people, upset conventional notions of dress and allow their wearers a profound change from their well-worn roles.

Like Leigh's earlier films on contemporary Britain, *Life Is Sweet* (1991), *Naked* (1993), and *Secrets and Lies* (1996), *Topsy-Turvy* creates a gritty sense of historical realism with constant reminders of Victorian class, colonial, and gender hierarchies. The film highlights details that emphasize the more sordid or painful aspects of life in 1885, including prostitution, dentistry, abortion, alcoholism, and drug addiction. Both racism and imperialism are obvious aspects of the film; in one scene, the male leads for *The Mikado* discuss the defeat of General Gordon by the Mahdi's troops at Khartoum; George Grossmith indignantly declares, "We bring them civilization and this is how they repay us!" As in his other films, Leigh worked with his cast extensively toward a psychological realism that can convey these more serious aspects of characters' lives. Leigh is noted for his careful development of actors in his films, which includes intensive discussion, improvisation, and research in order to develop interactions more organically. "You see, with all of my films, the way we rehearse is that the actors *don't* play themselves—it is character acting, and they learn how to *be* the character."[24] In one interview, Leigh describes the rehearsal process for the actors playing the Japanese inhabitants of the Knightsbridge Japanese Native Village:

> What is fascinating and awful about the genesis of the piece was that these Dutchmen actually did go to Japan, pulled out men, women, and children—many without exit permits—and shipped them over to London for something like 53 days. They stored them

in this hall near what is now the Imperial College and used them for this cultural exhibition. We didn't know much about it initially, but when we did some research, we found out that Kabuki Theater was part of the exhibition. And I thought, "God, yes! Fantastic!" Because that would help influence Gilbert. So, to answer your question, it wasn't so much because of Japanese cinema that we chose *The Mikado,* but once we were making it, it was a great gas to think, "Hey, we're making a Japanese movie here." In fact, there was a moment when I was working with the Japanese actors in the film—and I worked with them the same way I do everyone else; they're all London-based actors—and doing these improvisations in this dark basement for about two and a half hours, pretending that they were in this ship on this journey from Yokohama to London. And I just sat on the floor in a corner, watching them act in character, and I thought, "Wow, I'm making an Ozu film here." So, yes, it's all in the mix, but there are very few surface references.[25]

Interestingly enough, it is clear that Leigh wanted the same degree of psychological preparation for playing the Japanese characters, yet the potential for these characters to show any psychological depth remains unfulfilled. The presence of the Japanese characters is limited to their brief appearances in the exhibition, as viewed by Gilbert, and in the rehearsals for the "Three Little Maids," after which their presence is quickly upstaged by the brilliant Savoy performances. The depiction of the Japanese in the film, though rooted in realistic acting techniques, is ultimately not realistic but romanticized; they become enigmatic icons, part of the corroborative detail for the opera's genesis. In his depictions of the Japanese, then, Leigh returns to a familiar trope: a transformative experience of cultural contact between British artists and Japanese artisans. *The Mikado* turns into another example of how a racial fantasy of Japan revitalizes the West.

For white women in particular, Yoshihara comments, the consumption of Japanese and other oriental goods offered vicarious "adventure as well as cultural refinement."[26] In general, the film shows the most sympathy for its female characters, contrasting how creative genesis for men such as Gilbert and Sullivan turns on the thwarted female reproduction of their wives and lovers. In the final scenes of the film, following the celebrated success of *The Mikado,* Sullivan is told of his mistress's impending abortion, and Gilbert's wife vents her frustration with her husband by describing her idea for an opera in which neglected wives run after their inattentive husbands and nannies push empty perambulators. In keeping with this bitter reality, we see Leonora Braham drunk in her dressing room, ironically whispering Gilbert's lines to herself in a mirror, "Sometimes I sit and wonder, in my artless Japanese way, why it is that I am so much more attractive than anybody else in the whole world." Her words might well end the film, but the final moments of the film in fact move away from this tragic note. As she sings "The Moon and I," Braham is bathed in a radiant light; the camera moves back, then pans upward in a gesture of beauty, uplift, and transcendence. The musical and visual power of *The Mikado* seems to carry her away from an insecure and anxious life offstage. *The Mikado* again becomes exemplary of the pleasure of creative and racial transformation that imagines what is Japanese as a healing salve to the painful realities of 1885.

On the broadest level, the Christopher Renshaw productions and the Mike Leigh film show us two directions for *The Mikado*'s racial imagining. The first is the insouciant lightness of the opera, which plays Japanese through a willful fiction of spectacular objects; the other is a more profound yearning for a positive and transformative encounter with Japan. These two sets of productions show that what reanimates more contemporary *Mikado*s such as these is not simply habit or nostalgia (though both undoubtedly play a role in any Gilbert and Sullivan production) but rather an ongoing fascination with how Japanese difference might be staged. The seductive power of the opera's brand of racial transformation, of playing Japanese, rubs off on its viewers. Stepping into the imaginary space of Titipu, whether by viewing the opera, singing the music, or donning a kimono and fan, allows for the easy enjoyment of racial masquerade, a kind of fancy dress. Conversely, it might offer some relief from the weight of modern life through imagining alternative worlds of inspiration and creativity. Yet however compellingly light or transformative the touch of the opera, *The Mikado* still is freighted with questions regarding the representation of race, whether Japanese or, as we shall see in Part II, other subjects of racial imagination.

1938–39

· Chapter 4 ·

"And Others of His Race": Blackface and Yellowface

IN DECEMBER 1937, Harry Minturn, director of the Illinois Federal Theatre Project, wrote to national Federal Theatre Project director Hallie Flanagan, "We have a good deal of dancing and singing talent in the Negro group with which I think we can do something worth while," and expressed his interest in staging *The Mikado* with the "entire colored cast."[1] Minturn was quite familiar with the opera (he played Ko-Ko several times in a touring repertory company) and noticed early on when looking over casting records for his players that one of them, Maurice Cooper, had previously sung the role of Nanki-poo for the Verdi Opera Company (associated with Chicago Musical College, which trained African American musicians).

At first, Minturn dismissed the idea of casting African American performers in these roles incongruous. But then, he related,

> I began to see ... that it might seem strange casting to put Negro players into a traditional "Mikado" using all the hallowed Victorian costumes and stage-business that have invariably been employed from the time of the original production at the Savoy Theater in London under the eyes of Gilbert and Sullivan fifty-odd years ago. But if we changed the locale from Japan proper to some South Seas island (which made sense, because the Japan of "The Mikado" is not a real Japan, but a mythical barbarous land that Gilbert might just as well have called Zanzibar or Nyasaland), if we changed the costumes, the dances and even dared to tamper with the music by adding some primitive rhythms here and there—then there was some logic in it, then we had something to do for our Negro players."[2]

For Minturn, the fantasyland of *The Mikado's* Japan could be easily translated to a "mythical barbarous land" set on "some South Seas island," and embellished with both the "primitive rhythms" of swing music and "choruses danced as only a Negro cast could dance them."[3] Duncan Whiteside, technical director for Chicago's Great Northern Theater, suggests that the inspiration was not Minturn's alone. He recalls that this version of *The Mikado* was originally intended as a more traditional production, under the direction of Kay Ewing. During rehearsals of the opera, however, pianist Sammy Davis Sr. improvised tunes while "choristers tapped and trucked," and in this innovation the "whole course of the show was changed. And it was redesigned and redirected and everything else."[4] The Negro Unit of the Federal Theatre Project staged *The Swing Mikado*, which opened on September 25, 1938, at the Great Northern Theater. The opera, according to Minturn, was reset in a "mythical Japanese Island possession, with a note of the South Seas," and the Mikado arrived in act 2 "in a 26-foot war canoe, brightly painted in Island design, bearing lights and streamers."[5] The opera was performed with Sullivan's original score, but encores were reorchestrated. Nanki-Poo's "A Wandering Minstrel" included a tap dance performed in stop-time. "Three Little Maids" was performed in an "upbeat tripartite harmony" à la Andrew Sisters.[6] The third verse of the Mikado's "A More Humane Mikado" was performed in swing, and "My Object All Sublime" became a cakewalk. "The Flowers That Bloom in the Spring" had five encores that brought on a grand ensemble of tap-dancing and shagging couples. The "Titwillow" song became a spoken "Harlem lament."[7]

Whether initiated by the director's inspiration or the actors' improvisation or both, *The Swing Mikado* was a huge theatrical success. Arguably the biggest hit of the Federal Theatre Project, *The Swing Mikado* played in Chicago for five months to 250,000 people and made $35,000; in the weeks before Christmas, it grossed between $5,000 and $5,500 a week, a far higher gross than any other Chicago Federal Theatre Project production.[8] Although some reviewers claimed that the production fell short of Gilbert and Sullivan[9] and many wanted more swing orchestrations than the five numbers that were used,[10] by far the majority of reviews praised the production's innovative restaging of the opera.

In the history of the Federal Theatre Project, *The Swing Mikado* looms large as both an artistic and political milestone. Numerous offers were made to buy *The Swing Mikado*, of which Minturn was skeptical, in part because his actors had no guarantee of employment and the show continued to be sold out in Chicago. Interestingly enough, in deliberations that eventually led to the closing of the Federal Theatre Project, Congress cited the refusal to give commercial rights as evidence of mismanagement; they expressed their views that the Chicago production should have been given to commercial producers as soon as they expressed interest. *The Swing Mikado* finally did make its way to New York under Howard Hunter and Florence Kerr, both assistant administrators of the Works Progress Administration.

The popularity of *The Swing Mikado,* like its 1885 D'Oyly Carte predecessor, quickly inspired copycats. When his efforts to buy the rights for *The Swing Mikado* in New York failed, producer Michael Todd staged his own version, *The Hot Mikado,* directed by Hassard Short. *The Swing Mikado* moved to New York at the New Yorker Theatre on Fifty-fourth Street on March 1, 1939; *The Hot Mikado* opened at New York's Broadhurst Theatre on March 23 that same year. Where *The Swing Mikado* only embellished Sullivan's score with swing and other popular jazz and syncopated rhythms, *The Hot Mikado* "swung" all its songs. *The Hot Mikado* also tried to outdo its competitor with spectacular futuristic sets and costumes and an all-star cast that included the legendary tap dancer Bill Robinson as the Mikado and, as extras, Whitey's Lindy dancers from the Savoy in Harlem.

After sixty-two performances at the New Yorker, *The Swing Mikado* was sold to the commercial producers of Bernard Ulrich and Marvin Ericson of Chicago, who reopened it at the Forty-fourth Street Theater, right across the street from the Broadhurst where *Hot Mikado* was playing on May 1, 1939. It closed after twenty-four more performances, and the original company returned to Chicago for a return engagement and then to the San Francisco World's Fair, where it finally closed its curtains, along with Federal Theatre Project productions across the country, on June 30, 1939. *The Hot Mikado* ran a total of eighty-five performances on Broadway as well as playing at the 1939–40 World's Fair at Flushing Meadows and later on tour.

The examples of *The Swing Mikado* and *The Hot Mikado* loom large in the production history of *The Mikado* and force a reevaluation of how we understand the opera's racial politics. These productions transform *The Mikado* in order to comment on what seems to be a very different racial formation. The pleasures of playing Japanese are no longer the exclusive province of white performers. These productions were hailed as milestones in African American performance history. Other performances of *The Mikado,* as well as other African American performances of Japanese, have been used to articulate hopes for African American advancement and racial uplift. There is a long tradition of African American performers, such as the minstrel performer Thomas "Japanese Tommy" Dilward, who have long used cross-racial acting to gain some measure of expressive freedom. These freedoms, however, are closely circumscribed.

African American actors seem to promise a uniquely ironic take on the artifice of Japaneseness in the opera, destabilizing racial typecasting. Yellowface here seems to provide a liminal space in which African American performers can escape from the stereotypical renderings first established through blackface minstrelsy. This liminality does not, unfortunately, work in only one way. To many, the widespread acclaim of *The Swing Mikado* and *The Hot Mikado* signaled a broader racial progress, as African American artists could show their talents in performing previously all-white classics. Yet at the same time, *The Swing Mikado* and *The Hot Mikado* openly demonstrate the appeal of racial fantasies of blackness so characteristic of the negrophilia of the time. In some ways, *The Swing Mikado* and *The Hot Mikado* return to the very stereotypes their success supposedly left behind: to the "mythical barbarous land" and the "primitive rhythms" associated with black America and superimposed on a vision of Japan. As Brooks Atkinson, writing for the *New York Times*, vividly described:

> Every one, including Gilbert and Sullivan, declared a holiday at the New Yorker Theatre last evening in honor of "The Swing Mikado." In the program the Chicago chapter of the Federal Theatre politely dubs it "The Mikado," but no one need be deceived. For this is the Negro variation, not an impeccable Victorian theme, with the orchestra swinging some of the numbers and the performers swing the choruses with the grinning exuberance of night-club hot-cha. Among those present were Mrs. Roosevelt, for whom the audience respectfully rose; Mayor La Guardia, Harry Hopkins, who was once Mikado of the WPA, and Colonel Harrington, who is his successor. The Federal Theatre has never had such a gala opening in this preoccupied neighborhood. Leave it to the Negro minstrels to liven things up.[11]

The opera itself dictates a connection to blackface minstrelsy and suggests a much longer history of how yellowface performance is intimately related to blackface. These productions of *The Mikado* might allow us to examine interconnected and even contradictory racial constructions: the intimate associations of blackface minstrelsy and yellowface performance, the hope of racial uplift and progress for African American performers, and the imagining of racial utopias in which a fantasy of Japan provides a space for the meeting of black and white. What we will tease out of these productions and their theatrical legacies is a complex history in which multiple racial formations work in tandem or play against one another, demonstrating yet again how race is never simply a binary opposition.

"At Best Only a Monkey Shaved": The Shared Spaces of Blackface and Yellowface

All productions of *The Mikado* have a connection to blackface minstrelsy, some more direct than others. Gilbert's lyrics twice make reference to blackface minstrel performance, in lines inevitably altered for contemporary productions. Ko-Ko's original "little list" of "society offenders... who never would be missed" includes, along with others such as "pianoorganist" and "the people who eat peppermint and puff it in your face," "the nigger-serenader, and the others of his race." In "A More Humane Mikado," the Mikado states that the fitting punishment for "The lady who dyes a chemical yellow / Or stains her grey hair puce / Or pinches her figger" is to be "blacked up like a nigger / With permanent walnut juice." Though excised from contemporary productions, *The Mikado*'s specific connections to blackface minstrelsy are delineated through these casual mentions and accentuated by a striking "Bab" illustration (one of Gilbert's comic drawings, frequently accompanying his poems and lyrics).

By 1885, blackface minstrel performances were as popular in Victorian Britain as in the United States. Michael Pickering notes, "From their first wave of success in the late 1830s and early 1840s, minstrel acts, troupes, and shows figured as a staple item of the popular stage throughout the remaining decades of the century" and minstrelsy "continued to prove attractive to successive generations across all social classes, and among men and women of the large urban centres, provincial towns, and outlying rural areas alike."[12] Both Gilbert and Sullivan were quite familiar with blackface minstrelsy. Gilbert records at least one trip to see a benefit of Burgess and Moore minstrels,[13] and in a letter to his brother in 1860, Arthur Sullivan notes his enthusiastic participation in "a grand nigger performance" while a student in Leipzig.[14] In act 2 of their final collaboration, *Utopia Unlimited*,

Figure 11. Gilbert's "Bab" illustration for "As Someday It May Happen."

Gilbert and Sullivan include a song, "Society Has Quite Forsaken," in which characters arrange their chairs across the stage "like Christy Minstrels"; Gilbert's manuscript libretto calls for them to produce a banjo, set of bones, and tambourines to accompany their song.[15]

In the United States, most popular Gilbert and Sullivan operas inspired both blackface minstrel parodies as well as productions by African American performers. For instance, an African American version of *H.M.S. Pinafore* opened in the Globe Theatre in New York on April 28, 1879, not long after the London opening, of which the *New York Herald* remarked that the complexions of the actors "ranged from cream colour, through *café au lait* to strong coffee without milk, with various grades of less coffee and more milk."[16] Gilbert and Sullivan, with their satiric targets easily adapted to local settings, regularly provided new inspiration for American blackface minstrelsy. *The Mikado* spawned its own set of parodies. Thatcher, Primrose, and West Minstrels began a run of *The Mick-ah-do* on November 2, 1885, soon after the American production itself opened. Later in the year, they returned to perform *The Black Mikado*, likely the same show under a different name, which ran well into 1886.[17] Parodies of *The Mikado* were also performed by Haverly's, McIntyre and Heath's, and Carncross's Minstrels in 1886.[18]

Thus in a broader sense, the style of playing Japanese in *The Mikado* is put in place not only by British orientalism but also by blackface minstrelsy. Blackface minstrelsy formulated and formalized a way of representing African Americans as well as other racial groups. As Robert Toll and others have noted, the structure of blackface minstrel shows (and their later incarnations as variety or vaudeville shows) allowed for a quick succession of different ethnic types such as Chinese, German, Dutch, and Irish immigrants and American Indians.[19]

In America and Great Britain, blackface minstrels also made profitable use of Japanese tropes to add interest and novelty to their acts. Shows capitalizing on the popularity of Japanese acrobatics, whether incorporating actual Japanese acrobatic troupes or performed by their blackface imitators, were a frequent part of minstrel performances. Toll writes that touring Japanese acrobats inspired a host of minstrel portrayals of the "jap-oh-knees" between 1865 and 1867. At least eight major minstrel companies performed takeoffs on this new sensation, advertised as "The Flying Black Japs," in the most glowing rhetoric—"BALANCING, JUGGLING, TOP SPINNING, AND ENCHANTED LADDERS, HAM-SANDWICH-CELLAR-KITCHEN and his beautiful son ALL WRONG.[20] ... assisted by eleven or eight other 'japs,'"—or simply with the single bold word "jap."[21] In the early 1880s, J. H. Haverly presented a "Colossal Japanese Show" with jugglers, tumblers, and necromancers, from "the court of his Imperial Majesty the Mikado of Japan."[22] Musical and dance numbers were also popular; the loosely incorporative structure of blackface minstrelsy lent itself to introducing Japanese racial performances to lend an exotic flavor to familiar fare. In 1867, Burgess, Moore, and Crocker's Christy Minstrels show at London's St. James Hall included a "Mr. W. P. Collins" performing a "solo on the Japanese fiddle" to be followed, the program announced, "by a Christy's Burlesque on a Chinese Dance." The first part of an evening of song and ballads by the London-based Mohawk Minstrels in 1886 concluded with "a New and Original Japaneasy Absurdity by Harry Hunter and Edward Forman" titled "O Come Let Us Be Jappy Together."[23]

Blackface minstrelsy and its later forms such as variety and burlesque thus became one of the vehicles by which yellowface developed. The structure of blackface minstrel shows, with different sketches that did not require a common narrative thread, easily incorporated the oriental as a novelty act, adding interest and variety to the more familiar songs and patter of minstrelsy, providing an opportunity for grand spectacle, and giving performers the chance to show different talents.

As African Americans moved into the performance spaces of minstrelsy, they too adopted these familiar imaginings of Japanese and other orientals. Henry T. Sampson records the changing status of African Americans in theater during the late nineteenth and early twentieth centuries. For the most part, they were confined to roles that had been defined by white performers in blackface; however, they could also take advantage of the minstrel stage in order to showcase their considerable talents in music, dance, and acting. By the early decades of the twentieth century, African Americans were taking on roles that allowed them a limited measure of innovation. Minstrelsy, as James Weldon Johnson describes, served both to reinforce racial stereotypes and to afford new opportunities for the African American performer:

> Minstrelsy was, on the whole, a caricature of Negro life, and it fixed a stage tradition which has not yet been entirely broken. It fixed the tradition of the Negro as only an irresponsible, happy-go-lucky, wide-grinning, loud-laughing, shuffling, banjo-playing, singing, dancing sort of being. Nevertheless, these companies did provide stage training and theatrical experience for a large number of coloured men. They provided an essential training and theatrical experience which, at the time, could not have been acquired from any other source.[24]

Playing Japanese and other oriental characterizations, common in minstrelsy, allowed African American performing artists this opportunity to escape racist caricatures. Ethnic lampooning was a common feature of blackface minstrelsy, which stereotyped not only blacks but also a whole range of racial and ethnic types. African American minstrel performers were able to adopt, albeit in a limited way, the privilege of white performers to impersonate other races. Caricatures of immigrant Chinese as played by African Americans, for instance, were regular features of the vaudeville stage; as Krystyn Moon writes, impersonations of Chinese immigrants were quite popular among African American comedians from the 1890s through the 1920s:

> Through Chinese impersonations, African Americans were able to ally themselves with whites by marking the Chinese as different from the white norm, as they themselves had been marked. These characterizations, however, focused on both racial inferiority and the foreignness and inability of the Chinese to assimilate. This image contrasted with blackface caricatures that not only confirmed white perceptions of racial inferiority but also imagined African American culture as central to what it meant to be American.[25]

Moon asserts that if white performers of blackface minstrelsy depicted both black and Chinese immigrants on the stage "to reaffirm the inferiority of both groups" but also to "highlight the foreignness of Chinese immigrants," then one way of understanding African American performers of comic Chinese characters is that they worked to differentiate themselves from the Chinese, thus "asserting their role in the creation of American identity and culture."[26]

It is troubling to imagine the terms of African American racial uplift as simply a transfer of what had been formerly the privilege of white actors to impersonate a variety of nonwhite races in stereotypical ways. Thus in instances where African Americans perform in yellowface, we seek some kind of complexity, irony, or at least self-consciousness. It is tempting to read more deeply into anything that might indicate another dimension, as in this *Chicago Star* review of an October 1909 performance of noted African American comedian Sam Cook:

> Sam Cook, in the comedy Chinese-character impersonation, is the unique feature of a vaudeville bill entertaining practically throughout at the Grand this week. Ordinarily the announcement of a stage Chinaman is a signal to cringe, and when it is coupled with a sketch that suggests a laundry it means to cringe all the harder. But

Cook and his partner, Jim Stevens, who presents a Negro character that serves as an excellent foil to the Chinaman, make their sketch, "No Checkee, No Wash-ee," the hit of the bill. Cook, apparently, has discarded the traditional stage Chinaman in toto, has gone out into Chinatown and studied the Chinaman from life, and then has created and embellished a character true to life and, more important, to stage art. He gives to John Chinaman some little irresistible touches.[27]

The title of the sketch suggests that it does not deviate too far from conventional stereotype; at the same time, the reviewer at least finds this performance quite different from the conventional stage Chinaman. In dispensing with "the traditional stage Chinaman" and actually observing "the Chinaman from life," Cook gives his "John Chinaman" those "little irresistible touches." Perhaps there is a movement, however limited, toward challenging and dislocating not just stereotypes of African Americans but other racial groups as well.

Similarly, there is also a more complex interpretation of how African Americans performed American Indian characters in musical comedies such as *The Red Moon* (1909). Set in a government school, *The Red Moon* tells the story of Minnehaha, the "half-breed daughter of an Indian chief who fifteen years before had deserted her and her [African American mother] and returned to the wandering of his people and the Land of the Setting Sun"; this chief "suddenly returns and claims his child over the protests of the Negro mother and her friends"; the presentation of this story afforded, according to one contemporary report, "some splendid situations and brilliant lines, both comic and sentimental." *The Red Moon* employed a number of recognizable stereotypes of the stage Indian, as well as conventional minstrel numbers such as comedian Edgar Conner singing "Sambo."[28]

The portrayal of American Indian characters allowed African American actors to demonstrate their acting and musical talents. The *Freeman* praised "Arthur Talbot as 'John Lowdog,'" who "gave the public its first taste of Indian character work with merit by a Negro," and described that when J. Rosemond Johnson as Plunk Green and Abbie Mitchell as Minnehaha sang "The Red Shawl" song, the experience was "the neatest yet that has been offered in the form of Indian lovemaking. It made many young lovers in the house wish they were Indians." The play was acclaimed by the *Indianapolis Freeman* not only as musically worthy ("at last in the big league"; "the real goods"; with music "the best that was ever offered by Negroes") but also racially momentous: "This piece has crossed the line, 'no classic colored shows,' that has been drawn by the managers and press. They flatly turned back Abyssinia; now they are face to face with another."[29] But David Krasner points out that "while Cole and Johnson avoided stereotyping African Americans, they were not so generous to Native Americans."[30] "Cole and Johnson's relationship to Native Americans was certainly ambivalent: on the one hand, they cut against the grain of American ethnology that argued that mixing the races would lead to social collapse; on the other hand, they portrayed Native Americans as a rung below African Americans.[31]

While African American performers may have been lauded for their "true to life" characterizations of Chinamen and Indians on the stage, their portrayals of "Japanese" were evidently much less concerned with any notions of realism. Like the white minstrel companies, African American performers used Japanese acts for the most part to add a touch of fantasy as well as novelty to their shows. One example can be found in *Oriental America*, one of the earliest all-black vaudeville shows. *Oriental America* opened August 3, 1897, at Palmer's Theatre in New York City under the direction of John W. Isham.[32] The show was popular in New York, and subsequently toured in England.[33] According to the *Washington Morning Times*, this production included "a company of sweet singers and talented performers, the cream of the colored race," and highlighted both spectacle and the singing talents of the performers: "The several scenes in the each act have been given the benefit of very attractive and elaborate scenic and electric embellishment and especially is this so in the last act, where in are presented prominent scenes using appropriate costumes from well-known standard operas of the several schools, to which fully forty minutes were devoted." The reviewer notes, "Among the many features of the great show were a Japanese dance, cleverly rendered by Fanny Rutledge, Pearl Meredith, Alice Mackey and Carrie Meredith, who sang and danced equally well and were prominent in all the ensemble scenes of the performance. A quartet of cycling girls in bloomers and twentieth century maids, the maids of the Oriental Huzzars, led by Miss Belle Davis, as well as the hunting scene and opening chorus from the 'Bells of Cornville.'"[34]

How much the popularity of the show depended on its oriental content is certainly a matter for speculation. Despite the show's title, there certainly did not seem to be a sustained theme of any kind; later accounts emphasize its importance in the history of African American theater without any mention of the "Japanese dance, cleverly rendered" or the "Oriental Huzzars."[35] At the same time, the performance of these elements does raise a question of how we should read the playing of yellowface by African Americans. Is it substantively different from white actors playing yellowface? Of white actors in blackface minstrelsy? On the positive side, it does clear a space for the advancement of African American performers beyond their own racial caricatures; beyond that, the best we might hope for is that it also dislocates both racial stereotypes of "blackness" and "yellowness" through playing on the disjunction of the actor's body and the racial stereotype.

Yellowface by African American rather than white performers does create a sense of uncertainty insofar that it dislodges the exclusive hold that whiteness has over the enactment of other races and exposes all of these representations as artificial rather than natural. Like African American performers first forced to black up in order to inhabit the stages of blackface minstrelsy, African American performers of yellowface are inevitably compared to their white counterparts. However convincing their renditions, their bodies never fully dissolve into the roles they take on. What is foregrounded is precisely the imitative and performative mechanisms and actions of yellowface; how they act, rather than inhabit, a role.

Japanese Tommies

Scholarship on blackface minstrelsy often highlights either a straightforward racist stereotyping or the complex mechanisms of substitution and surrogation that go on between white minstrel performers and the black bodies they emulate. I would suggest that the workings of yellowface inevitably disrupt both of these processes, resulting in much more uneasy identifications. This is amplified in the case of African American minstrel performers whose roles include yellowface.

One striking example might be the career of the African American performer Thomas Dilward (also spelled "Dilworth" or "Dilwerd"), who took as his stage name "Japanese Tommy." Dilward was the second African American performer (the first was the renowned dancer Henry "Juba" Lane) to gain success performing with white minstrel companies. Dilward began his career in 1853 with Christy's Minstrels (the same year that Commodore Matthew Perry opened Japan to American trade, which may have inspired his stage name). Subsequently, he went on to play in a range of companies, including the mostly white Dan Bryant's Minstrels, Woods' Minstrels, Morris Brothers' Minstrels, and Kelly and Leon's Minstrels, as well as with African American troupes such as the Original and Only Georgia Minstrels Slave Troupe, managed by Charles B. Hicks.[36] Dilward made appearances around the world, including a tour of Ireland and other parts of Great Britain, in 1869–70, with Sam Hague's Great American Slave Troupe.[37] His career lasted quite a few years, as evidenced by his appearance with Hiscock and Hayman's Australian Federal Minstrels, who visited at the Free Trade Hall in Manchester from October 1880 until spring 1881.[38]

Dilward's success is measured by his relatively long career as well as by his star billing. He played the violin, sang, danced, and appeared in sketches; his short stature was also part of his attraction, and he was compared with such acts as P. T. Barnum's Tom Thumb and Bryant's Minstrels' Little Mac.[39] A playbill for the performance at the Grand Circus Pavilion, Swansea, in the week of March 29, 1869, has the headline "The Great American Slave Troupe and Japanese Tommy" and describes him as "The Tom Thumb of Africa, 36 Years of Age and only 35 inches in height."[40] His funeral notice described him as "a popular songster and a contortionist" who "appeared in both male and female parts" (not unusual, since cross-gender casting was common practice in minstrel performance).[41] A photograph taken between 1855 and 1865 seems to indicate a fairly prosperous as well as genial man. Nonetheless, at his funeral it was reported that "but few friends were present."[42]

It is not clear to what extent "Japanese Tommy" cultivated any particularly Japanese aspects to his act. Neither photographs nor reviews indicate any particular affinity for Japanese dress or characterization, although he may have appeared with George W. Harding, the stage manager for the Boston Dime Museum and dialect comedian and vocalist, to present the skit "Fun in a Chinese Laundry."[43] In one photograph included in Harry Reynolds's *Minstrel Memories,* he is dressed in a rather vaguely oriental way but is carrying a broom (a prop that Dale Cockrell suggests is connected both to blackface minstrelsy and mummer plays).[44] Yet his name and one particular reference indicate that he clearly capitalized on playing Japanese as a marketable identity. Importantly, curiosity about Japanese Tommy is prompted by both his size and the racial mobility that his performance affords him.

There was also at the Bryants' the "Japanese Tommy; or What is it?" some three feet six inches in height, and as great a puzzle for physiologists as the "What is it?" at Barnum's. We sat with open mouth and dubious soul while gazing at this nondescript. We marveled at how he was made, and questioned in our minds as to what theatrical manufacturer had begotten him. Whoever it is, he has turned out an unmistakably well finished article, and such a one as admirably answers the purpose of those who engage him."[45]

The "What is it?" asked of Japanese Tommy, and his long-term success with a range of audiences otherwise unwelcoming of African American performers, might point to some possibility of escaping the rigid artistic and economic limitations placed on African American performers. In becoming the exotic object of Japanese curiosity, Dilward can escape the tedium of enacting standard minstrel fare and earn praise as "an unmistakably well finished article" and, evidently, an admirable performer.

Dilward may indeed have developed his moniker to capitalize on the fame of another "Japanese Tommy," a member of the first Japanese embassy to the United States in 1860. Tateishi Onojirō Noriyuki, a teenager traveling with his interpreter uncle, became a minor celebrity during his visit to the United States.[46] He was nicknamed "Tommy" after his childhood name Tamehachi and was called "a darling fellow" and a "Japanese prince" by U.S. newspapers.[47] The praise of Tommy was consistent with racializations of the Japanese as more white than other Asians, calling the Japanese "the British of Asia" *(Harper's Weekly)* or asserting that "no nation possesses so many elements of the Anglo-Saxon mind as the Japanese" *(Washington [D.C.] Evening Star)*; the *Philadelphia Press* included a description of Tommy as "almost Caucasian in his complexion."[48] Still, this interpretation of the Japanese as almost white is premature, as seen in a satirical cartoon that appeared in *Harper's Weekly* on June 30, 1860.[49] The "Colored Gentleman" waiting tables refuses to hear the gentleman's demand of "Here, you Nigger, come here!" and replies "Nigger!—no Nigger, Sar; me Japanese, Sar!" In the second frame, "Tommy," dressed in kimono and described as "a little how-came-you-so," looks drunkenly through a pile of bricks, hiccupping, "One of dem (hic) is my Hat me know; but me be (hic) if me can tell which him is." Titled "Natural Mistakes," the picture draws attention to the "natural" confusion between characterizations of African Americans and Japanese. The "Natural Mistakes" cartoon provides a framework for thinking about Thomas Dilward's "Japanese Tommy" as well as Tateishi Onojirō Noriyuko; it points out the ridicule underlying the social elevation of the Japanese man and accuses the African American of asserting a Japanese identity in a vain attempt to escape being a "nigger." There is little difference between the "What is it?" and the "a little-how-came-you-so"; the alter ego of both is the colored man who seeks to move beyond his station.

This makes clear the conflicted nature of African Americans taking on other racial roles: while these roles allowed them some measure of artistic freedom and even some claims to being American by virtue of this racial masquerade, at the same time it also accentuated their debased status as black. White minstrel performers, although perhaps stained by their racial impersonations,[50] could remove the mask. African American performers were marked differently through the confluence of their own authentic blackness and by their association with other "coloreds." Their racial masking could show their talents, but it could not allow them the privilege of being the "neutral" white body, on which a host of racial others might be played.

Figure 12. "Natural Mistakes," Harper's Weekly, June 30, 1860.

Thus the performance by African Americans of these other racial types was one of both association and disavowal. They mocked immigrants such as the Chinese, whose unintelligible gibberish and manners marked them as inexorably foreign, and enacted barbaric or primitive characterizations of Indians or Africans. At the same time, they themselves were in danger of losing the distinctions they might be trying to make between themselves and other Others. On one level, playing Japanese imbued the African American body with the value of becoming a fashionable novelty. But within this act of playing, the African American body does not gain the privilege of disappearing into the role. Rather, the body of the actor is marked by its blackness and measured by its ability to play "yellow": in terms of audience, there is at times little difference found between the two.

African American *Mikado*s and Racial Uplift

Late nineteenth- and early twentieth-century African American performances of operas, including *The Mikado,* provided a much clearer opportunity for African American performers to demonstrate both their talent and their dignity. The early part of the twentieth century saw the rise of a black middle class for whom *The Mikado* was popular, for a variety of possible reasons. Reginald Kearney describes the success of a 1905 Indianapolis production, attributing it to a particular kind of racial solidarity between African Americans and Japanese:

> When the black citizens of Indianapolis decided to put on the opera *The Mikado* for the benefit of the St. Philips Episcopal Mission building fund, the event was acclaimed as "one of the most successful from the standpoint of merit and attendance ever given by the colored people of the city." People from Marion, Muncie, Anderson, and Evansville joined "the city's representative colored people" in making the event a success. Tickets for the opera were to go on sale at eight o'clock Monday morning at Pink's drug store, but an irritated music lover complained that she and several other ladies had arrived before the appointed time only to find that others had queued up from midnight of the previous night, and 75 percent of the tickets had already sold out.[51]

Kearney argues that some deeper political affinity of African Americans for Japanese people and culture might underlie the choice of *The Mikado* as entertainment; his larger thesis implies that such cultural choices may have been dictated by what Vijay Prashad calls "polyculturalism" or Bill Mullen describes as "Afro-Orientalism": the admiration and affinity for Asian countries such as Japan, India, and China held by African American writers such as W. E. B. Du Bois and the shared activist struggles of those of African and Asian descent "to escape the prison house of racist capitalism."[52] It is difficult, however, to find radical solidarity expressed through these African American productions of *The Mikado*. Upon investigation, they seemed predictably light orientalist entertainment in much the same vein as the Savoy productions, and thus one might dismiss them as part of what Mullen calls a "secret history" of cultural fetishization.[53] However, there is something interesting about how African American productions that, even in embracing the commodity racism of decorative orientalism, also invested *The Mikado* with their own desires for African American racial uplift.

For instance, on May 27, 1914, a production of *The Mikado*, described as "a Japanese comic opera," was reviewed by L. P. Williams in the *New York Age*. This production was performed at the Star Casino on 107th Street, New York, by members of the choirs of St. Benedict's Church and accompanied by the New Amsterdam Orchestra under the direction of H. G. Marshall. Politics or cross-racial solidarity were far from Williams's mind; instead, his review highlighted the singing (particularly Mrs. O. L. Hooper in the role of Katisha, "the feature of the evening") and praised the costumes, which were clearly featured in the staging: "After the performance the whole cast escorted front and rear by the ushers gave the public a better view of their Japanese costumes by parading in a grand march."[54]

Another review of a production of *The Mikado*, the previous year, begins by echoing these terms. The reviewer, R. G. Doggett, a student at Howard University, reported that the packed performance of *The Mikado*, by the Choral Society of the Washington Conservatory of Music at the Howard Theatre on March 1, "scored an instantaneous success, both on account of its melodious and well scored music, as well as its playful satire." He congratulated Mrs. H. G. Marshall on the "choice of this opera as a medium for the exploitation of the excellent talent of the members of the choral society" and had warm praise for the conductor Jesse Shipp ("one of the race's greatest producers and stage managers"), the scenery ("there has been nothing seen on the Howard stage this season that has surpassed the gorgeous and bizarre taste in which this opera was mounted"), and many of the leads.[55]

However warm Doggett's praise, he did criticize some of the leading players, such as Louis Howard as Pooh-Bah ("a charming performance" but "a miserable failure from a vocal standpoint"). Interestingly enough, he also criticized the inadequacy of the racial makeup, chiding the performers for failing to represent the supposed uniformity of the Japanese "type" even while acknowledging the variety of skin tones that the African American performers presented:

> Very few took advantage of the opportunity to properly make up so as to look the type they were supposed to impersonate. Instead of a large company of Japanese the audience was presented to a set of faces resembling every color in the rainbow, with a few additional studies in black to complete the spectacle of many colors.

According to Doggett, "The best Japanese in the company [was] Miss Edith Chandler, a member of the chorus. The greatest offenders of all in the way of make up were seven or eight members of the male chorus who made a piteous spectacle."[56]

This review came under fire when, two weeks later, Lester A. Walton, critic for the *New York Age*, took Doggett to task for his more unkind assessments. Walton cited defensive comments from others who attended the production, such as Howard University senior Adolph Dodge, who saw the production as "the most artistic, elaborate, and successful affair ever given in the Howard Theatre," and was angry at Doggett's "scathing, unjust, and incompetent criticism," and Dr. A. P. Albert, who resented the "faint praise intermixed with harsh criticism" that Doggett provided in his earlier review and voiced the "general opinion... that the 'Mikado' was very creditably rendered and that it was greatly enjoyed by the audience was clearly shown by the frequent and, at times, prolonged applause." Moreover, Albert states, "The columns of The Age should be used to encourage rather than to dampen the ardor of the members of the race in their efforts making for the uplift of the race."[57] These reviews and responses suggest that the popularity of African American productions of *The Mikado* was deeply connected to the hope of racial uplift; the successes of African American performers who could perform classics such as Gilbert and Sullivan were meant to inspire all the race.

Many African American responses to *The Swing Mikado* and *The Hot Mikado* were consistent with this directive. Some hailed *The Mikado* as part of a larger racial project that insisted on equal rights and dignity for African American performers and audiences. Tenor Maurice Cooper, who played Nanki-Poo in *Swing Mikado,* declares, "The Federal Theater is tearing down the antiquated idea that the Negro in theater is a buffoon. He has been given a chance to display his ability as a serious artist."[58] Reviewing *Swing Mikado* for the *Chicago Defender,* Nahum Daniel Brascher predicts that "this production will demonstrate to the nation that audiences will go to the theatre and see living people perform, and that it will not only have a long run in Chicago, but will equal 'Green Pastures' [Marc Connelly's Pulitzer Prize–winning 1930 play] in general interest nationally." Brascher gives credit to the production as "the supreme achievement in Federal Theatre production" and notes:

> One of the true inspirations to me is in my knowledge of the fine ambitions of so many of the men and women, trained in the best schools and colleges of the country, and fitted for the very work they are so efficiently doing, but present national economic conditions had to open this new "Door of Opportunity" for them. These people are not amateurs, novices. They rise to the occasion because they love their work, and because they have a vision of a new day for demonstrating to the world their ability to bring entertainment and appreciation to the American public.[59]

On the one hand, *The Swing Mikado* and *Hot Mikado* were clearly employed in the service of racial uplift, using the performance of Japanese as a way of proving that African Americans perform musical classics in ways that demonstrated their talents and rendered their skin color moot. On the other hand, these productions made use of rather than challenged racial clichés about African Americans, casting them as primitive and sexualized. Praise by reviewers of *The Swing Mikado* are particularly rife with stereotypes of blackness:

> But just as you are becoming reconciled to another cut-price Gilbert and Sullivan revival, the performers grin and strut and begin stamping out the hot rhythms with animal frenzy. "Za-zu-za-zu," the three little maids from school say huskily, breaking down into a smoking caper. All this is something to see and hear. If they are going to swing, let them swing the whole thing with abandon, for

these are the folks who can do it.... The chorus includes some dusky wenches who can dance for the Savoyard jitterbugs with gleaming frenzy, tossing their heads in wild delight. There are also some corpulent dames, whose loose construction puts swing into the category of perilous professions.[60]

Did you know that Sir Arthur Sullivan's melody, "Flowers that Bloom in the Spring," is so primitive in its elements that it can be reduced to a jungle beating of tom-toms?
   Or that "Three Little Maids from School Are We" is so pagan, despite its surface innocence, that it calls for a dozen encores when a little brown girl in the chorus winds it up with climatic movement of a Mata-Hari dance?
   Or that song about letting "Punishment Fit the Crime" can be gradually speeded up so that, toward the finish, it is a perfect orgy of bacchanalian dancing?
   If not, you haven't seen the All-Negro version of "The Mikado" being presented by the Federal Theater at the Great Northern.[61]

Musically, *The Swing Mikado* contrasted each straight rendition of Sullivan's songs with swing versions, thus suggesting that the performance of the classic might pave the way for a more truly "black" performance to follow; in converting the entire score to swing, *The Hot Mikado* capitalized further on the popularity of seeing African Americans perform their "natural" rhythms. Ronald Radano has describe how, at the beginning of the twentieth century, American public culture embraced

> a radically new conception of black music that gave special emphasis to qualities of rhythm. While rhythm had always been associated with African and African-American musical performances, it now seemed to overtake other aspects, identifying what many believed to be the music's vital essence. Black music's propulsive and seductive "hot" rhythm—a term linked etymologically to forms of excess—seemed at once underdetermined and saturated with context specific meaning.[62]

The change from Sullivan's orchestration to the "hot" rhythms of swing clearly gave the audience license to imagine *The Mikado* transformed into what Radano describes as "a hot fantasy of racialized sound" that links its African American performers with "animal dances" and a "savage" jazz animated by "jungle rhythms."[63]

This view of the music in these productions was clearly highlighted by reviewers as the animating force that revealed the true nature of their African American performers. *The Swing Mikado* South Seas setting effectively fused stereotypes of black primitives and brown exotic natives; for Lloyd Lewis, this is a "Mikado Malayed":

> Gilbert and Sullivan's "Mikado" has been transplanted to an island in the Pacific, a South Sea welter of brown skins, totem poles, grass collars and red sarongs. . . . Japan was all gone from the scene and the songs—all but the fans, and these didn't last long into the play. The male principals were made up like comic artists' impressions of cannibals, the Mikado wearing the stereotyped plug hat and Ko-Ko wearing an outlandish pattern of rubber balls over his strong robes and colossal headdress.[64]

In *The Hot Mikado* the costumes and scenery created a fantastic and opulent space that only vaguely echoed Japan: for Rosamond Gilder, "the play is left in a highly imaginary Japan, decorated with street lamps made to look like dice against a striped backdrop suggesting Fujiyama."[65] The addition of such favorite acts as the Lindy Dancers from the Savoy Ballroom in Harlem further reinforced that the fantastic sets and costumes of *The Hot Mikado* did not reference Japan but the more familiar nightclubs of Harlem. Thus *The Hot Mikado* openly evoked how African American musicians and dancers became "hot" racial commodities for white consumers; Langston Hughes vividly describes a time when "the Negro was in vogue," with "the growing influx of whites toward Harlem after sundown, flooding the little cabarets and bars where formerly only colored people laughed and sang," and when "strangers were given the best ringside tables to sit and stare at the Negro customers—like amusing animals in a zoo."[66] Hughes takes more direct aim at *The Swing Mikado* in his "Notes on Commercial Theatre":

> You've taken my blues and gone—
> You sing 'em on Broadway
> And you sing 'em in Hollywood Bowl,

And you mixed 'em up with symphonies
And you fixed 'em
So they don't sound like me.
Yep, you done taken my blues and gone.

You also took my spirituals and gone.
You put me in *Macbeth* and *Carmen Jones*
And all kinds of *Swing Mikados*
And in everything but what's about me—
But someday somebody'll
Stand up and talk about me,
And write about me—
Black and beautiful—
And sing about me,
And put on plays about me!

I reckon it'll be
Me myself!

Yes, it'll be me.[67]

The Mikado's Crossover Roles

Apparently, according to promptbooks, neither reference to "niggers" in the original text of the opera seems to have been changed for either *The Swing Mikado* or *The Hot Mikado,* despite other changes to the dialogue. In addition, these productions actually highlighted their use of minstrel traditions. Bob Parrish, *The Hot Mikado's* Nanki-Poo, performed "A Wandering Minstrel" with a banjo instead of a Japanese samisen.[68] Edward Fraction, *The Swing Mikado's* Mikado, the only non–African American performer, was known as an experienced minstrel performer,[69] and his cakewalk with Katisha (Rosa Brown) in the second act was one of the hits of the production.[70] Michael Rogin has noted how the increasingly liberal attitudes of the 1920s and 1930s were not incompatible with the continued popularity of blackface minstrelsy; in fact, blackface was thought by many to be an essential element of African American culture:

> Outside the NAACP, almost no whites questioned it. White liberals mostly assumed that blackface was another instance of crossracial sympathy. Eleanor Roosevelt and the cosmopolitan journal-

ist and Socialist Heywood Broun loved Amos 'n' Andy. Rhapsody in Blue, with its left-wing screenwriters Elliot Paul and Howard Koch, brought back the blackface Jolson. Larry Parks, who played him in the Jolson biopics, was the Communist leader of the left wing of the Screen Actors Guild (which opposed "discrimination against Negroes in the motion picture industry" and the stereotyping of African Americans).[71]

The reviewers' constant comparison of the old version with its new swing incarnation suggests that they see it as infused with a primitive life and the abandon characteristic of "Negroes." "For it is an original notion," Brooks Atkinson claims, "to slide 'The Mikado' into the groove of black and hot rhythm, and this dark company is full of high spirits. When they give 'The Mikado' a Cotton Club finish they raise the body temperature considerably."[72] However "original" this notion, the "dark companies" mentioned by Atkinson are preceded by a long history of "blacked-up *Mikados*" that associates blackness with primitive energy, sexuality, and comic release. These versions point out deeper parallels between the original opera and blackface traditions. It is not so much that blackface minstrelsy might have influenced Gilbert and Sullivan (although undoubtedly it did) as it is that the unruliness—and with it an associated idea of race—inscribed into productions of the opera can easily find an expression through the characteristic forms of blackface minstrelsy.

Blackface minstrelsy, of course, construed black bodies as barely civilized and exploited the humor that lay in their malapropisms, jokes, gesticulations, and rude gestures; these were funny precisely because they disrupted the confines of proper language and deportment. The Japanese figures of *The Mikado,* despite their carefully regulated and correct behavior, also demonstrate a propensity for such titillating transgressions. In the context of the opera, these racial epithets associate the "blacking up" of minstrelsy with debasement and the bodily grotesque. In the lyrics of Ko-Ko's "little list," minstrel performers, white as well as black, are placed into the same "race"; all are guilty of the same social annoyance that is worthy of execution. In the Mikado's song, white women who dye their hair or corset their waists deserve the permanent stain of blackface. While in chapter 1 I suggested that the guiding mode of the opera is to look at what is Japanese solely in terms of an obsession with objects, I would suggest here that another—and not unrelated—dimension of the opera

Figure 13. Program, Michael Todd's Hot Mikado, *New York World's Fair (1940).*

is its presentation of characters whose beautifully wrought and objectified exteriors barely disguise what is beneath: a primitive, irrational and ultimately cruel race. Within the characterizations of *The Mikado* there is the constant shifting from the image of refined beauty to its opposite, grotesque savagery, from which arises the irony of the Mikado, who praises himself for being "humane" yet rejoices in the most horrible punishments for transgressions.

At first the opera's proposed punishment either for "blacking up" or by "blacking up" seems quite different from, say, act 2's making-up of the bride-to-be Yum-Yum. A much prettier picture emerges in "Braid the Raven Hair," where "Art and nature thus allied, / Go to make a pretty bride." However, a much more grotesque image is shown by Gilbert's "Bab" drawing for the lyrics "Paint the pretty face— / Dye the coral lip," which show a squatting Yum-Yum being painted by a simian Ko-Ko.

As we have seen in the discussion of the Japanese Native Villages, racial categorization still portrayed actual Japanese people as barbaric, primitive, and inferior (despite their ability to produce beautiful items for consumption). Rotem Kowner notes that in the latter half of the nineteenth century, Darwin's theories were frequently used to categorize nonwhite races as apelike: "This theory, once used to describe only Africans (and Irish), was now applied to any non-white people, wherein the Japanese were no exception. . . . For many writers and artists, the Japanese were at their most simian when they were trying to be modern." Kowner notes, "Toward the end of the century, an increasing number of writers, even the prominent

Figure 14. Gilbert's "Bab" illustration for "Braid the Raven Hair."

John Ruskin, Pierre Loti, and Charles Baudelaire, adopted ad nauseum simian images when describing Japanese features and behaviour."[73] This is clearly shown in Frenchman Georges Bigot's caricature "Monsieur et Madame vont dans la Monde," which pictures a Japanese couple in modern dress looking into a mirror; their reflection shows them as monkeys in human dress.[74]

Gilbert's lyrics and "Bab" illustration for the song "A Lady Fair, of Lineage High" in the opera *Princess Ida,* immediately preceding *The Mikado,* also conjures up a similar image of a monkey with aspirations toward civilization:

> He bought white ties, and he bought dress suits,
> He crammed his feet into bright tight boots—
> And to start in life on a brand-new plan,
> He christened himself Darwinian Man!
> But it would not do,
> The scheme fell through—
> For the Maiden fair, whom the monkey craved,
> Was a radiant Being,
> With a brain far-seeing—
> While a man, however well-behaved,
> At best is only a monkey shaved!

The Mikado presents a world of animated objects, familiar-yet-exotic commodities that were an inseparable part of the domestic space of Victorian England and America. Inherent even in those performances, however, was a different force that equally figured in productions of the opera. Comic moments provided opportunity for emphasizing an anarchic, sexual, and youthful energy. It is this energy that becomes coded as raw, primitive, disorderly, and "black" in blackface minstrelsy. The core of blackface's appeal, then, lies not only in the racial impersonations taking place but also in the disorder that is suggested by this impersonation.

Thus the orientalism of *The Mikado* seems only on the surface to be a spectacular yet dignified and refined patrician experience. Underneath are more riotously comic and/or fearfully debased characterizations and actions. These, I suggest, draw not only from the English burlesque tradition, with figures such as the oriental despot and the Widow Twankay,[75] but also

Figure 15. Georges Bigot, "Monseiur et Madame vont dans le Monde" (1893).

from the riotous performances of blackface minstrelsy. Two characterizations in particular offer interesting resonances with some of the familiar types of blackface minstrelsy. The role of Katisha is transformed from a caricature of aging white femininity directly descended from English comedies of an earlier century (Congreve's Lady Wishfort, for instance), to the strong, mature, and sexually rapacious black woman whose "devilish" appearance inspires both fear and admiration. Comparisons might well be made between the role of Katisha and the male drag performances of minstrel, particularly "funny old gal," who with the more seductive "wench" was one of the staples of blackface minstrelsy. The reference in the Mikado's song to the "lady who dyes a chemical yellow / or stains her grey hair puce" is often linked to Katisha (who in many productions has bright "puce" hair); thus her fate is to be figuratively blacked-up in punishment. Katisha, confident that she is attractive and worthy of love, in spite of her advanced years and grotesque appearance, resembles some of the figures of blackface minstrel songs such as "Miss Ebony Rose," in which an equally aggressive female of dubious attractions threatens to chase down and punish her errant lover. Like Katisha's accounts of her "left shoulder-blade," "right elbow," and "circulation," Miss Ebony Rose names her various attractive parts for the audience and flaunts them openly and seductively.

> I is Ebony Rose, as you may see,
> From de iseland call'd Timbuctimbee—
> Me ramble up and down dis town,
> To look for de nigger what dey calls Jim Brown.
>
> And if me cotch dis ole Jim Brown,
> Dat plays dem cimbles about de town,
> Me fust hit him up, and den hit him down,
> Me play de berry debil wid dis ole Jim Brown.
>
> Oh, I'se de gal what makes dem grin,
> Wid de white-wash teef and de blackball chin—
> Lips ob red, and turn-up nose,
> I'se de beauty—Ebony Rose.[76]

Significantly, *Hot Mikado* reviewers often praised a similar racial typecasting of Katisha: Rosa Brown became "a Katisha who is no black-toothed hag but a Harlem siren, a Cotton Club Sadie Thompson, a *cafe-au-lait*

Mae West, who has insinuating songs to sing."[77] Brooks Atkinson relates, "When Rosa Brown sweeps in as Katisha toward the end of the first act, things pick up immediately, for she is the most torrid of these sepia troubadours and a blues singer of quality."[78] *Time* magazine describes her as an "eye-rolling, hip-shaking, torch-singing Red Hot Mama,"[79] and *Variety* praises her singing of the "I, Living I" number as "a smoking torch song."[80] For Richard Watts, this translation of the role of Katisha is the most welcome improvement on the original *Mikado:*

> All of Gilbert's meanest and most vindictive streak went into this malicious satirization of an ugly, aging woman longing for youth, and the result is as cruel and mean-spirited as it is dull and ineffectual. . . . It is all the more astonishing, therefore, to find that Katisha suddenly becomes one of the greatest virtues, rather than the outstanding drawback, of "The Hot Mikado." Because Miss Rosa Brown, a gay and mischievous young woman with a look in her eye, plays the hitherto frightening matron with humor and sings the role in the manner of the hottest of torch singers, Katisha becomes the desirable one of the tale, and poor Yum-Yum is forgotten by everybody, probably including Nanki-Poo. In at least one way I find it difficult to describe this Miss Brown. The easy thing would be to call her a sepia Mae West, but she is so much superior to the estimable Diamond Lil that the comparison might be confusing.[81]

The tailor Ko-Ko, too, both in his false elevation to the status of Lord High Executioner and in his insistence on playing the heroic lead ("Must I never be allowed to soliloquize?" he mourns), seems to borrow from a standard role in blackface minstrelsy, the upstart Zip Coon, who was ridiculed for his pretensions to upper-class behavior. Whether or not they openly recalled Zip Coons of the past, both Herman Greene of *The Swing Mikado* and Eddie Green of *The Hot Mikado* echo minstrel performances in their performances. According to one reviewer, Herman Greene played Ko-Ko "as Bert Williams might have."[82] *Hot Mikado's* Eddie Green is praised as "vastly amusing as Ko-Ko—melancholy, shuffling, putting his voice through the traditional jumps of the Negro comic."[83]

It was perhaps impossible for African American performers to escape the inevitable comparisons with popular minstrel shows. Nonetheless, both *The Swing Mikado* and *The Hot Mikado* openly capitalized on the comic energies associated with blackface minstrelsy to enlarge the opera's inherent sense of racial unruliness. The all-white productions of *The Mikado* that preceded them, as we have seen, incorporated corporeal humor from the start. The presence of African Americans intensified this in particular ways. Freed of the restraint of the Savoy style, what Audrey Williamson has described as "a traditional spirit avoiding vulgarity,"[84] these versions of *The Mikado* turn blackness into a trope for release. Eric Lott suggests, "The minstrel show as an institution may be profitably understood as a major effort of corporeal containment—which is also to say that it necessarily trained a rather constant regard on the body." If, as Lott states, blackface minstrelsy embodies the "twin streaks of insurrection and intermixture, the consequences, to white men's minds of black men's place in a slave economy,"[85] *The Mikado* could also harness the incendiary powers of racial desires and anxieties projected through bodily display. Marshall and Jean Stearns relate a story about the Lindy dancers hired to perform in *The Hot Mikado* at the New York World's Fair:

> Making the best of an old stereotype, the male dancers in the troupe, who wore tight jersey trousers, padded their supporters with handkerchiefs (a trick that has been known to happen in ballet) and executed an occasional slow, stretching step facing the audience. It was a private joke. Eventually Mike Todd noticed it with horror. "If this isn't stopped, I'll never be able to put another show on Broadway." He ran to the wardrobe mistress to ask whether the dancers were wearing supporters. When assured that they were, he decreed that thenceforth each must wear two supporters.[86]

The double standard is clear when the roles of Katisha, Ko-Ko, and others are inhabited by African American performers. While a racialized eroticism and a queer and quaint deviance are suggested in *The Mikado*'s original incarnations, casting these roles with African American performers intensifies these sexual references; Katisha is transformed into a "hot mama" and the Ko-Ko who can only fantasize about the use of his "snickersnee" moves between Zip Coon and Sambo. If the white performer can flirt with this racialized deviance as a form of harmless fun, the African American performer marks it as irretrievably aberrant.

Once again we recall earlier comments made in Doggett's 1913 review of *The Mikado* in the *New York Age*. When Doggett criticizes the Howard University company for presenting "a set of faces resembling every color in the rainbow" instead of presenting a convincing "Japanese type," he is only upholding the standards of racial impersonation that made the Savoy players so popular. His hope and expectation is for the African American performer to be able to do as the white performer does, to make a convincing racial transformation. However, the greater challenge was the prejudices facing African Americans, who were inevitably thought of in terms of an essentialized blackness. In the case of *The Mikado* this "inherent" primitivism was seen to bring out what was already considered queer about playing Japanese, the titillating sexual deviance and sense of transgression that underlay certain roles in *The Mikado*.

This appears in the two contrasting portrayals of the Three Little Maids that appear on 1885 advertising. The first, the "Trois Petites Mamans," emphasizes youth, innocence, and virginity; these "mamans" have the solemn expressions of childish Madonnas. Just as easily, however, the Three Little Maids can translate into a grotesque blackface version. Their books, slung carelessly, suggest the insouciance of the song itself; their elaborate hats and bouquets belie their tattered clothing, bare feet, and slouching posture. Both show the appeal of this trio, whose ebullient energy and "girlish glee" flaunt a degree of independence and sexual license even while insisting on virginal maidenliness. As Mari Yoshihara suggests, orientalist racial cross-dressing enabled white women to enjoy a measure of liberty that was crucial to the formation of the New Woman: "It was not coincidental that the proliferation of white women's performances of Asian heroines and the emergence of New Women overlapped. The freedom to cross racial, class, cultural lines—even if it was temporary 'play'—was part of being 'modern' American women, particularly new Women."[87] The first *Mikados* played up the fine line between an acceptably domesticated form of female allure and a more dangerous disorder, as suggested in Jessie Bond's story of her oversized obi. The Three Little Maids as performed by white actors are granted the safety of youthful white female allure even while evoking racial typecasting of Japanese women as erotic geisha. African American performers, however, are seen to embody a transgressive sexuality of their own that makes the eroticism unmistakable.

Figure 16. "Trois Petites Mamans" and "Three Little Maids from School," trade cards, circa 1885.

These illustrations make clear how easily the types created by the opera translated into minstrel parody as well as idealized image, into Topsy as well as Little Eva. Perhaps this contrast is not unexpected; Karen Sánchez-Eppler describes the topsy-turvy doll widely popular in the nineteenth-century United States, which presented "two dolls in one: when the long skirts of the elegant white girl are flipped over her head, where her feet should be there grins instead the stereotyped image of a wide-eyed pickaninny." This doll, missing pelvis and legs, reveals a familiar relationship of race and gender whereby white and black femininity are tied together: "the sexual fears and desires of the white woman are figured on the body of the black, while the black woman presents her sexual experience in the terms sanctioned by white models of feminine decorum."[88] What is Japanese about the three maids seems to do a kind of vanishing act to reveal a more familiar American preoccupation, whereby virginal Madonnas easily become the incorrigible and unruly children of blackface minstrelsy.

Through tracing this shared history of blackface and yellowface, we have seen how through performing *The Mikado* African Americans gained the privileges and freedom of yellowface impersonation, successfully transforming themselves into versions of the opera's spectacular Japanese. But perhaps they could do so only because what is Japanese is by no means racially neutral but is already marked as bearing some affinity to the deviance and primitivism of blackness. Thus *The Swing Mikado* and *The Hot Mikado* are vehicles in which audiences might see African American performers as both successfully integrated yet still indelibly confined to essential notions of blackness.

The myriad black versions of *The Mikado* that have since emerged demonstrate a continuing relationship between yellowface and blackface minstrelsy. In these *Mikado*s, the former is never reworked without the latter's close proximity; the opera's complex racial presentation of Japanese holds the door open for blackness as well. There have been multiple attempts to reproduce the commercial success of *The Swing Mikado* and *The Hot Mikado* with other black versions of Gilbert and Sullivan, including a 1940 "tropical" *Pinafore*, performed by an African American cast. At least according to its *Time* magazine reviewer at least, this version fell short of its *Mikado* forebears. Set in "a banana-bright Caribbean isle," it opened "with a jungle chant that Sullivan neglected to write" and "burst into syncopation when a huge, black, big-bosomed Little Buttercup appeared, called Dick Deadeye picklepuss and shaking her gargantuan hips." In spite of its jazzed-up score, "gone-native" setting, and "singing that not only the Swing Mikado, but even the D'Oyly Carters, might envy," the disappointed reviewer finds that the production registered "little of the genuine high spirits that lifted *The Swing Mikado* high off its feet" and "went over on its rich husky Negro singing rather than as a shagging Harlemquinade."[89] Without the workings of yellowface already in place, these versions of Gilbert and Sullivan productions are clearly seen as lacking.

Minstrelsy continues to haunt black versions of *The Mikado*, such as *The Black Mikado*, which premiered at the Cambridge Theatre in London in 1975, directed by Braham Murray. Reviewers of *Black Mikado* praised the musical arrangements and choreography; Derek Jewell in the *London Times* mentions the "soul-rock, reggae, blues, calypso and splendid jazzy touches from the stage band Juice, like the flugelhorn solo in 'The Sun and I,'" and "the feeling of improvisation and joyous exuberance [that] is there all the time, in the dynamic dancing as well as the music."[90] But these descriptions again suggest that what was exciting about this production was its hot and primitive rhythms; here blackness might serve as the curative for a staid Victorian culture obsessed with cold oriental objects.

> Into the cherry blossoms and frozen peaks of Japan it imports, just as Dionysus himself came into Greece, from an alien place, the maddening sunshine, the drumbeat and the tribal dances of the West Indies, transforming Sullivan's pleasant teacup tunes with a blaze of colour and life. It is more continuously and rapturously at one with the disturbing and dangerous Thracian god . . . and the flash of the brown arms and legs in its wild dances is electrifying.[91]

The album cover evokes both blackface and yellowface: a geisha figure with a half-white, half-brown face wears a bone, a Jemima-style kerchief, and chopsticks in her hair.

Recognizing the production's links to the earlier *Swing Mikado* and *Hot Mikado*, Clive Barnes for the *New York Times* finds:

> It is "Carmen Jones" time again. People have tried to stage a black hepped-up version of the Gilbert and Sullivan operetta, where any number of British blacks are revealing to the world that they too have natural rhythm. Perhaps my antagonism to the piece can at least in part be attributed to my dislike, bordering headily on hatred, for Gilbert and Sullivan as such. But possibly Savoyards would be more turned off by this jokily travestied version than ordinary people. Who can tell?
>
> One thing that certainly makes this one of the hits of London is the playing of the cast. Whether or not one thinks this "Black Mikado" worth doing, it must be admitted that it is being done superlatively well. Derek Griffiths is resourcefully witty as Ko-Ko, and Michael Denison reveals an easy, lazy style as Pooh-Bah. But—oh dear—does one really have to produce Gilbert and Sullivan as an alternative for a musical theater? Even in blackface?[92]

Ultimately the *Swing Mikado* and *Hot Mikado* revealed a range of spectators who valued these productions for different reasons, and whose understanding of what is Japanese about *The Mikado* seems to be subsumed under other racial agendas. For many, the worth of these productions was not reducible to the primitive stereotypes that entranced so many of

Figure 17. Album cover, The Black Mikado *(1975).*

the reviewers. In contrast, many affirm that through these productions a kind of racial progress—at least in the form of the recognition of African Americans as performers in the larger sphere—was being made. Alain Locke notes *Swing Mikado,* along with Federal Theatre Project's *Voodoo Macbeth* (1936), directed by Orson Welles and set in Haiti, was "refreshing and revealing Negro versions of familiar classics" that to him manifested what he called "the compound gain of the distinctive cultural hybrid" and the "experimental ventures of the powerful appeal of Negro idioms in dignified and unstereotyped contexts."[93] It is this kind of experimentation that for Locke pushes African American art beyond the "romantic and jazz exoticism" that made Harlem a "fashionable fad" or the "subservient imitativeness" of more general trends in contemporary American art and literature such as aestheticism, realism, regionalism, or proletarianism.[94] More recently, Susan Gubar celebrates, "Such exuberant transformations of white scripts redefine the color line that W. E. B. Du Bois saw as the central problem of the twentieth century as an inspiring opportunity for aesthetic innovation."[95] Rena Fraden gives a more guarded assessment:

> Clearly the *Swing Mikado*'s cast cannot be said to have exploded the song and dance discourse that surrounded them then. But in the tentative groping to an identity as a unit, perhaps (who knows?) one actor of two may have stepped from behind the screen of minstrelsy to some other part history hasn't recorded for us. And certainly it is also possible to read this episode deliberately (as I have tried to do here at the end) as a self-conscious attempt to call attention to the artifice of their role, forcing an audience or a reader to consider the boundaries of propriety, property, the appropriate, which, if not exactly revolutionary, may be a liberation of sorts— if not then, then now.[96]

The appearance of African American performers certainly did leave room for the expression, however momentary, of more barbed political sentiments. A questioning of the overall social status of African Americans could be tucked into performances of *The Hot Mikado*, such as in this moment where Bill Robinson as Ko-Ko makes his list:

> There's the Radio Comedian
> Whose jokes are thick with mold
> And the Glamour Girl of Sixty
> Who refuses to grow old
> All Men who start each statement with
> "Now I'm not prejudiced."
> I've got them on my list.
> They'll none of them be missed.[97]

Finally, productions did provide a way for two large casts of African American performers to find work, even a measure of success, in a field that was otherwise tightly circumscribed even in more prosperous times. There were few alternatives to the minstrel stage. For experienced performers such as Bill Robinson or Maurice Ellis, these productions confirmed their ability to enter into a range of classic roles. For younger performers, such as tap dancer Cholly Atkins, it was a practical choice and provided a stable environment in which to refine abilities for the future. Atkins describes his mixed reaction when he was asked to replace a dancer at the 1939 World Fair production of *The Hot Mikado:*

> I spoke with Chink Lee, captain of the Cotton Club Boys, and he arranged for me to go out to Queens and watch the show for a couple of nights. Then Honi (Coles) and I talked it over again. He said, "These guys are not the greatest dancers in the world, but they get a lot of gigs and it will keep you busy until you find something else to do." That's pretty much the way I was thinking about it, too, so I decided I'd definitely give it a shot.
>
> After all, it was a stable job and would at least put some bread on the table. I went in, rehearsed with them a couple of days, tried on the new costumes and everything. That's all it took.[98]

Atkins's pragmatic approach to the job has little to do with its being a breakthrough role or even an artistic challenge. He recalls that the "Lindy Hoppers had some real wonderful spots in the *Hot Mikado,*" including the "Three Little Maids," where, dressed "in yellow tights and light green jackets," "The Cotton Club Boys played the wandering minstrel band. Our dances were all tap routines—different wardrobes, different sets, different music, but all tap." Still, Atkins concludes, "Although the musical arrangements were fabulous, the choreography was pretty elementary."[99] During the tour of *The Hot Mikado,* he uses the opportunity to develop alternatives for the future:

> On tour at the beginning of 1940 I could see that the Cotton Club Boys had a lot of real talent mixed up in there, so early on I started planting the seeds that would change them into a real act. Let's face it, there were not too many Broadway shows that black dancers could get into, so I was starting to think about how we could prepare ourselves for other performance options, like appearances with jazz bands.
>
> I said to the guys, "Look, we could be great and we could get a lot of work, but we're going to have to do more interesting things." Periodically, I would hold rehearsal sessions when we went into a city for two or three weeks during the Hot Mikado tour. These

were not mandatory all the time, but we did a lot of rehearsing, getting things in shape to build a better act.[100]

What is clear from Atkins's account and others is that these African American *Mikado*s were important stepping-stones to a future career.

However, in the face of acclaim for African American performers, the discussion of yellowface tends to drop out. Instead, *The Swing Mikado* and *The Hot Mikado* in particular are often used to claim a kind of universality for the opera, whereby the African American performance of it confirms its status as a classic and negates any charges of racism against the Japanese.

The Mikado occupies a space of particular racial sensitivity within the Gilbert and Sullivan oeuvre. Part of the interest in redoing *The Mikado* lies in redeeming it from its suspect racial representations of Japan and resetting it as an African American opera comes from an inherent awareness of its racism. Such versions seem to promise an escape from the pitfalls of the representations of Japan, not only through casting African American performers as Japanese characters but in billing this change as triumphant racial uplift. In other words, the inherent racism of *The Mikado* toward the Japanese can be erased because these productions demonstrate the democratic *staging* of the opera for African American visibility. These versions both establish a difference from the D'Oyly Carte authorized versions (to make a case for artistic freedom) and reinterpret the opera's racial politics in order to re-inflect it as a black performance. Both are related, promising a break from the opera's Victorian past toward a new multicultural future whose locus is the United States. In other words, such productions reposition the opera, moving it from a Victorian England obsessed with a consumable Japan to a United States actively working to solve its racial problems. These new versions of *The Mikado* carry with them the hope that the performance of artistic classics, far from being the property of a cultural elite, might provide a place of common access in a multicultural society. However, this reinvention of *The Mikado* is enabled by the very logic of commodity racism that we saw earlier, a dynamic of consumption in which what is Japanese is simply a style, an invention, an act without consequences. These swinging *Mikado*s only become an invitation for all races to participate more equally in the pleasurable masking of yellowface.

· Chapter 5 ·

Titipu Comes to America: Hot and Cool *Mikado*s

Gilbert and Sullivan's tuneful fantasies have become a symbol of a very English Englishman's ironic humor. But not until the all-Race version of their most popular work is heard will Chicago theatregoers realize how American their operas can be.

Publicity report for The Swing Mikado

The *Swing Mikado* and *The Hot Mikado* reveal not only the close ties of blackface and yellowface but also how the racial dynamics of the opera depend on an imagined locale. Its new settings—an imaginary South Pacific island or a slick gold-and-silver futurism à la *Hot Mikado*—seem far away from the commodity-laden Titipu of 1885, but there is a similarly therapeutic effect in each, whereby racial play offers novelty, pleasure, liberation, and escape. The infusion of swing music and the pointedly African American casting of *The Swing Mikado* and *The Hot Mikado* specifically relocate the opera from a fantasy of Japan to one of the United States, where blackness defines the hip new commodities of choice. The Japan of *The Mikado,* a space of exotic locale, fantastical characters, and tempting commodities, becomes the backdrop for the imagined amalgamation of black-and-white.

As we have already seen, there is actually a much longer history of innovative *Mikado*s in the United States. Blackface minstrel parodies from 1885 onward adapted *The Mikado* to satirize American politics, such as in the characterizations of Carncross's Minstrels: Alvin Blackberry, a "smart Coon, chairman of the Ward Committee"; Whatdoyousay, a Japanese "Black and Tan"; Grover Tycoon Cleveland, the "big Fly Coon from Washington"; a Japanese "no account"; and "as a special curiosity," a "few honest New York Aldermen."[1] An advertisement for one of the several versions of *The Mikado* simultaneously running in Chicago in October 1885 listed Haverly's Home Minstrels performing "Mr. R. N. Slocum's new local burlesque on THE MIKADO," *High-Card-O!,* whose characters included the "High-Card-O of Chicago, not so contented with life as he might be, because of the harrassin' circumstances attending a late municipal election"; "Yankee-Pooh, his son, disguised as one of Haverly's Minstrels"; "Ko-Ko-Nuts, a West Side Pawnbroker, High Sheriff of the Ninth Ward"; and "Waukesha, a middle-aged damsel from Wisconsin."[2]

These early parodies all used the comic unruliness of blacked-up performers to satirize figures of authority. Minstrel burlesques of *The Mikado,* like other parodies of European opera, appropriated and mocked high art forms from Europe.[3] From the 1890s onward, wayward productions of *The Mikado* increasingly emphasized a tension between the yellowface classic and the riotous and "barbaric" energies of blackface minstrelsy. These productions played openly on the possibilities for different racial contrasts of yellow and black: foreign and domestic, decorous and unruly, unintelligible and all too familiar. In doing so, they resituated the fantasy of Japan in the United States. More serious spin-offs, such as Mathews and Bulger's 1899 "ragtime opera" *By the Sad Sea Waves,* described as "a mixture of airs from *The Mikado* and popular 'coon' songs,"[4] also associate Gilbert and Sullivan's quintessentially English opera with specifically American forms and locales.

Versions of *The Mikado* reset in the United States also circulated in Europe. One of the more notorious is described by A. H. Godwin in the *Gilbert and Sullivan Journal* as an "appalling travesty," seen in a Berlin theater in December 1927:

> Imagine Nanki-Poo Yankee-ised in flannels and blazer! Imagine Katisha entering in a real motor-car and in a tailor-made of bewildering pattern! One gets resigned to anything. Thus, the Charleston is jogged by a troupe of semi-clad damsels as the first act curtain falls. It rises on the second act to show an absolutely naked girl bathing. Clearly, she is meant to be Yum-Yum, and her conspicuous ablutions precede her adornment in bridal attire.... Usually Sullivan's airs are used very much as we know them until they reach the sound and fury of a kind of ultra-jazz "tail piece." This sends the trumpets and saxophones and other tortuous instruments crashing. In fairness I must say that the orchestral playing, like much of the chorus work, was at times unusually good, and some num-

Figure 18. Poster, Mathews and Bulger's By the Sad Sea Waves *(1898). Library of Congress.*

bers I have never heard made half so impressive (and artificially impressive) in England. . . . In the "Wandering Minstrel" song a line of fantastically dressed girls indulge in a high-kicking parade. Evidently they are meant to be the troops of Titipu.[5]

Although its cast was white, this version bears more than a casual resemblance to the later *Swing Mikado* and *The Hot Mikado*. Through the incorporation of jazz and African American–inspired dance forms such as the Charleston, *The Mikado* is liberated from its Victorian contexts and relocated to a fantasy of a black-and-white America.

The Swing Mikado and *The Hot Mikado* have a special place in this relocation. In the opening lines of *Swing Mikado*, the chorus of men defining themselves as "gentlemen of Japan / On many a vase and jar" changes to "high-steppers of afar / On many a screen and star." *The Mikado* is transformed by its employment of recognizable bodies and tropes that have been already established as part of a black American context. In *Hot Mikado* the casting of tapper Bill T. Robinson also functions as such an icon; says one reviewer, "Bill Robinson's rolling eye and beaming smile, his masterly dancing, his kindliness and his vitality climaxes a gay evening and gave it that extra lilt which comes from the presence of one of Broadway's most engaging and beloved comedians."[6] Thus the opera highlights a new racial message in which the "primitive" swing performed by African Americans both remodels a now-staid Victorian commodity and attests to visions of a "new world" of American racial harmony. Stephanie Batiste astutely remarks that both "'Negro' exoticism and swing" suggested that *The Swing Mikado*'s blackness was "a carrier of an American modern sensibility": "both permitted the Federal Theater to mark *The Swing Mikado* with a particularly American stamp."[7]

That both swinging *Mikado*s received such warm success is no accident. Their black reimagining of Titipu is consistent with what Christina Klein describes as the larger cultural workings of Popular Front liberalism in the 1930s and 1940s; numerous musical classics were revised in what was deemed an American idiom, with such examples as Oscar Hammerstein's *Carmen Jones* (an African American adaptation of George Bizet's *Carmen*) declared a "people's triumph."[8] This liberalism opened the door for African American performers on mainstream stages and redefined the racial dynamics of American popular culture in fundamental ways.

What happens to the fantasies of Japan in this relocation? The swing versions of *The Mikado* were seen as hip improvements on an overly repressed classic, even as New Deal America with its more liberal race politics saw itself as improving a racist America of the past. As one reviewer of the *Swing Mikado* exalted in 1939:

In effect, the old "Mikado" becomes a juvenile antique. It should be stuffed and put in a museum, for now it's as dated as a kiddy's kite alongside of an Atlantic Clipper. Yes, sah! Harlem's got Gilbert and Sullivan on the list—and they never will be missed.⁹

Left out of this equation, of course, are not only the problematics of blackface minstrelsy that we just illustrated but also any questions about the ethics of yellowface. If in the 1885 production one was hard pressed to find anything authentic about the Japanese Yum-Yum, Nanki-Poo, or Pooh-Bah, *The Swing Mikado* and *The Hot Mikado* banished Japan even further. Given the obsolescence of Gilbert and Sullivan's quaint fantasy in the face of widespread anti-Japanese distrust and anti-Asian sentiment (the fear of the yellow peril that we will later describe in more detail), the emergence of this new Harlem-based Titipu seems fortuitous for fans of the opera. It allowed for the continued enjoyment of yellowface in a newly hybrid form, which embraced a fetishized blackness as the new soul of *The Mikado*.

Popular Front liberalism of the 1930s and 1940s drove the success of the 1938–39 swinging *Mikado*s, but this type of adaptation had some striking reincarnations later as well. These are characterized by related spatial and musical shifts: Titipu becomes an Americanized racial playground in which interracial conflict can be romantically resolved, and the music is correspondingly reorchestrated to swing, blues, and other popular African American musical styles.

This distinctive racial reimagining of the opera does not confine itself to the 1930s. In this chapter, we will look at two striking examples of later productions with this same theme. *The Swing Mikado* begot *The Hot Mikado,* and a new spate of *Hot Mikado*s, beginning with a production at Ford's Theatre (Washington, D.C.) in 1986, has kept this new vision of *The Mikado* as racially liberated very much alive. The newer versions of *Hot Mikado,* collaborations between director David Bell (who also adapted the book and lyrics) and composer Robert Bowman, openly cite the 1939 Michael Todd version as their inspiration. These new versions now seem to rival the popularity of the original in the English-speaking world. These new *Hot Mikado*s stage themselves as racially liberal productions, prominently featuring black-and-white interracial romance and multicultural casting. Yet, as we will see, these productions also run into the same tensions suggested earlier insofar that they harbor some of the legacies of blackface minstrelsy as well as present stock images of Japan as a perpetually foreign and decorative entity.

In this chapter I cannot resist using as my other example a film that few (aside from diehard Gilbert and Sullivan fans) still remember and most think is better forgotten: *The Cool Mikado*. Set in a Japan still obviously under American cultural and military influence, this 1963 film also restages *The Mikado* with cool jazz rhythms and fosters fantasies of Japan as a space of racial recreation for the liberated American. What is fascinating about this obscure example is that once again the image of a hip and racially liberated America subtly informs the interactions, orchestrations, and dance sequences of the film's blatantly revised and reorchestrated *Mikado*. Both these hot and cool *Mikado*s pay tribute to a newly liberal understanding of race, mobilized in order to celebrate the benevolence and superiority of new racial orders, from the U.S. cold war influence in Asia to 1980s multiculturalism.

Hot *Mikado*s, 1986 and After

In 1986 director David Bell staged the first of these contemporary productions at Ford's Theatre in Washington, D.C. "I always liked the idea of a hip, multicultural version of 'The Mikado,' and I knew about the two competing versions that were created in 1939," Bell told reviewer Hedy Weiss. "But when [musical director] Rob Bowman and I started to do research, we realized that there were no orchestrations or complete script to be found. And we really had to set about re-creating the wheel."[10] Bowman rewrote and developed his own arrangements with other rhythms in addition to swing, such as blues, gospel, rock, and soul. The 1986 *Hot Mikado* had critical success, and its revival at Ford's Theatre in 1994 yielded a 1995 production at the Queen's Theatre in London's West End as well as plans, later aborted, for a Broadway run. Numerous professional and amateur *Hot Mikado*s have since been produced widely throughout England, Scotland, Australia, New Zealand, Bermuda, and the United States.

Although they do not use either the book, score, or any design elements of the 1939 version, these contemporary *Hot Mikado*s claim Michael Todd's production as well as *The Swing Mikado* as their point of origin rather than the 1885 *Mikado* of Gilbert and Sullivan. Within their advertisements, program notes, and reviews, *The Swing Mikado* and *The Hot Mikado* are hailed as better progenitors for these more multicultural times. In a review of a 2006 Watermill Theatre (Newbury, U.K.) production of Bell and Bowman's *Hot Mikado*, Lyn Gardner makes this characteristic point:

> "If Gilbert and Sullivan could see me now," cries one of the hoofers in David Bell and Robert Bowman's musical mugging of the 19th-century operetta. If they could it seems unlikely that they would entirely disapprove. Their timeless tale of Yum-Yum and would-be husband Nanki-Poo has been transposed to a Titty-poo [sic] that is more American than Japanese, where the three little maids seem to be gearing up for careers in pole dancing, southern-fried sushi is the dish of the day and the characters constantly seem surprised that they can read Japanese.[11]

These productions delve into the celebratory fantasy of a multicultural America in which African Americans are fully empowered to play both established classics and other races. Here both the subtle yet pervasive fetishism of African American hip culture as well as the playing of Japanese style (maintained as foreign and exotic) is an integral part of seeing African Americans as the true originators of culture. No longer is Titipu confined to Japan; instead, its association with other spaces, such as 1939 Harlem, with blackness, and with "exotic" and unrepressed spaces such as the nightclub and the streets, turns it into a much more familiar contemporary racial fantasy. Like its 1885 counterpart, this fantasy, rife with deviant sexuality and danger, is at the same time safe for domestic consumption.

However, there are important differences between the new *Hot Mikado*s and their 1939 predecessors. Whereas the casts of the 1938–39 *Swing Mikado* and *Hot Mikado* were almost exclusively African American (*Swing Mikado*'s Edward Fraction being the exception), these more recent *Hot Mikado*s have a pointedly multiracial cast, with white performers featured strategically in lead roles. This multiracial casting is not color-blind but carefully managed for effect. Rhoda Koenig writes, "In tune with today's liberal multiculturalism" white actors were included in the 1995 London West End production, including a "charming Paul Manuel as Nanki-Poo," whose father was played by African American Lawrence Hamilton, who coolly explained to the audience, "There's not much family resemblance."[12] Thus these productions used strategic casting of these leads to reference (slyly) an imagined multicultural America family and more pointedly a fantasy of interracial romance, with the pairings of Nanki-Poo and Yum-Yum and Ko-Ko and Katisha portrayed by black-and-white couples.

Responses to these productions confirm how in these *Hot Mikado*s much of the focus stays on the portrayal of a harmonious marriage of black and white. If some of the attention is on African American performers who, as in the 1939 *Hot Mikado*, are thought to infuse Gilbert and Sullivan with new life and new rhythms, others note the ability of white performers to cross over into music imagined as quintessentially black, as in this assessment of the West End production: "[Sharon] Benson and [Alison] Jiear are the musical stars of the show. Jiear, who is white and plump, gives the kind of uninhibited full-throttle singing you still expect only blacks to deliver in hot jazz. Benson, who is glamorous and black, is fabulously authoritative in everything except the first half of her Act Two solo."[13] Occasionally there are Asian American cast members, such as Paul Matsumoto as Pish-Tush and chorus member/dancer Kiki Moritsugu in the 1994 Ford's Theatre revival; however, these choices are nearly entirely overshadowed. These *Hot Mikado*s still capitalize on the novelty and the implied racial progress inherent in staging black versions of *The Mikado* and in turn can avoid uneasy questions about the underlying racial representations of the Japanese. "Here was what 'The Mikado' needed," writes Steven Winn of the San Jose, California, 1998 version, "an irreverent steam cleaning with lots of jazz, swing, blues, gospel and jitterbugging dancers in loud zoot suits."[14]

It is perhaps not surprising, then, that these contemporary *Hot Mikado*s, like their 1930s predecessors, seem to invite the same terms of racial commentary as *The Swing Mikado* and *The Hot Mikado* and even present new connections back to the traditions of blackface minstrelsy. For instance, in reviewing a 1993 Chicago production, Richard Christiansen describes how Felicia P. Fields as Katisha, in growling "Come over here, fool" to her terrified lover, is a "flashy red-hot mama";[15] and Alastair Macaulay describes Sharon Benson's "big black-mama entrance" at the end of act 1.[16] Rhoda Koenig finds that all the female roles have been similarly sexualized as well as racialized by "ghosts" of former performances:

> On the female side as well, the casting alone does away with the coy, prissy sexlessness of G&S and their assumption that women over 40 are hideous viragos. Paulette Ivory, a delectable teddy-clad

Yum-Yum, anticipates her marriage by wriggling voluptuously through "The Sun and I." Sharon Benson's Katisha has clearly stayed unmarried because she is too much woman for the men of Titipu. Mae West couldn't improve on the way she tells us about her lovely left shoulder blade. The jitterbugging Little Maids shake everything shakeable and the arrangements are saucy and sensual—"Braid the raven hair," as close as G&S ever get to foreplay, gets a lot closer as a rhumba.[17]

The playing of Katisha and Ko-Ko in these new *Hot Mikado*s invites some of the same commentary as did *The Swing Mikado* and *The Hot Mikado*, foregrounding racial and gender typecasting familiar from blackface minstrelsy. As Eric Lott describes, these moments reflect the "white men's fear of female power" characteristic of blackface performance and the "bold swagger, irrepressible desire, sheer bodily display" of the "minstrel man."[18] Other comments on the new version of the *Hot Mikado* evokes the specter of blackface as well; director David Bell praises the performance of Ross Lehman as Ko-Ko as "an homage to such great vaudeville comedians as Bert Lahr and Eddie Cantor, whose work Roo [Lehman] captures so brilliantly."[19] Like other Jewish stars of vaudeville and film, Eddie Cantor got his start in blackface minstrelsy; born as Israel Iskowitz, Cantor created his first blackface character, Jefferson, in 1912 for Gus Edwards's *Kid Kabaret*, a show that earned him the attention of leading Broadway producer Florenz Ziegfeld. One of Cantor's acts for the Ziegfeld Follies paired him with African American comedian Bert Williams. Cantor played Williams's son; both men wore blackface.

While seemingly transformed into a multicultural romp, or even offered as a tribute to a history of African American performance, the contemporary version of the *Hot Mikado* does not run far from the minstrel mask. But its subtle associations, like so many contemporary reminders of blackface minstrelsy, are lost to most audience members. Such contemporary racial signifiers are carefully managed in order to avoid any offense. Blackness is staged in terms of its value as spectacle rather than as social commentary; these "hot" commodities might be easily displayed alongside those that point back to the japonaiserie of the 1885 *Mikado*. These *Hot Mikado*s have not lost their addiction to fans, screens, pagodas, and other familiar objects, which become revamped along with the music. Reviewer Rhoda Koenig wrote of the West End production: "The fun starts right away, with a gang of hipsters in lime, fuchsia and tangerine zoot suits slinking out to stare the audience down. Then they whip out what look like flick-knives, which with a snap, become fans for the gentlemen of Japan."[20] Humor relies on the clever juxtaposition of exotic Japanese and African American signs and mannerisms. In the 1994 Ford's Theatre production, the entrance of Ted Levy's Mikado is signaled by a gong, but his first line is "Yo, what's up?" Levy tap dances à la Bill Robinson but wears a cape with an oriental symbol. Returning from lunch, he sighs contently, "Southern fried sushi is what's happening." As Jeremy Kingston notes in his review of the West End production:

> One of the jokes is the extreme remoteness of these Brooklyn and Harlem characters from anything oriental. When Paulette Ivory's delicately provocative Yum-Yum wonders about her beauty "in my artless Japanese way," the sheer madness of the phrase is achingly absurd. The dialogue Gilbert gave to Ko-Ko and Pooh-Bah was rooted in English nonsense, and so there is a further, er, disorientation when a New York Jewish comedian and his black partner twitter on about the First Lord of the Treasury and the Lord Chief Justice.[21]

Thus racial meanings seem compounded, with the interracial marriage of black and white characters and music pointing the way toward a multicultural, even global America.

However, what is black and what is Japanese are still figured in very different ways, rather than as equal partners in contemporary multiculturalism. One of the many striking posters for the 1999 production of *Hot Mikado* by the Burgess Hill Operatic Society in Sussex, England, features a Statue of Liberty turned geisha, holding a trumpet and a fan and posed against a backdrop of rising sun, pagoda, and skyscrapers. The image of the Statue of Liberty suggests America as a nation of immigrants, yet its transformation into the geisha figure and its containment within the iconography of the Japanese flag undo any sense that what is Japanese might equally inhabit or define the national space of America.

If *Hot Mikado* serves as a vehicle for the celebration of a multicultural America, it does so by perpetuating clichés about Japanese foreignness. What is Japanese is still seen as exotic and unassimilable, in stark contrast

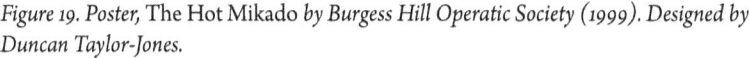

Figure 19. Poster, The Hot Mikado *by Burgess Hill Operatic Society (1999). Designed by Duncan Taylor-Jones.*

to a melting pot of black and white. Reviewing the 1994 revival at Ford's Theatre, J. Wynn Rousuck notes:

> Granted, the characters are obviously American—not only in their speech and mannerisms, but also in their dress. Costume designer Jess Goldstein clothes the men in jewel-colored zoot suits and the women in kicky knee-length dresses. Bell explains this seeming incongruity with a joke. Handed an official document, Ko-ko, the Lord High Executioner, exclaims, "It's in Japanese!" Then, after a head-scratching moment, he remembers, "We are Japanese."[22]

It is difficult to catch anything more than a fleeting glimpse of a more substantive message about race. Although they claim to be their direct descendents, these *Hot Mikado*s seem to erase the racial tension that so clearly informed the 1939 productions of *The Swing Mikado* and *The Hot Mikado*. As the increasing prevalence of new *Hot Mikado*s with all-white casts suggests, any deeper message about racial uplift, reconciliation, or triangulation is suppressed in favor of the staging of multiculturalism as a collection of shimmering costumes and memorable mannerisms. These *Hot Mikado*s freely play with both blackface and yellowface as styles of dress, gesture, and dance, creating a musical version of the melting pot replete with hip black music, a nostalgic 1940s nightclub setting, and chic new versions of japonaiserie. This postmodern mixture of styles, with its "flashy '40's zoot suits wrapped with obis (sashes) for a neon kimono look" and "women dressed like the Cotton Club-comes-to-Tokyo,"[23] does not seem to carry with it any history or political weight. This sets the stage for a purely stylistic hybridity, a pastiche seemingly devoid of any deeper meaning, as suggested for instance in Dan Hulbert's review of a 1997 Alliance Theatre production:

> We get a ravishing Daniel Proett nightclub set with a neon pagoda, gleaming chrome footbridge and trees made of Japanese parasols and fans; zoot suits and other 1940s costumes (by Nancy Missimi) of fantastic cuts and hues; opulent lighting by Diane Ferry Williams; gospel numbers in the Olympian voice of Atlanta's Chandra Currelley; a top-banana comic turn by Tony Award nominee Joel Blum, with deft takeoffs on Jack Benny and W.C. Fields; and a tap

solo by Joey Hollingsworth in the elegant tradition of Charles "Honi" Coles, backed by a thundering tap chorus. . . .

At this point you may wonder what this grab bag of wonders has to do with Gilbert and Sullivan, the clever gents who penned "The Mikado" in 1885. The short answer is, nothing. The longer answer is, who cares? Once it becomes clear that the G&S comic opera—itself a spoof of Victorian England in the guise of a storybook Japan—is just a flimsy excuse for Bell's multicultural good time, you can stop trying to figure out "Mikado" and just go with its Colorado River-Style flow.[24]

Postmodern pastiche seems to leave *Hot Mikado*s free to borrow from the legacies of both yellowface and blackface but without any apparent memory of their earlier meanings. The result is a sexier, hipper, presumably guilt-free *Mikado*. It is only after following a long and complicated history that one concludes that this erasure is not complete; that task done, the singing and dancing of the new *Hot Mikado* reveal a succession of more troubling ghosts.

The Cool Mikado

The recent spate of new *Hot Mikado*s marks a transition to the new racial regime of multiculturalism, which makes itself legitimate by carefully managing certain kinds of racial visibility. Displays of cross-racial casting or of interracial romance, for instance, support ideals of the United States as a liberal and tolerant nation. The movement from 1885 to the 1938–39 *Swing Mikado* and *Hot Mikado* and to the *Hot Mikado*s of the 1980s reveals a noticeable shift between different versions of racial utopias, from an exotic Japan to the "hot" settings of the South Seas to a black-and-white America defined by 1940s Harlem nightlife, zoot suits, hot dancing, and cool music.

Looking at the 1963 film *The Cool Mikado* helps us trace this movement back to an imagined Japan. The contemporary versions of *Hot Mikado* suggest that what is "hot" about this *Mikado* is its ability to celebrate American diversity; the performance of interracial harmony reworks the tired old opera, just as racial uplift and multiculturalism suggest the ability to overcome a history of violence and segregation. As the United States takes on the role of global power after World War II, this image becomes particularly necessary. As *The Cool Mikado* shows, post-occupation Japan can be refigured to serve as a kind of contemporary racial playground as well as a nineteenth-century "elf-land." As with the "swinging" *Mikado*s, music plays a key role in this transformation. The hot rhythms of swing have been modified into the cool styles of popular music, such as the jitterbug, cha-cha, and twist; nonetheless, this reorchestration adds a layer of eroticism and hipness onto the image of a modern Tokyo envisioned as a center of pleasure and opportunity for knowledgeable white visitors.

Serving mainly as a star vehicle for English and American comic actors Frankie Howerd and Stubby Kaye, who played Ko-Ko Flintridge and Judge Herbert Mikado, respectively, *The Cool Mikado* was largely panned by critics and dismissed by fans.[25] With its awkward modernization of Gilbert's plot and its sadly dated swinging sixties renditions of Sullivan's music, it is no wonder that the film has been largely forgotten. But though dreadful by all accounts, it nonetheless demonstrates the ways that the racial utopias of *The Mikado* have been updated to reflect the image of the United States as a new superpower spreading its message of liberal tolerance around the globe. Melani McAlister argues that after World War II, a new "post-Orientalist" model for representing the Middle East emerged for American audiences. This was clearly affected by the radical expansion of U.S. political and economic interests abroad; the Middle East became seen as a kind of new American frontier, and U.S. intervention in that region was justified as a kind of "benevolent supremacy" that would replace older European models of direct colonial rule.[26] Given this new context, no longer could simple models of orientalism as binary oppositions—East–West, masculine–feminine, foreign–domestic, us–them—hold explanatory power for encountering the Middle East.

In many ways, the older models for understanding Japan have likewise been fractured by World War II and the postwar occupation of Japan. The Japanese setting of *The Cool Mikado* is clearly unlike the japonaiserie of an earlier day, but elements of the queer and quaint still persist. The film was mainly made on a soundstage, with stock footage of Japan used to establish atmosphere at key moments. In the opening credits, different location shots are used to show both the quaint and modern sides of Japan: rural landscapes are interspersed with urban settings, and images of beautiful Japanese women wearing bathing suits and other Western-style clothing as well as kimonos bring the viewer into a setting that is both similar to the familiar decorative Japan and much more up-to-date.

Different attitudes toward Japan define the characters of the film. In the opening, Hank Mikado (the romantic lead, played by Kevin Scott) and Yum-Yum (Jill Mai Meredith) are regaled with tales of tourist adventures by the loud Charlie Hotfleisch (also played by Stubby Kaye). Charlie's loud stories about tourist attractions and geishas clearly mark him as the ugly American, boorish and uneducated about Japan's true charms. He is finally embarrassed into silence by Hank, who casually mentions his own considerable experience living in Japan. The remainder of the plot loosely follows the story (now following a gangster theme) and score of *The Mikado*, all the while exploring the differences between those who, like the ignorant Charlie, still cling to outdated clichés about Japan and those who, like Hank and Yum-Yum, are in the know. Through our introduction to Charlie, who doesn't appear in the rest of the film, the film makes its defining distinction between the old images of Japan given over to tourists and the new cultured and cosmopolitan Japanophile.

The film suggests how characters such as Hank embody another kind of yellowface; though they do not dress as Japanese, they are associated with insider knowledge of Japanese culture, language, and custom. This contrasts with other comic characters in the film. The tourist Charlie Hotfleisch is joined in his boorishness by Hank's friend Bernie (played by Bernie Winters), an Army soldier who loudly proclaims his erotic fascination with Japanese women, sings loudly in Japanese gibberish, calls Mount Fuji "Mount Fugo," and forgets to take off his boots before entering the house, eventually putting his foot through the floor. If the film pokes fun at Japanese culture, it does so through these comedians, who mimic bows, bang gongs, and abuse local people. This satiric treatment of the ugly American is extended to the British soldier who does not bother to learn anything about local culture or customs. Both are contrasted with the suave urbanity of Hank, who moves confidently through the various locales and mixes easily with the locals, even singing "A Wandering Minstrel" with a group of "traveling musicians" that he has presumably found despite their growing scarcity. Ironically, that these traveling musicians, with guitars in hand, are played in yellowface suggests that they are meant to be "natives." The other band members—white, black, and occasionally Japanese—who appear in the film do not wear racial makeup.

Likewise, Yum-Yum's bleached blond hair and blue eyes conspicuously marks her as white, but at the same time she is shown as easily blending into her Japanese surroundings. The Three Little Maids wear dresses that are identical except for color, and Yum-Yum's banter with Pitti-Sing (Chinese American Tsai Chin) and Peep-Bo (Japanese Canadian Yvonne

Shima), played by performers with conspicuously Asian features but no Japanese accents, suggests little difference among them. When Yum-Yum in her boudoir tells Pitti-Sing about Hank, the latter's slangy reply is "Ask him if he's got a friend for me" and then "I know love is here to stay, but put some clothes on first, huh?"

Whether singing "The Sun Whose Rays" poolside in a tiny blue bikini or posed on the decorative bridge at the Mikado Nightclub, Yum-Yum too has gone native. As Hank waxes rhapsodic about his courtship with Yum-Yum, he suggests that both of them find common ground in their affection for this "adoptive" country: "We both had Japan." Both hero and heroine show a cosmopolitan air that is in contrast to the smirking tourist Charlie Hotfleisch, the dopey Bernie, or the snide racisms of Ko-Ko, who treats the Japanese with contempt.

This emphasis on the superiority of the white Japanese cultural insider does not mean that the film has lost any traces of racism. Openly stereotypical portrayals, such as the buffoonery of Kenji Takaki in the supporting role of Ho-Ho, are certainly one of the reasons the film is so painful to watch. Like the sexism, embodied in the overdone role of the bombshell Katie Shaw (Jacqueline Jones) who does a striptease in front of Japanese male reporters, the racism is as flat and predictable as the bad cutout of Mount Fuji in the background. Each of these roles, whether of the different Japan experts—including comedian Tommy Cooper in a brief stint as Pooh-Bah, Private Detective—or of their unsophisticated, fresh-off-the-plane counterparts, lacks subtlety.

Nonetheless, the overriding preoccupation of the film with the urbane Japan insider who passes for Japanese says something interesting about this image of Japan as a new racial playground. In one of the film's many departures from the opera, a fascinating split happens in the character of Nanki-Poo. The film reincarnates the romantic lead in the character of Hank but also inflects him through the new character of Nanki, played by dancer, choreographer, and television personality Lionel Blair. At first, Nanki might be seen as simply one of the many feeble attempts at yellowface; played with a painfully stereotypical accent by Blair, he serves as a sidekick and go-between. But Nanki also seems key to what is considered cool about *The Cool Mikado*. In two of the most memorable song and dance sequences, the "Three Little Maids Cha-Cha" and the "Titwillow Twist," he and his "Lionel Blair dancers" have a prominent role.

Whether shimmying up to the camera, cavorting with a fan, or kissing one of the chorus girls, Nanki is given a much more interesting role than just serving drinks or telling Hank that his courting of Yum-Yum is "vewy dangerous." Likewise, his local coffee bar, called a "real swinging place" by Hank, similarly evokes the image of Japan as the hip new racial playground, inviting a host of not simply racial but also sexual transformations. Robert Lee has suggested that the depiction of Japan as "polymorphous, transgressive, and exotic" in a film such as *Sayonara* (1956) invests its leading characters with "a sexuality that is transgendered and unpredictably dangerous"; furthermore, oriental sexuality itself was often more generally "constructed as ambiguous, inscrutable, and hermaphroditic."[27] Nanki never gets the girl, but there is a similar polymorphous perversity in the sight of him dressed in tight vest, necktie, and pants and doing the same moves as his all-female chorus. Nanki's appeal builds further on the imagining of Japanese sexual deviance. Nanki-Poo mutates into Hank and Nanki, the heterosexual American Japan expert and the somewhat more sexually ambiguous Japanese sidekick; in the glamorous Tokyo of the film, both emerge triumphant, and the racial playground of this *Mikado* is refigured in terms not just of the quaint but also of the queer.

Perhaps the most memorable part of *The Cool Mikado* is its timely take on the practice of yellowface and Japan as a space of play for the liberated Westerner. It features a vision of a new opening of Japan that was made possible by U.S. victory and postwar occupation, by the airplane, and by a new racial sensibility. One short scene suggests a particularly American basis for how Tokyo can become this new racial playground. Even though by the time of the filming of *Cool Mikado* the American occupation of Japan had ended, the action takes place in a Japan where the presence of American military is omnipresent. Thus one of the most striking moments of the film is when a chorus of white American army officers sings "If You Want to Know Who We Are." Following the song, their claim that "we are gentlemen of Japan" is explained by Hank: "They've been over here so long they've gone native." Thanks to the U.S. military (still very much present), this post-occupation Japan has been transformed into a place that might attract tourists but holds its real rewards for those who "go native."

To do Japanese is to partake of what also might be seen as an American vision of race. In both the hot and cool *Mikados*, Titipu becomes the racial playground in which a liberal conqueror teaches old racial regimes how to swing.

Contemporary *Mikados*

· Chapter 6 ·

"The Threatened Cloud": Production and Protest

PARTS I AND II show two very different directions for the racial history of *The Mikado*, yet there is something consistent about the productions described in them. Both parts build on the opera's use of a spectacular and engaging decorative orientalism that fuses racial fantasy with the consumption of commodities. Both employ an easily imitated style of racial transformation whereby one can become Japanese with minimal effort; thus one can imagine a Japanese effect even in a swinging *Hot Mikado* set in 1940s Harlem. Both also articulate the seductive power of the very act of playing Japanese. These racial transformations can be seen as part of a much longer tradition of yellowface acting by white performers or as a form of racial triumph for African American performers who were formerly denied the ability to step out of their own skin.

Viewing the opera, singing the music, or creating one's own Mikado room allows for the easy enjoyment of racial masquerade in the imaginary spaces of Titipu. *The Mikado*'s racial playground, whether located in imagined Japan, the South Seas, or Harlem, can easily escape more complicated questions about the ethics of representing Japan through a claim to a kind of lightness. At the same time, *The Mikado*'s relationship to racial representation is vexed. There is a long tradition of pointing out that the opera's dialogue, satiric targets, performers, and songs (save one) are recognizably English; the claim that *The Mikado* is really about England, not Japan, is often mustered in defense against any charges of misrepresenting the Japanese. But *The Mikado* has also *defined* what is Japanese in a variety of ways and to a multitude of audiences. Though it bills itself as a fanciful invention and source of innocent merriment, it also represents Japan both metaphorically and metonymically through its creation of Titipu and its characters and through the prominent display of Japanese objects and costumes onstage.

The meaning and circulation of the opera throughout its long life is caught between questions of its representational fidelity and its capacity to operate as a thing unto itself. At times, *The Mikado* seems to act as a marker of an offstage Japan; at other times it seems to elude any such significance. Throughout the opera's history, its compelling vision of a fantasy Japan, played out through the seductive charms of yellowface, have never fully banished the representational power of the "real" that inevitably lurked behind the innocent merriment. The history of *Mikado* production has been dogged by reminders of this power, from the fear of outright censorship to nagging concerns about spoiling the fun. However compellingly light the touch of the opera, it still carries the weight of having to stand for Japanese people and Japanese culture.

In Part III, we will consider this aspect of the opera's racial history: how it operates not only as harmless divertissement but also as a touchstone of racial sensitivity. This chapter begins with an account of the 1907 censorship of the Savoy revival and how this event affected Gilbert's later reworking of the opera into the children's book *The Story of the Mikado* in 1908. Gilbert's impatience with how the growing diplomatic influence of the real Japan hindered the performances of his opera translates into a kind of hostility that is only barely disguised in the fairy-tale tone of this version of the opera's story.

We will examine protests of the opera along with other examples that demonstrate the opera's power to represent Japanese and other orientals. Nowhere is this influence more obvious than when the opera is put to use to disseminate a much darker fantasy of Japan. As the various images of Japan changed throughout the twentieth century—from "elf-land," to imperial power, to enemy aggressor, to defeated and occupied nation—so did what was represented on the opera stage. *The Mikado* framed its Japanese as queer and quaint, a racial stereotype that seems innocuous in comparison with other racial stereotypes of orientals as inherently untrustworthy, evil, diseased, and invasive. Yet the opera, as we shall see, also becomes a vehicle for much more open and virulent anti-Japanese and anti-Asian sentiment.

Censorship at the Savoy (1907)

At the end of April 1907, Mrs. Helen D'Oyly Carte, who managed the D'Oyly Carte Opera and the Savoy following her husband's death in 1901, received a notice from the Lord Chamberlain informing her that beginning August 4, performances of *The Mikado* would be forbidden. This took place under Regulation 20, part of the Theatres Regulations Act of 1843, which stated, "No offensive personalities or representations of living persons to be permitted on the stage, nor anything calculated to produce riot or a breach of the peace."

As Antony Best relates, this incident was part of an overall pattern in which British officials tried to determine the correct course of diplomacy with Japan. After perceived slights to Japanese royalty on previous official visits, Japan was sensitive to any suggestions of offense. For instance, British officials had debated over whether to present the Meiji Emperor, a non-Christian, with the Order of the Garter, the most prominent decoration that the British king could give a fellow monarch. Eventually, the award was given when Japan proved itself a rising world power in its defeat of Russia in the Russo-Japanese War (1904–5). After Japan's victory, a new alliance between Britain and Japan was marked by increasingly preferential treatment. In 1907 Prince Fushimi visited London in order to express the Emperor's gratitude at receiving the Garter; shortly before he arrived, officials at the Japanese embassy in London expressed their concern about the impending *Mikado* production to the Lord Chamberlain's Office. Likewise, these officials feared that "conductors of military bands might well think that tunes from *The Mikado* might provide an appropriate welcome to the Japanese prince. A hint to the contrary was therefore urgently conveyed to the Services."[1] The ban covered all professional and amateur productions as well as concert performances and even arrangements for band or orchestra. The Secretary to the Admiralty forbade naval and marine bands to play selections from the opera. The license of the Lyceum Theatre in Sheffield was withdrawn after a D'Oyly Carte company performance was staged there in defiance of the order.

An angry Gilbert wrote that he learned "from a friend, who had it from the King, that the Japs made the objection to *The Mikado* and that it was on their instance that it was suppressed." Gilbert blamed the British as well as the Japanese for his financial losses: "I suppose you have read that the king (with his unfailing tact) has forbidden that the Mikado shall ever be played again. That means at least 500 pounds out of my pocket. It is so easy to be tactful when the cost has to be borne by somebody else."[2] Many ridiculed the decision; one editorial in the *Pall Mall Gazette* declared, "Really, this withdrawal of 'The Mikado' licence, after twenty years of inoffensive fooling, seems to argue a lack of sense of humour somewhere, and does set people asking how many classical English plays may have to disappear unvenerably at the capricious hest of an excessive diplomatic delicacy."[3] The subject was raised on the floors of the House of Commons, and even the Prime Minister took part in the subsequent debate about the responsibility of the Lord Chamberlain to the House of Commons. However, *The Mikado* remained barred until April 28, 1908.

The censorship of the 1907 revival of *The Mikado* at the Savoy Theatre reflects both the opera's continued popularity and its seeming incongruence with the changing status of Japan on the world stage. The "excessive diplomatic delicacy" of the 1907 censorship was born out of uneasiness at how to deal with Japan in its new status as a world power. Japan could assert cultural influence as well as military power on the world stage. Suddenly, playing *The Mikado* was seen as an overtly political act, and its representations became subject to scrutiny from new perspectives. K. Sugimura, the Japanese special correspondent of the Tokyo newspaper *Asahi* and sent to England to cover the Prince's visit, was invited to the Sheffield performance to assess the situation. He reported that the opera was, in fact, humorous rather than offensive, and that "the only part of the play to which objection might be taken by some is the presentation of the Mikado on the stage as a comic character."[4] Yet even this slight was, according to Sugimura, excusable:

> This would be impossible in Japan, where my countrymen regard the person of the Emperor as too high for such treatment. Yet, even with us, one of our most famous novelists, Saikako, of the Genroku period, did treat the figure of the Emperor humorously, describing one of his characters as the Emperor Doll. That novel is still circulated in Japan. It has not been prohibited there.[5]

Sugimura finds censorship unnecessary, giving approval to the opera's "bright music and much fun" and declaring that "the English people, in withdrawing this play lest Japan should be offended, are crediting my country with needless readiness to take offence." Nonetheless, he also undercuts the arguments that the opera might be purely innocent merriment by taking the opportunity to point out inaccuracies and misrepresentations:

> I cannot understand from what part of Japan the author got the names of characters. Yum-Yum I thought at first to be Num-Num, an incantation to Buddha. Real Japanese girls would not be called

Yum-Yum or Peep Bo. The name of the man Pooh-bah is not a
Japanese name. Of course, the play shows quite an imaginary
world, not in the least like Japan. The characters embrace and kiss
quite publicly. In my country this would be quite shocking. No
properly brought-up young lady like Yum-Yum would ever dream
of doing this.[6]

In Sugimura's terms, *The Mikado* does bear comparison with a real Japan; its misrepresentations, such as the names Yum-Yum and Peep-Bo and the overt kissing, define it as "an imaginary world, not in the least like Japan." It is the English who are presumptuous in their assumption that Japanese people lack humor or the ability to differentiate between "a comic character" and "real insults."[7]

Though he is primarily employed to counter charges that the opera is offensive, Sugimura importantly does not read the opera as pure fantasy, insisting instead on the relevance of *The Mikado* as a representation of Japanese people. His comments highlight how *The Mikado* never truly succeeds in escaping the responsibility of representing Japan or Japanese people. Even in claims that it is pure invention, the opera retains a certain power to signify, to stand in for, and to speak for Japan.

The Mikado and the Yellow Peril

Throughout the twentieth century, certain understandings of the opera registered the tensions between Japan as a construct of pure imagination and Japan as a military force rivaling the European powers and the United States. This is evident in Gilbert's rewriting of *The Mikado* as a children's story in 1908. Still smarting from the censorship of *The Mikado* revival the previous year, Gilbert begins by poking fun at what he sees to be the pretensions of modern Japan even while defending the depiction he offered in *The Mikado*:

> It has recently been discovered that Japan is a great and glorious country whose people are brave beyond all measure, wise beyond all telling, amiable to excess, and extraordinarily considerate to each other and to strangers. This is the greatest discovery of the early years of the twentieth century, and is one of the results of the tremendous lesson the Japanese inflicted on the Russians, who attempted to absorb a considerable portion of Manchuria a few

years ago. The Japanese, however, attained their present condition of civilization very gradually, and at the date of my story they had peculiar tastes, ideas and fashions of their own, many of which they discarded when they found they did not coincide with the ideas of the more enlightened countries of Europe.

Gilbert's biting commentary is aimed not just at the Japanese but at what he sees to be the excessive deference given to Japanese influence by the British government.

> It is important to bear this in mind, because our Government being (in their heart of hearts) a little afraid of the Japanese, are extremely anxious not to irritate or offend them in any way lest they should come over here and give us just such a lesson as they gave the Russians a few years ago. My readers will understand that this fear is not entertained by the generality of inhabitants of Great Britain and Ireland who, as a body, are not much afraid of any nation; it is confined mainly to the good and wise gentlemen who rule us, just now, and whose wishes should consequently be respected.[8]

Gilbert disconnects the world of *The Mikado* from the real Japan recently victorious over Russia and now asserting an imperial hold over Korea, China, and other parts of Asia. In doing so, he takes the opportunity to mock Japan's "present condition of civilization" as well as the "peculiar tastes, ideas and fashions" of their past. Interestingly enough, he does not relegate "the story of the Mikado" to the realm of pure fiction but rather claims it as an account of history, "the Japan of that time." In his children's tale, Gilbert does not bother to correct any inaccuracies of detail previously invented for his opera; in fact, he adds more, such as describing the song "Miya sama" as the "Japanese National Anthem."[9] As the story unfolds, what was invented for the opera is described to his young readers as customs and practices of Japan. In its revision into fable, *The Mikado* loses its overt connections to yellowface and instead passes for a real Japan that, even with its fairy-tale elements, comments subtly on a darker and more threatening vision of Japan, ruled by a Mikado with "a habit of punishing every mistake, however insignificant, with death" (3). Gilbert's anger at the 1907 censorship and his deprivation of the privilege of representation and the profit it entailed translate into a subtle gloss over the Titipu he initially created.

This serious counterpoint to the lightness of *The Mikado* is not wholly unexpected. As Japan gained increasing military and diplomatic influence in the first decade of the twentieth century, so did its image change. At the turn of the century, some described Japan as a cherry blossom toyland and the Japanese as a childlike people in images familiar to *Mikado* audiences;[10] others, like Japan scholar William Elliot Griffis, assessed the Japanese as "honorary whites," superior to other Asian ethnic groups.

> Like all great nations the Japanese are a composite of various stocks. The ancestral homes of the various tribes had been in both continental and insular Asia, in Tartary, Korea, Formosa and the southern Pacific islands; while in the northern half of Hondo and in Yezo dwelt the Emishi, or the Ainu, whose characteristics and language point to their being a branch of the Aryan family. At the base the Japanese are as truly a "white" as they are a "yellow" race.[11]

Other, much more negative, images of Japanese also associated them with the frightening archetypes of the Mongol; these racial images proliferated with Japan's rise to power on the world stage. Gina Marchetti suggests that the stereotype of the yellow peril may have first arisen at the time of Genghis Khan and the Mongolian invasions of Europe. According to Marchetti, "The yellow peril combines racist terror of alien cultures, sexual anxieties, and the belief that the West will be overpowered and enveloped by the irresistible, dark, occult forces of the East."[12] Colleen Lye adds, however, that a more particular understanding of this term emerged in the mid-nineteenth century with the rise of Japan as a military and imperial power and with a large-scale migration of Asian labor to white settler colonies around the Pacific Rim.[13]

In 1904, Jack London cautioned that the Japanese seizure of Korea and Manchuria signaled a new race war, a "menace to the Western world which has been well named the 'Yellow Peril.'" Even if China was weak politically, through its huge population alone it still represented a threat, particularly under the influence of the Japanese, a "race of mastery and power, a fighting race through all its history, a race which has always despised commerce and exalted fighting": "The menace to the Western world lies, not in the little brown man, but in the four hundred millions of yellow men should the little brown man undertake their management."[14] Such imaginings were broadly promoted in popular culture. While the stereotype of Japanese femininity, familiar from *The Mikado* but popularized even more by versions of *Madame Butterfly* for the stage by David Belasco and Giacomo Puccini, remained alluring and exotic, visual representation of Japanese men became demonic, inhuman, and monstrous. These visions of yellow-skinned, slant-eyed, and buck-toothed figures did not wholly supplant earlier renditions of japonaiserie; rather, they worked in tandem with familiar images of a more quaint and decorative Japan, as in a 1905 French postcard depicting a Japanese rickshaw running over figures representing the European powers Russia, Britain, France, and Germany, and which reads "Place aux Jaunes" (Make Way for the Yellows). The Second World War intensified the contrast of these various images. If depictions of the Japanese as evil enemy conflicted with the queer and quaint depictions of *The Mikado,* later military conflicts and alliances with China, Korea, and different countries in Southeast Asia made depictions of the "exotic" East even more fraught. Popular media representations of allies and enemies fluctuated between positive and negative images, often presented as two sides of the same coin.

Fears of Japan as a world power and threat from the outside were com-

Figure 20. Postcard by "Mille," "Place aux Jaunes" (Make Way for Yellows) (1905). Leonard A. Lauder Collection of Japanese Postcards, Museum of Fine Arts, Boston. Image copyright 1905 Museum of Fine Arts, Boston.

bined with anxieties about Asian immigrants as internal threats to racial homogeneity and domestic peace. As we have already seen in our discussion of the "coolie Chinee," the idea of the yellow peril was not only applied to Japan as the evil invader from outside but also evoked in tensions about immigrant labor. In the United States, the yellow peril served to illustrate both the threat of world domination by nonwhite races and fears of Chinese, Japanese, "Hindoo," and Filipino coolie labor. Chinese immigrants were targeted for racial exclusion and socially ostracized; other Asian immigrant groups were subsequently subjected to similar laws and marginalization. Multiple restrictions on immigration, naturalization, and property ownership, such as the 1917 Immigration Act that prohibited immigration from persons whose ancestry could be traced to the Asiatic Barred Zone on the Asian continent and Pacific Islands, were accompanied by prevalent images of multiple Asian ethnic groups, including the Japanese, as debased, sexually deviant, untrustworthy, and unassimilable.

The Mikado's alluring and decorative Japanese fantasy seems at first quite removed from these much more violent and hostile representations, but there is a marriage between the two in a series of wartime propaganda cartoons by American satirists. The first cartoon, by Edwin Marcus for the *New York Times,* captioned "Let the punishment fit the crime," responds to reports during World War II that the Japanese were killing captured American airmen. It depicts the Japanese as a brute ape, to be executed by a gun wielded by "Civilization."[15] The second, by Richard Quincy Yardley for the *Baltimore Sun,* is captioned "The Lord High Self Executioner."[16] Commenting on the Japanese rejection of the terms of unconditional surrender to the Allies, it translates the "Jap militarist" into a Japanese samurai impaling himself on a giant sword while "Uncle Joe" Stalin watches from the East, and figures representing the United States, Britain, and China wave from the West. Again, the quaint types of the opera are evoked, but a very different vision emerges of a Japan of kamikazes and brutal imperialism.

These edgier forms of *Mikado*-humor with their virulently anti-Japanese images reveal the violence and brutality latent in the opera itself. As Beatty-Kingston first pointed out in his assessment of the opera as "the grimmest subject ever yet selected for treatment from the comic point of view," the opera turns on depictions of inhuman punishments and despotic rule, which it renders plausible through its Japanese setting.[17] Thus despite its light-heartedness, *The Mikado's* maniacal motivations and violent deaths have never been far from the racial typecasting of the Japanese as not only radically foreign but also inherently inhumane. The character of the Mikado, with his demonic laughter and thirst for execution, is consistent with how Japanese rulers were thought to fit into the more generic characterization of the despotic oriental emperor. German physician Philipp Franz von Siebold, who described the despotism of "the sovereign authority ruling Japan" as "one of its greatest evils," wrote: "Liberty is, indeed, unknown in Japan; it exists not even in the common intercourse of man with man; and the very idea of freedom, as distinguished from rude licence, could, perhaps, hardly be made intelligible to a native of that extraordinary empire." Japanese despotism, according to von Siebold, resides not in a particular emperor or demagogue but rather in law and established custom, which "unvarying, known to all, and pressing upon all alike, are the despots of Japan": "Scarcely an action of life is exempt from their rigid, inflexible, and irksome control; but he who complies with their dictates has no arbitrary power, no capricious tyranny to apprehend."[18]

Anti-Japanese sentiment grew in the first half of the twentieth century along with Japan's rise to world power and intensified with World War II. Perceptions of Japan were also affected by anxieties felt over Asian migration, particularly to the United States, where exclusion laws had by 1924 virtually barred immigration from the Asia-Pacific Triangle. But it is not until relatively recently that a more direct anti-Japanese sentiment was allowed free expression in *The Mikado*. A larger sea change in Gilbert and Sullivan productions happened after the expiration of the D'Oyly Carte's copyright in 1961, and the demise of the original D'Oyly Carte Company in 1982 provided more opportunities to unleash Gilbert and Sullivan. As Peter Davis remarks, this allowed companies in the U.K. to follow the lead of the earlier, pirated U.S. versions:

> In point of fact, the United States has never been much bothered by Gilbert and Sullivan traditions, ever since the "pinafore" craze of 1879, when innumerable versions of that operetta were playing the length and breadth of the land. And, come to think of it, perhaps this is a good thing, too. Consider that bastion of G&S convention, the D'Oyly Carte Company, which has reverently preserved every bit of original business laid down by W. S. Gilbert a century ago, from the patter singer's raised left eyebrow to the tenor's dulcet expressions of modified rapture. The D'Oyly Carte productions have become so mummified in recent years that most Britishers have

become completely soured on the subject of G&S. The company is apparently even threatened with extinction through lack of audience support. These operettas can withstand almost anything, it seems, except the stifling weight of their own traditions.[19]

Contemporary Commodity Racisms

The commodity racism of Gilbert and Sullivan's *Mikado* sets the stage a century later for a vision of a Japanese economic, technological, and cultural invasion. If the Japan craze of 1885 inspired white viewers to partake in playing Japanese, its counterpart a century later also inspired versions of *The Mikado*. However, attitudes toward this new japonaiserie were much more negative. Frederik Schodt notes that starting in the 1980s, U.S. popular opinion toward Japan began to shift. "Instead of regarding Japan as America's star pupil in democracy and capitalism (an 'economic miracle')," Schodt describes, "more and more people began to worry that Japan might be operating under a very different set of assumptions about trade and national security," and Japan became seen as a potential economic threat.[20] The U.S. trade deficit and accompanying economic problems, coupled with Japan's new technological prowess and increasing economic influence worldwide, led to new imaginings of Japan as a seductive and attractive place of new and enticing objects and as a potentially invasive force, a new yellow peril.

This mixture of admiration and anxiety regarding Japan's economic dominance clearly dictated new *Mikado*s, some more experimental than others. At the Paper Mill Playhouse, Millburn, New Jersey, in 1990, *The Mikado 2001* inserted a subplot that included, according to reviewer Alvin Klein, a robotic "geishanette," an automated office lady, as well as evoking through Thomas Ikeda's Mikado "a Far Eastern Howard Hughes" who, in the finale, assures us that humanity "cannot be measured in microchips."[21] Reviewer Mark Mobley described how the Virginia Opera's 1993 *The Not Mikado*, a 90-minute version orchestrated in a variety of musical styles including doo-wop, country, ragtime, and rock, significantly revised lyrics to the opening song: "If you wanna know who we are / we are techno of Japan / We make all your compact car / your transistor and your van." These lines are sung by the men as the women recite names of Japanese corporations, and the whole group then sings, "Our outlook once was rocky / You Yankees very cocky / We remember Nagasaki / Ah!"[22]

One of the most striking contemporary productions inspired by this new commodity racism and its attendant anxieties was directed by Peter Sellars at the Lyric Opera of Chicago in 1983. During the overture, young women dressed as flight attendants instructed audiences on the use of seat belts and oxygen masks during their imagined flight to Tokyo. Act 1 took place in a corporate boardroom with neon signs for Fuji, Seiko, Minolta, Toshiba, Sony, and Coca-Cola flashing in the background. Reviewers recognized the conspicuous references to Japanese electronics, cars, and computers: describing the production for the *New Yorker*, Andrew Porter noted, "Japonaiserie of another kind surrounds us today; we tell the time by it, listen to music through it, hear it being on the hour in our concert halls, ride in it."[23] The chorus of Gentlemen of Japan were identically dressed in business suits, sunglasses, and black wigs. Reviewers described how the Mikado, "bemedalled like a South American dictator,"[24] makes his entrance in a red Datsun, with a full contingent of security men, and how Pish-Tush is staged as "a J. R. Ewing-type tycoon" and Pooh-Bah as "a snooty chairman-of-the-board"[25] who employed "sly Nixonesque overtones in his characterization."[26]

Titipu is transformed into a place of multinational companies and commodities, highlighting the inseparability of Japanese and American influences. Remarked one reviewer, "This *Mikado* is set in our own time—in a Japan so smitten with Western society that it has joined it."[27] The Sellars production thus suggested a different direction for the opera's racial mimicry. Instead of yellowface as the straightforward impersonation of Japanese by white performers, here white performers enact a Japan that imitates the United States and vice versa. However, this interpenetration of Japan and the United States is weighted in different ways; while the production caricatured Japanese corporate power, American global influence was represented not as repressive capitalism but as irrepressible and ebullient popular culture. Nanki-poo was transformed into a celebrity rock star with an electric guitar in hand whose comic turns, as one reviewer described, "suggested a cross between the late John Belushi and the Fonz"; he rode a motorcycle onto the stage for his initial entrance into the corporate boardroom that was "filled with Japanese clone-like businessmen."[28] Yum-Yum becomes a mini-skirted Valley Girl with a Snoopy on her bed, and the Three Little Maids "boogied clumsily to the beat of a transistor radio."[29] Katisha's performance of "There Is Beauty in the Bellow of the Blast" in a nightclub echoed swinging *Hot Mikado* settings. The avid consumption of American culture by the Japanese suggests that the tables have been turned and that the Japanese now have not only technological prowess but also disposable income; at the end, reviewer Robert Jacobson notes, "We journeyed back to Chicago amid a swarm of Japanese visitors armed with flash cameras."[30]

This is not to say that in Sellars's production the cherry blossoms and other vestiges of traditional *Mikado* production went away entirely. In fact, Sellars reused a stock 1920s set from Chicago performances of *Madame Butterfly* (recognizable from the 1955 production of *Butterfly* with the title role sung by Maria Callas)[31] and cast a D'Oyly Carte veteran as the Mikado, Donald Adams, who was known to many reviewers as having done more than two thousand performances of the role. These reminders of old-style *Mikado*—the queer and quaint Titipu of exotic customs, beautiful objects, and alien inhabitants— provided an immediate contrast with this picture of contemporary Japanese whose performances of American culture and capitalism reversed the traditional racial mimicry of yellowface.

Though clearly presented in a lighthearted style, this double mimicry also suggested some of the complex fears behind the modern version of the yellow peril: Japan as not just the slavish imitator of the United States in business and popular culture but its rival and even superior. Those who had been pictured by Georges Bigot as monkeys dressing up in human clothes—the modernized Japanese—had now produced a superpower that could outdo its European and American counterparts at its own game. George Knox, a British writer and long-time resident in Japan, summed up succinctly this aspect of the "problem" with Japan at the end of 1904, a time when its astounding victory over Tsarist Russia seemed certain. Knox admitted:

> In our superficial way we have classed Asiatics together and we have assumed our own superiority. It has seemed a fact, proved by centuries of intercourse and generations of conquest, that the East lacks the power of organization, the attention to details, and of master over complicated machinery. Japan upsets our deductions by showing its equality in these matters, and, on the final appeal, by putting itself into the first rank of nations. . . . Here is a people, undoubtedly Asiatic, which shows that it can master the science and methods of the West.[32]

Sellars's *Mikado* suggests how, with its 1980s "economic miracle," Japan might be the Asian model minority that threatens to make its Western counterparts obsolete.

Racial Humor and Pastiche

Susan McClary notes that many contemporary productions of classic opera engage in self-conscious and deconstructive presentation: "rather than transmitting them as sacred objects, they are deconstructing them—laying bare their long-hidden ideological premises—and yet reenacting them, so that one experiences a shared heritage and its critique simultaneously."³³ While the Sellars production provided a coherent conceptual framework for using these new racial images, many updatings of *The Mikado* cannot be credited with encouraging such a radical space of self-critique. These productions do not provide a system for using these racial stereotypes but rather include them as part of a hodge-podge of amusing devices.

That even blatantly hostile racial images can pass as innocent humor seems in keeping with that peculiar quality of the opera that we have been describing all along. Placed in the context of a work so presumably fantastical and light, these casual references can escape the charges attached to any serious racial representation, hence even brazen racial stereotyping declares itself to be harmless fun. The deeper significance of any of these yellow peril images often escapes any notice; reviewers seldom mention these references, even though they are far from indirect.

Tradition is clearly dispensed with in radical revisions such as *The Gentlemen of Titipu*, an animated children's feature directed by Leif Gram for Australian television in 1972.³⁴ The show seems similar to that of many cartoon versions of classic literature, theater, and opera remade for a young audience. In this version, the Mikado, Pooh-Bah, Pish-Tush, Katisha, and Nanki-Poo arrive at Titipu for the Cherry Blossom Festival; Ko-Ko winks at Katisha and is sentenced to death. The remainder of the plot, though greatly truncated, is similar to the original. The songs have been revised and reorchestrated in a seventies pop rock style, and the action contains plenty of pratfalls, including the arrival of the Titipu town band and a musical scene in a dungeon, complete with burly executioners. There are some holdovers from the conventional stage, such as Anna Russell, noted for her parodies of grand opera, who voices over an oversized and strident Katisha; however, much of the original *Mikado* has been excised in favor of the familiar slapstick of cartoons. What is interesting is that these transformations include a host of racial stereotypes added on to the familiar cherry blossom scenery (redone in the bright color schemes typical of early 1970s animation) and characterizations of the opera. Some are nods to Gilbert's nonsense, with characters such as Om-pah-pah (the leader of the town band), Bow Wow (a servant to Nanki-Poo), or Miss Tut-tut (a schoolteacher to the Three Little Maids). Others, such as the heavy accents of a number of characters and the buck teeth of Pish-Tush, seem more akin to stereotypes familiar from films such as the 1961 *Breakfast at Tiffany's*, which featured Mickey Rooney's caricature of a Japanese neighbor to Audrey Hepburn's Holly Golightly.

In this cartoon, what identifies the characters as Japanese combines the features of *The Mikado*'s Titipu and racial caricatures borrowed from film and television. Like the hip reorchestrations of what it packages as an "animated children's classic," these newer images update the opera for new and young audiences, remaking *The Mikado*'s fantasy of Japan in ways that easily incorporate other stereotypes. We might identify a number of these that have become standard fare for contemporary *Mikado* audiences. Gilbert's nonsensical names—Yum-Yum, Nanki-Poo, Pish-Tush, and the like—inform the naming of multiple extras, such as the cast list for the 1998 production of *Hot Mikado* by the Catchment Players of Victoria, Australia, with chorus members such as Yucki-Poo, Ping-Pong, Bing-Bang, Sushi, and Kinki-Lee.[35] Toward the end of the first act, Gilbert's libretto calls for the repetition of the nonsensical "O Bikkuri shakuri o" to drown out Katisha's proclamation; contemporary performers of *The Mikado* often ad lib with similar faux-Japanese phrases. These jokes verbally typecast Japanese as unintelligible or infantile. Similarly, male and female characters racially identify themselves not only through the mincing steps, bowing, and giggling of Gilbert and Sullivan's staging, but also through gestures borrowed from other stereotypically oriental characters. Players of the Gentlemen of Japan and Ko-Ko often throw in some improvised martial arts moves à la Bruce Lee movies or revert to elaborate and ridiculous bows and salutes.

This racial typecasting is a standard part of the new *Mikado*s of the 1980s and after. One such example comes from the 1982 Stratford (Ontario) Festival production, directed by Brian Macdonald, which was broadcast by the Canadian Broadcasting Corporation in 1986 and later revived at the Virginia Theatre in New York in 1987. With its vigorous and athletic choreography and Broadway musical delivery, it seems influenced by other popular Gilbert and Sullivan productions such as the well-known New York Shakespeare Festival's *Pirates of Penzance,* directed by Joseph Papp, which came to Broadway in 1981. The Stratford *Mikado* production, praised for its innovation and casting, did not cast celebrities nor did it rock the orchestration; however, it did depart from a more traditional D'Oyly Carte staging in some notable ways. The Japanese aspects of the opera were established primarily through an elegant use of intercultural design and aesthetics. Fans, kimonos, parasols, and other oversized objects remained prominent in the opera, but the staging also used devices from traditional Asian performance forms, including a circular ramp reminiscent of the *hanamichi* of Kabuki theater, stagehands dressed in black (like Kabuki's *kuroko*), and acrobats and ribbon dances reminiscent of Beijing opera.

There are also several notable departures from the standard yellow-face look of D'Oyly Carte. Katisha has red hair, and Nanki-Poo appears in a ponytail and without the exaggerated eye makeup typical of the role. Thus important aspects of the production moved away from the familiar racial exaggerations of more traditional *Mikado*s. However, this more neutral take on racial impersonation was counteracted by repeated references to racial types of other kinds. At every mention of the Mikado, characters responded with exaggerated bowing and high-pitched cries. The demonical laugh of the Mikado so often used in Savoy productions became, with Gidon Saks's performance, a strange high-pitched voice so heavily accented at times that it became unintelligible gibberish. Most strikingly, Richard McMillan as Pooh-Bah worked a variety of references to racial stereotypes into his comic mugging. In his multiple impersonations, ranging from Canadian politicians to movie stars, he frequently employed Fu Manchu and Charlie Chan accents and gestures, fake martial arts moves, and repetitions of stock phrases such as "chop-chop," "ah so," and "hi-ya" to highlight his role.

In many contemporary productions of *The Mikado,* modernizing the opera means referencing a variety of contemporary racial allusions. Many of these are clearly derogatory, commenting on specific images of the Japanese or other Asians as evil threats or unwanted immigrants. However, some productions apply such an amalgamation of racial stereotypes that these subtle distinctions become lost. Such was the case when Simon

Gallaher's Essgee Entertainment of Queensland, Australia, produced an updated version of *The Mikado* for Australian and New Zealand audiences in 1995, after their success with a modernized version of *Pirates of Penzance* in 1994. Their *Mikado* was a great commercial success, leading them to produce *H.M.S. Pinafore* later. Like their version of *Pirates*, Essgee's *Mikado* included considerable revision of the libretto, reorchestrations of the songs to contemporary rock and pop rhythms, vigorous choreography, and lots of comic improvisation. The women's chorus was transformed into a trio of three women, the Fabulous Singlettes, who also take on all the parts of Pitti-Sing and Peep-Bo. The men's chorus was full of young, virile men who exposed plenty of skin. The opera featured dance numbers, closing with a Vegas-style reprisal of songs complete with flashing lights, video display, fireworks, and other pyrotechnics.

Though performers wore kimonos and headbands and carried fans and swords, their extravagant characterizations bore little resemblance to *Mikados* of the past or anything remotely resembling Japan. Instead, this production suggested a postmodern pastiche that seemed to neutralize any effort at racial representation, a popularization that featured handsome young leading men without any hint of yellowface makeup in nearly all the leading roles. But this energetic adaptation also recycled any number of racial jokes: incessant bowing at every mention of the Mikado, the humorous mimicking of martial arts movements, references to familiar stereotypes from stage and screen. The Mikado was played by David Gould who, though dressed fantastically in a futuristic suit with flags protruding from his shoulders, nonetheless delivered his lines in a familiarly stereotypical manner, punctuating his heavily accented lines with utterances of "so sorry" and "come, come, grasshoppers." In the finale, Gilbert's dialogue is punctuated by random utterances of Japanese product names such as "hibachi" and "Nintendo." This version of "Miya sama" is rewritten to end with phrases such as "Sayonara" and "Miss Saigon," changing the only real Japanese song into yet another list of new Asian commodities. During the final curtain call, the Fabulous Singlettes engaged the audience in how to speak Japanese, which consisted of asking them to say words such as "karaoke" and "Mitsubishi" and ended with the pronouncement of "raw fish—bleah!" These evocations of Japanese brand names seem to be part of the standard mockery of Japanese language that takes place in many productions; nonsensical words and names are often used to reinforce the sense of foreignness associated with what is Japanese.

What happens when *The Mikado* is inhabited by these buck-toothed, myopic, unintelligible, hysterical characters reminiscent of the Japanese enemy of World War II Hollywood films, Mickey Rooney's Mr. Yunioshi, or Fu Manchu? These references to racial stereotypes introduce an overtly representational and racially hostile take on *The Mikado* that troubles the nostalgic lightness of the opera. These new additions seem strangely retrogressive in light of the new racial politics that have converted *The Mikado* into a multicultural *Hot Mikado* that celebrates racial harmony. Yet even the recent *Hot Mikado*s have their share of racist humor. A reviewer of a *Hot Mikado* that played during March 2004 in the Fulton Opera House in Lancaster, Pennsylvania, suggested, "Between the death-penalty humor and Asian jokes, the musical is rather politically incorrect."[36] Similarly, a reviewer for a Musical Theatre West production of *Hot Mikado* in the Carpenter Performing Arts Center, California State University–Long Beach, during February and March of the same year, reflected that the show's "blazing abandon should electrify Broadway babies, but attendees allergic to Asian jokes are alerted, as are purists."[37]

These overt racisms can seem very much at odds with what traditional fans of Gilbert and Sullivan feel to be the spirit of the opera. One reviewer, weary of what he saw to be the antics of Sellars, even confessed to feeling a certain longing to return to the D'Oyly Carte tradition:

> In fact, when Donald Adams, who was the lovably bloodthirsty Mikado of some 2,000 performances in his D'Oyly Carte days, appeared in this production and did his familiar turn, I found myself thinking kind thoughts about the tradition he represents. Mr. Adams made me realize how much I would like, once more, to see a genuine unashamed D'Oyly Carte performance.[38]

As I've suggested earlier, modernizing *The Mikado* and the use of new racial images go hand in hand. The strict limits on improvisation set by the D'Oyly Carte's model kept racial representation within the limits of decorous behavior. While Savoy performers, for instance of Ko-Ko, such as George Grossmith, Henry Lytton, and Martyn Green, did indulge in some authorized ad-libbing,[39] for the most part, the tight control of Gilbert kept ruder improvisation at the Savoy under restraint. Audrey Williamson writes of the Ko-Ko role, "The part is full of opportunities for mime and therefore, unfortunately, equal opportunities for clowning. Amateurs fall for the last more frequently than professionals, for in spite of occasional accusations by the die-hards both Lytton and Green [the Savoy's Henry Lytton and Martyn Green], the principal exponents in our time, seem to me to have preserved a certain 'style' in the part which avoided mere rough-and-tumble excesses."[40] Thus in most versions, anything that might openly give offense was suppressed in favor of a more genteel portrayal of Japanese racial difference. In the traditional D'Oyly Carte style, Williamson lauds "Gilbert's ruling of a traditional spirit avoiding vulgarity";[41] what seems to have happened after the end of the D'Oyly Carte's influence is that the decorous stagings of the Savoy's yellowface have given way to broad exaggeration that includes a much more open use of racial stereotype.

The Mikado in an Age of Cultural Sensitivity

In much the same way as it became imbued with the vocabulary of blackface minstrelsy in twentieth-century America, the racial language of *The Mikado* can easily take on elements of racial humor familiar to contemporary audiences. What is most interesting in these recent productions is that they are played in venues where stronger racial representations, such as the openly racist humor of blackface, have become taboo. These overtly hostile gestures and references exist not just as the nostalgic and accidental remnant of an old vocabulary, but as a demonstration of a new and alarming racial backlash. While it seems as though current sensitivities about expressing racism should make these references to the Japanese as the yellow peril less rather than more likely, perhaps it is the very opposite, whereby the release of racism in front of presumably liberal audiences accentuates the fun.

The derogatory term "nigger" is finally officially excised from *The Mikado* in 1948. Rupert D'Oyly Carte explained the changes to the D'Oyly Carte libretto in the *London Times*:

> We found recently in America that much objection was taken by coloured persons to a word used twice in *The Mikado*, a word which I will not quote but which your readers may easily guess. Many protests and letters were received, and we consulted the witty writer [A. P. Herbert, who coined the substitutes most often used] on whose shoulders the lyrical mantle of Gilbert may be

said to have fallen. He made several suggestions, one of which we adopted in America, and it seems well to continue doing so in the British Empire. Gilbert would surely have approved, and the alteration will be heard during our season at Sadler's Wells.[42]

His comment affirms the necessity of the opera's conforming to a new climate of racial sensitivity and suggests that even Gilbert, so intransigent on other details, "would surely have approved" of this change. As J. M. Balkin and Sanford Levinson suggest, this assumes ignorance rather than evil in Gilbert's use of this racist term. Rupert D'Oyly Carte was

> practicing an altogether justifiable principle of charity in interpretation: he assumed that Gilbert was a man of his times; the original lyrics manifested mere parochialism rather than conscious malevolence. Surely, it might be argued, a decent person would change a lyric when its offensiveness was brought to his attention, and if the person in question is dead one ought to act on this assumption in the interests of charity. Indeed, if Gilbert were alive today, he would probably never have written such racist lyrics in the first place.[43]

Thus a work such as *The Mikado* might easily be cleaned of casual racisms for contemporary audiences, substituting "banjo serenader" and "painted with vigor" for the clearly derogatory lyrical references. These changes are easily made; lyrics to the two songs in question (Ko-Ko's "Little List" song, "As Someday It Might Happen"; and the Mikado's song, "A More Humane Mikado") are often altered.

If the word "nigger" has been thoroughly and neatly excised from productions, why then the addition of new racial insults? One explanation is of course that anti-Asian racial humor and yellowface are not perceived as publicly offensive in the same way that anti-black racism is. Some might say that "yellow" is relatively ignored in racial terms while racial representation has been dominated by discussions of black and white. However, simple parochialism doesn't seem in itself to be enough of an explanation. What is it about *The Mikado* that not only its original queer and quaint yellowface but also its even more egregiously offensive racial stereotypes are allowed to be played in front of presumably liberal audiences time and again? If the objections "by coloured persons" to the use of the word "nigger" successfully motivates even the D'Oyly Carte Opera Company to change Gilbert's libretto, why is the same attention not given to anti-Asian sentiment?

One answer might be that these racial insults exist in a much more veiled form, as momentary gestures. Again, *The Mikado* deflects any sustained commentary on its racial politics, with some claiming that it is thoroughly English, following G. K. Chesterton's famous remark, "There is not, in the whole length of *The Mikado*, a single joke that is a joke against Japan. They are all, without exception, jokes against England, or that Western civilization which an Englishman knows best in England."[44] For them, the Japanese setting of *The Mikado* can be thought of as just another topsy-turvy setting for the linguistic and musical genius of W. S. Gilbert and Arthur Sullivan; the world of *The Mikado* is no different from any of their other settings — a pirate ship, Gothic Scotland, South Pacific islands — that serve as a colorful backdrop for a satire on late-Victorian British life. However, this move only accentuates the extent to which the representation of Japan actually enables this particular mode of satire. The racial fantasy bolsters the sense of who the English are; as Chesterton added in his own remarks:

> This sort of English caricature requires a Japanese frame; that, in order to popularize a criticism of our own country, it is necessary to preserve a sort of veil or fiction that it is another country; possibly an unknown country. If the satirist becomes more of a realist, he enters the grosser native atmosphere in which he is expected to be a eulogist. The satire bears no sort of resemblance to an Englishman criticizing Japan. But it has to assume a certain semblance of a Japanese criticizing England. Oliver Goldsmith discovered the same truth, when he found he could only talk truthfully to his countrymen in the stilted language of a Chinaman.[45]

Chesterton's additions notwithstanding, an interpretation of *The Mikado* as "only about the English" has become a commonplace. A certain anxiety about race is inevitably tied up with this assertion. Many have claimed the thoroughly English nature of the opera precisely in order to dispute any claims that it has any troubling racial content. A contributor to the Gilbert and Sullivan discussion list comments on her own experience with producing *The Mikado* at Oberlin College:

Oberlin was a difficult venue in which to produce *Mikado*. We had barely any budget (says the Treasurer), and a very politically sensitive student body (my soprano quit because of a single word). So I went into directing the *Mikado* with the idea that these are English people putting on a show which is set in a country whose culture they don't really understand. This saved us a lot of money on makeup and hair, as well as keeping us safe from the boycotters. If anyone complained, I could point to the style of the production and say, see, we're making fun of the English! Isn't it clear?[46]

The Oberlin production, of course, is but one of many productions that cite the Englishness of the opera in hopes of deflecting any criticism of its racial representation. This strategy inspires a variety of production choices, such as the introduction of quintessentially English objects—bowler hats and umbrellas instead of fans and parasols—sometime even in productions that are otherwise staged in full yellowface of the D'Oyly Carte variety.

One of the most de-Japanned of these productions is Jonathan Miller's 1986 production at the English National Opera, which was also brought to Los Angeles and Houston and filmed for Thames TV. Miller sets his version of the opera in the foyer of a grand hotel; Titipu becomes an English seaside resort in the late 1920s. The whitening of *The Mikado* is literally carried through with Stefano Lazadiris's opulent white-on-white design for the stage. The male chorus wears full morning dress, monocles, and carnations; Nanki-Poo is in flannels and straw boater hat; Katisha is glamorous in furs and evening gown. Dance numbers with butlers, valets, and maids erupt spontaneously, echoing Hollywood musicals of the 1930s. The staging includes little of the familiar scenery, costume, and props; Japanese fans and swords are transformed to lacrosse sticks, tennis rackets, billiard cues, and lollipops.

Miller is open about his intention to move away from the faux Japanese of the D'Oyly Carte, stating, "The piece had been completely embalmed up till then in this literal Japaneserie."[47] He borrows liberally from Marx Brothers movies, the Ascot scene from *My Fair Lady*, and Hollywood extravaganzas. This concept was clearly attractive to performers, such as Eric Idle (of *Monty Python* fame), whom Miller asked to play the role of Ko-Ko. When Miller told him, "I'm going to get rid of all that Japanese nonsense for a start," he recalls, "that just hooked me—if he was going to take the

Japanese stuff out of *The Mikado,* I wanted to know how on earth he was going to do it!" Idle finds, "Once Jonathan had liberated the piece from its Japaneserie, it was suddenly free of years and years of accretions and jokes that had been built into it by each generation. Consequently we were able to approach it as if it was a totally new text, without worrying about everything that had gone before, and this gave us tremendous scope with Ko-Ko."[48]

But however complete the transformation, this Englishness is nonetheless still disturbed by certain reminders of the Japanese origins of the opera. In Miller's exuberant staging, Japaneseness seems reduced only to a vague echo in the kimono designs of the black-and-white dressing gowns, an outline of Mount Fuji outside the window, and the occasional black bob. These are in-jokes, anticipating the audience members' previous expectations of *The Mikado*. What is most interesting, however, are not these sustained stylistic choices but the seemingly more casual racial references. As the men's chorus sings "we are gentlemen of Japan," they pull the corners of their eyes back; at other times, they make karate chop motions. These gestures are repeated at various points, when Eric Idle as Ko-Ko comments on the "typical Nipponese attitude" (paraphrasing Gilbert's "characteristic Japanese attitude") and when the chorus sings "O ni bikkuri" to drown out Katisha's revelations.

As fleeting as these moments seem, such gestures convey multiple meanings. The familiar and exhausted racial vocabulary of insult has been reduced to a minimum, yet these movements still signal both yellowface and racial insult. Even the most de-Japanned version of *The Mikado* can still make room for the racist gesture. The inclusion of this gestural mockery seems all the more troubling because of its gratuitousness. Miller's white-on-white production seems to bypass all the pitfalls of racial representation by following through on the insistence that the opera satirizes England, not Japan. Compared, for instance, with recent *Hot Mikado*s in which casual anti-Asian jokes seem somewhat corralled, however tenuously, by the overall spirit of good multicultural fun, in this glamorous production the intrusion of the racial gesture is much more blatant.

In terms of anti-Asian racial slurs, the "slant-eyes" gesture is the equivalent of fighting words. How do we understand this openly antagonistic gesture if the point of the production is to de-Japan *The Mikado*? Are these insulting yet vague gestures meant to reflect on the snobby tuxedoed characters who make them, to reinforce their privilege as white? Or is it that in order to claim the artistic innovation, Japan must be reduced to barely recognizable gestures, like the glimpse of Mount Fuji through the window?

Miller's production only highlights the puzzling reiteration of openly caricatured racial stereotypes that appear with regularity throughout contemporary productions of *The Mikado*. One way is to read them as precisely a response to the anxieties of race that have presumably been erased by the whitening of the opera. These casual gestures mark the privilege of whiteness—to take the gesture lightly and to make it with impunity—they also register the dare of a new age of cultural sensitivity. This racial version of flipping off, like so many other instances of momentary insult, are symptomatic rather than atypical of the racial tensions that surround multiculturalism; they are inspired by the perceived policing of free speech and the loss of the apparent privileges of playing fast and loose with race.

This and other references to the hostile imaginings of the yellow peril are used strategically in *The Mikado* not to offend openly but to give contemporary productions of the opera an irreverent and edgy quality. Challenging what many perceive as the tyranny of political correctness, these productions have a go at a barely sustained, yet perhaps momentarily thrilling, expression of racism. One of the most interesting aspects of the contemporary racial insult is its buoyancy. Disguised as part of the innocent merriment of the opera, it can evade protest even as its meaning is powerfully antagonistic and, to its intended targets, unmistakable.

Pomona College Protests (1990)

As these modern versions all suggest, the revitalization of Gilbert and Sullivan lies in innovative restaging, youthful performers, and energetic performances. Unfortunately, in the case of *The Mikado*, this also entails a revisiting of stereotypes—the foreign invader or the immigrant coolie—that hammer home an overtly hostile and racist message. These moments reveal how *The Mikado* can never really disguise its own power to represent Japan and its connections to a political orientalism that exists within its patrician fantasy. These aspects of the opera fuel protest against its production. The 1907 censorship of *The Mikado* demonstrated how the opera was judged in light of diplomatic relations between England or the United States and a foreign Japan. In the past few decades, a new perception of racial injury informs protests of the opera.

In 1990, faculty, staff, and students at Pomona College protested a production of *The Mikado* by Opera à la Carte, a professional company specializing in Gilbert and Sullivan, staged at the Claremont Colleges. In her book *About Face*, Dorinne Kondo describes her reaction to an announcement of the opera:

> I groaned inwardly as I looked at the listing. Not again. The last production of *The Mikado* I remembered was in Boston, where the Emperor's Court had metamorphosed into a Japanese company populated by Japanese businessmen, conjoining the Oriental despot trope with that of the corporate soldier. Not again—facing the situation that women, people of color, gays, and lesbians face all too often when oppressive stereotypes recirculate in forms that the dominant considers harmless fun. And as in all such occasions, one must decide what to do. Make a fuss? So much effort, and I just got here. Let it go? Then I would hate myself for being the "silent Asian" who allows an egregious event to slip by without a whisper of protest.[49]

Kondo emphasizes several ways in which the opera gives racial offense. There is first the opera's perpetuation of stereotypes, "the problematic Orientalist tropes that permeate the text: nonsensical and offensive renders of Chinese (not Japanese) names, Oriental exoticism and despotism, Oriental proclivities for suicide, and Oriental women as either submissive lotus blossoms or witch-like dragon ladies." Anticipating the well-worn defenses of the opera, "that *The Mikado* is a cultural classic; that it is simply a satire; that Gilbert and Sullivan were 'really' writing about England," she argues, "We must ask: for whom is *The Mikado* a cultural classic?" For her, calling the opera satire "merely excuses the continued circulation of racist and sexist tropes. In this regard, the choice of Japan as the setting for this satire was overdetermined given the contemporary discourses of Orientalism and Britain's imperialist project." Also, *The Mikado* was chosen over newer works that might enlighten viewers with regard to racial topics, and this lack of attention to newer work reflected an ongoing institutional racism: "the choice to stage *The Mikado* at the Colleges effectively preempted the performances of Asian American plays written and performed by Asian Americans, echoing an institutional history that had failed to confront Asian American issues."[50]

The occasion of the opera's production became transformed into an arena for racial consciousness-raising. What might have otherwise been an unremembered revival instead transformed Gilbert and Sullivan's work into a forum for activism. Kondo records that faculty, staff, and students formed a Coalition of the International Majority/National Minority that staged a teach-in preceding opening night and organized protests at performances, with signs that read "El Mikado es un pecado" (The Mikado is a sin).[51] As a result of these protests, the college administration moved to establish an Asian American Resource Center. So this *Mikado* actually inspired some concrete institutional change, though it certainly was not the effect that the opera's devotees intended.

What is interesting as well, however, is that this open disapproval produced backlash as well as open minds. The protest did not result in a boycott or cancellation of the production. Although the protest clearly moved the hearts and minds of those who participated in it, the opera went on as planned. One contributor to an online Gilbert and Sullivan discussion list posted a very different recollection of this event:

> Opera à la Carte's *Mikado* was boycotted once in Claremont, California by an ethnic student group who felt it was racist and sexist. There were picket signs out front. It would have been funny except that it was so pathetic. We think they missed the point. As the overture began we were warned there would be a "walkout." As promised, on the initial downbeat approximately 6 people got up and left the otherwise filled-to-capacity auditorium. I think they would have done well to involve some students of management. WE could not resist a hasty response. In the list song when I sang "Likewise, you know who" our Pooh-Bah obstinately crossed behind me with a large picket sign saying "DOWN WITH OPERA." Cheap, I know. Hey, it got a laugh.[52]

There is a striking disconnect between this dismissive account and the heated concerns of those protesting the opera. Here the writer glories in the "cheap" laugh generated at the expense of the protestors, who, he claims, "missed the point." In this rebuttal, as well as the protest, it can be seen how in contemporary settings the opera has become part of a deeper uncertainty associated with race. This uncertainty manifests itself not in any openness, let alone consciousness-raising, but in an even more obstinate denial that the opera has anything to do with racism. Even while providing a "hasty response," it was clear that those producing the opera were ill-prepared to engage in any level of debate about who or what their production actually represented.

The question of what this means haunts productions of more than just *The Mikado*. Many operatic and theatrical revivals must deal directly with questions of racial representation. Whether they rely on racial provocation or try to avoid direct confrontation with the questions they provoke, the questions remain the same. Instead of engaging directly with issues of race, power, and representation, such productions displace the tension and anxieties of racial representation into small gestures of defiance against political correctness. This response can be read as naughty rather than racist, performed through hasty responses or insulting gestures that can easily be disavowed as humorous. Given the opera's own celebration of flirtation in defiance of royal edict, some might see a censorship of racial slurs to be part of the larger control of the state over individual rights of self-expression. Thus they might see the opera as encouraging a roguish spirit of rebellion or feel relief at getting away with racist language and behavior.

Debates about political correctness become arguments for the artistic right to free expression. But when playing *The Mikado* ironically becomes a bold statement about artistic freedom, this in turn suppresses deeper questions about the continued privileges inherent in yellowface and other forms of racial performance.

· Chapter 7 ·

Asian American *Mikados*

THIS BOOK BEGAN by describing *The Mikado*'s elusiveness: how, under the guise of nonsense, the opera seems to disavow any intentional hurt or misrepresentation. Thus its productions, whether quaintly queer or more openly hostile, provide little footing on which to pin charges of racial malice or injury. The opera's versions of Japan, excusably pure invention, escape largely unscathed from protests. Even when confronted with direct criticism, playing *The Mikado* seems a habit that is hard to break. Yet, as we have seen, there are ways of disrupting this placid history. The preceding chapter focused on how *The Mikado*'s Japanese productions responded to political and popular perceptions of Japan as a nation. Here, we might also reinforce the opera's significance as a *racial* fantasy with a representational power that extends well beyond national and ethnic lines.

Critics of the opera are not only from Japan. We also have protests of *The Mikado* from the West, emphasizing the fact that the West is itself not a homogeneous entity. Events such as the Pomona College protest of the Opera à la Carte production in 1990 establish the racial sensitivities of the opera: its power to represent not only the Japanese but also Americans of Asian descent. This chapter concentrates on several instances of *The Mikado* as directed or performed by Japanese Americans and other Asian Americans. As we will see, there is no uniformity of approach in the Asian American *Mikados*, nor has there been a concerted large-scale attempt at a revisionist reworking of the opera. However, even in these singular instances we learn something about how this opera might work on the contemporary stage in ways that are quite different from Victorian nostalgia or contemporary anti-Japanese or anti-Asian sentiment. The engagement of Asian Americans highlights particular questions of racial visibility within the United States at a moment of multicultural awareness.

On Western stages dominated by white actors, the practice of yellowface—the playing of oriental characters by non-Asian actors—marks the privilege to represent. Whiteness has traditionally been granted the power of racial transformation: white actors could successfully enact a variety of colored others, whereas nonwhite performers, as we have seen with the black performances of *The Mikado,* were invariably marked by what was seen to be the indelible and natural features of their race. Even when allowed more artistic freedom than as a quaint curiosity or display of brute primitivism, the nonwhite performer was rarely credited with the ability to transform into a full range of characterizations. *The Swing Mikado* and *The Hot Mikado* might well be considered milestones insofar as they seemingly extended the power of playing Japanese characters to African Americans. But in the eyes of white mainstream audience members, these productions did not fully allow African American performers to embody the vision of Titipu and colored *The Mikado* musically and theatrically with what were thought to be an essentially black music and style.

This history raises a similar question with regard to the employment of Asian Americans in *Mikado* productions. Might this be taken as a sign of a more general racial progress, in that the stage includes more directors and performers of color? Or is it a continuation of the very limited roles given to Asian American performers in stage and film, whereby Asian American performers run the risk not only of reproducing racial stereotypes but of affirming them as authentic with their very participation? This chapter looks at how an awareness of Asian American racial consciousness plays out in the history of this opera. These examples, while quite different in style and effect, all address how the opera represents a living people, whether Japanese or others of Asian descent who are inevitably associated with them. In other words, these productions, no matter how lighthearted, do not simply assume that *The Mikado* bears no responsibility for racial and ethnic representation.

In her study of contemporary Shakespearean production, Susan Bennett describes the dilemma of "whether there are, in fact, new ways to play old texts.... Theatre is, anyway, generally and rightly regarded as a conservative art form, and the devotion to Shakespeare a manifestation of that inherent conservatism." Yet she asks also whether there might not be possibilities in new productions that are not entirely fettered by the past: "can a new text, by way of dislocating and contradicting the authority of tradition, produce a 'trangressive knowledge' which would disarticulate the terms under which traditional gains its authority?"[1] Translating Bennett's inquiry to *The Mikado,* we ask whether there are elements of the opera that can be so transformed. Is there another way to understand the participation of Asian Americans in such works as *The Mikado*?

At the heart of Asian American discontent with a history of orientalist images and practices, such as have been amply demonstrated in *The Mikado*, is a desire for stage presentation to reflect some offstage authenticity, usually imagined as the laboring bodies of the disenfranchised. This was clearly voiced at the conclusion of the 1990 protest of the Opera à la Carte production when Pomona College students and faculty read lines from a poem by Carlos Bulosan.[2] The poem's title, "If You Want to Know What We Are," echoes the opening lines of the opera; however, Bulosan gives the words sung by the "gentlemen of Japan" living "on vase and jar" to the voices of immigrants and working-class laborers ("We are multitudes the world over, millions everywhere; / in violent factories, sordid tenements, crowded cities"). The very coolies so conspicuously absent from the opera now appear in Bulosan's words as "the living testament of a flowering race." Their riff on Gilbert's lyrics becomes the starting point for their poetic utterances of hope for a new future:

> We are the desires of anonymous men everywhere,
> who impregnate the wide earth's lustrous wealth
> with a gleaming florescence; we are the new thoughts
> and the new foundations, the new verdure of the mind;
> we are the new hope new joy life everywhere.
> . . . .
> If you want to know what we are—
> WE ARE REVOLUTION![3]

The juxtaposition of Gilbert and Sullivan's quaint opera with Bulosan's writing presents a startling contrast between the decorative orientalism of light bourgeois entertainment and the earnest representation of Bulosan's protest literature depicting Asian Americans and other immigrant workers. As I suggested earlier, the 1990 Pomona College protest provoked resentment and backlash from devotees of the opera, but it also made the opera meaningful in a different way by making us think about how *The Mikado* might be reappropriated by those heavily invested in the history of racial exclusion and questions of racial representation.

Not all the examples we might consider are radical restagings of the opera—in fact, far from it. The 1990 reworkings of Gilbert's line into Bulosan's words contrasts dramatically with another college production several years later at the Wisconsin–Madison University Theatre and University Opera in 2003. The Wisconsin production, from the remarks of one reviewer, was received as yet another familiar cherry blossom spectacular; he comments:

> William S. Gilbert would have loved the Union Theater's current production of "The Mikado." ... The moment the curtain went up Friday night, the audience reacted with audible delight. And with good reason. The set, designed by University of Wisconsin Professor Joe Varga, transformed the Union Theater from an ordinary Western-style stage into a gorgeous Japanese theater.
>
> A temple-like structure and backdrop of painted cutouts depicting cherry blossoms, Japanese houses and mountains framed the stage and created a sense of mystery and exotic beauty. The men's chorus (otherwise known as the gentlemen of Japan), onstage as the curtain went up, resembled beautiful plumed birds with their vivid kimonos, elaborate hairpieces and brightly colored fans.[4]

Interestingly enough, comments made by director David Furumoto on certain aspects of the production, while not challenging a conventional interpretation of the opera, ask us to read the production as somewhat different from a purely nostalgic oriental fantasy. Furumoto declared his intention to use *The Mikado* to correct misperceptions of Japanese culture. For him, the racial stereotyping of the opera lay not in its yellowface but in its ethnic confusion: "When you talk about stereotyping, the biggest thing that gets to me about the typical performance of Gilbert and Sullivan is that it's a mishmash. They throw Chinese and Japanese things together." His production made a considerable effort to correct such inaccuracies of movement, props, and language:

> The choreography of other productions has bothered me. Because they were done by Western choreographers, there's been an odd kind of movement that isn't authentically Japanese. What I'm trying to do is return it to authentic Japanese dance. We'll use the classic "mie" (pronounced MEE-ay) pose being struck.[5]
>
> I also made a special trip to Japan to make sure we had enough authentic dance fans and parasols—not the oversized Chinese ones that so many other productions use. They help to express the emotion in the story.
>
> Will there be accents? If anything, you'll hear more of an

authentic Japanese tone for the actual Japanese words that are actually used in the text. I'm trying to get the cast to pronounce them authentically.⁶

Through a careful incorporation of the movement and aesthetic of Japanese performance styles, Furumoto tried to redeem *The Mikado* from charges of racial insensitivity: "I think it will be a beautiful production to look at and listen to.... And maybe I can change some people's minds who felt 'The Mikado' was insulting to the Japanese. Maybe this production will take away some of the negativity." Furumoto attempts to redeem the opera from charges of misrepresentation and to frame it instead as a prototype for contemporary intercultural experimentation, in which his own training as a Kabuki performer becomes significant.

Thus Furumoto's production *The Mikado* references less the 1885 Savoy's strategic use of "real" Japanese objects and gestures than the more contemporary idea of interculturalism. In one interview, he spoke of his desire to incorporate elements of Kabuki into the production as well as make the objects and setting more authentically Japanese. Commenting, "I want to return it to the country where it's based," Furumoto stated his hope of showing what *The Mikado* might have looked like if Gilbert and Sullivan "had access to people who really knew kabuki theater": "I want to show that 'The Mikado' still works as a Japanese play.... There's a lot of correlation between Japanese society and British society. Hopefully, we'll be able to show that these cultures have a lot in common."⁷

The move to make *The Mikado* an intercultural work echoes the attempts to authenticate the vision of Titipu in the 1885 Savoy productions by strategically borrowing elements of design and gesture. Furumoto's attempt to make his 2003 production more authentically Japanese runs the risk of again reducing "Japanese" to certain predictable icons and gestures of yellowface. As critic Michael Billington described: "The key question is whether you go for Japanese authenticity or quintessential Englishness. The solution here is to keep a foot in both camps so that the result is a kind of Kensington Kabuki: white make-up and pigtails are prevalent, but so too are bowler hats and lace underwear."⁸ Such intercultural *Mikado*s intensify the risk that interculturalism faces in general, "fixing on easy cultural markers or signs of cultural difference as a shorthand that precludes research or cultural understanding and reduced culture to a stageable sign,"⁹ what Una Chaudhuri calls "museum interculturalism" that "literalizes difference itself, reducing it to the grossest and most material of conceptions."[10] Robert Young has suggested that European imperialists have long marked bodies by rigid classifications of race and gender in order to justify colonial enterprises.[11] Julie Holledge and Joanne Tompkins have extended this to describe a "taxonomic" version of intercultural theater, whereby performing bodies are imagined as being isolated from one another by rigid and inflexible boundaries of nation, framed by "supposedly pure and authentic cultural essences." This approach to intercultural performance seems to celebrate a blending of world cultures, but in fact represses certain "anxieties generated by globalism": "On the one hand, the fear of conflict was ameliorated by a utopian vision of global collaboration and harmony, and on the other, economic injustices and inequalities were justified by a re-affirmation of the innate and essential differences between races and cultures."[12]

While intercultural exchange could be viewed as a "'two-way street,' based on a mutual reciprocity," Rhustom Bharucha suggests that "in actuality, where it is the West that extends its domination to cultural matters, this 'two-way street' could be more accurately described as a 'dead-end.'"[13] Producing *The Mikado*, with its attendant illusions of lightness, weightlessness, and lack of representational responsibility, is particularly rife with such dangers. Thus the care with which *The Mikado* is made authentically Japanese for a Madison, Wisconsin, audience in the end only seems to confirm a pleasing vision of aesthetic foreignness that in fact covers over any more complicated understanding of exchange, commodities, labor, and commerce.

However, one aspect of Furumoto's attempts to redo the opera as authentically Japanese may be of further interest, and that is his perhaps tongue-in-cheek claim to fit the opera by virtue of his own hybrid identity: "Ethnically, I'm a mixture. My father is a second-generation Japanese-American born in Hawaii and my mother is of Scottish and English descent. So what more perfect show for me to do than 'The Mikado'"?[14] On the one hand, we might read this statement as being in keeping with his intercultural sensibility, in which Furumoto claims affinity with different cultural essences that correspond to what is Japanese or British in the opera. On another level, though, this ethnic mixture points to a different relationship both to what is Japanese in the play and to the labor of making it authentically Japanese.

The Mikado seems to be most immediate in reinforcing national affinities; Japanese spectators and commentators as well as performers (the subject of our next chapter) have a distinctive investment in who *The Mikado* represents and in what way. Furumoto's comments, however, identify a related but also distinctive *racial* investment in the opera. Asian Americans have a stake in the accuracy of *The Mikado*. Like the native informants so often appealed to for their opinion of the play's accuracy, they are called on to either discount the opera or to claim its verisimilitude. Their relationship to the opera also suggests a certain weightiness or gravity that belies *The Mikado*'s lightness; with their presence, attention again shifts to the opera's depiction of Japanese as a human interaction. Titipu becomes a world overrun with not only objects but also people whose presence cannot be ignored.

Thus there is a certain logic as to why Asian Americans might want in fact to participate in *The Mikado* rather than just protest against it. To do so is to recognize the enormous yet subtle power that this comic work has and to begin to move this power in other directions. That Furumoto's intense interest in reclaiming some dimension of authentic Japaneseness in his personal history is significant, for it claims, however humorously, that an element of Japanese heritage allows him to have an edge in making a better version of the opera. His statement mocks a racial association—how we might assume an instant affinity between a second-generation Japanese-Scottish-English man born in Hawaii and the Japanese of the opera—but it also promotes it as a way of correcting racial misrepresentation. In the end, Furumoto's production of *The Mikado* seemed to use authenticity in much the same way as the original Savoy production did, to support a predictably decorative vision of Japan. At the same time, his words point to a somewhat different perspective, whereby his production of the opera serves not only as a familiar re-creation of a Gilbert and Sullivan fantasy but also as a way of thinking about how certain racial identities make themselves visible and legible.

This emphasis on using the opera to think through Asian American identities and affinities appears with another *Mikado*, directed by Henry Akina at the Hawaii Opera Theatre in 2004. In many ways, this production also does not fall far from the D'Oyly Carte tree. Unlike an earlier adaptation, *Kabuki Mikado*, directed by James R. Brandon at the University of Hawaii at Manoa in 1996, Akina did not radically alter the lyrics or plot of the opera. This led to praise from reviewer John Berger, who interpreted Akina's production as an "anti-PC" stance against "self-appointed guardians of political correctness" who might find *The Mikado* offensive. Berger contrasted Akina's production with the 1996 "bowdlerized version" at the University of Hawaii–Manoa's theater department:

> A professor and four students changed the characters' names, eliminated everything they took issue with in the "quaint (yet racist) libretto," and restaged it as kabuki. Well, here comes Hawaii Opera Theatre's production, and artistic director Henry Akina doesn't buy into the racist argument.
>
> "It's really sort of a comedy about human frailty . . . and basic human absurdities," he explained, calling from his office last Friday morning. Akina is directing the company's precedent-setting, first-ever, summer production of "The Mikado" that opens this weekend, and he promises that it will be faithful in form and spirit of the story that Gilbert created in 1885.

Berger quotes Akina as saying that "We take 'Mikado,' I would say, pretty straight" and notes that the production, while updated in some ways, stays "pretty close to what Gilbert wrote." Akina comments on how productions of *The Mikado* should not be affected by the racial sensitivity of contemporary times:

> Political correctness is sort of an issue of the '90s—the idea of people being offended by various things has reached a fevered pitch in our age—and we didn't really want to deal with that (because) "The Mikado" is not supposed to be offensive to the Japanese or to the British.[15]

He reprises the argument that Gilbert was "satirizing the manners and mores of late-Victorian England," and that potentially insulting misrepresentations, such as the names of the characters, might be dismissed as pure English fun: "As for the characters' names, they weren't intended to be Japanese at all, but were simply in-joke references to various slang terms and products that were in vogue at the time."

However, casting Akina as a brave keeper of Gilbert and Sullivan tradition mistakes the extent to which so much of the energy of this production focuses on making *The Mikado* enjoyable to his contemporary audiences in Hawaii. For Akina, the vision of Gilbert and Sullivan's Japan is intrinsic to the opera; at the same time, with the substantial Japanese American population, ties to Japanese culture, and the visible presence of Japanese tourism in Hawaii, the production opera needed to highlight its own incongruities:

> It didn't seem to me that it would be right to go in the direction of the New York City Opera or the English National Opera ... and ignore the whole Japan thing. Productions like that have been very fashionable nationwide, but that's not exactly the way I wanted to do it and I don't think that's something for Honolulu. On the other hand, we know that the way these (characters) act is not terribly Japanese, and so we've put in points of confrontation in the performance where things that are sourced on authentic Japanese things are used.[16]

Akina inserted multiple allusions to political figures, community, and culture that referenced local Japanese American communities and the Japanese presence in Honolulu, enlisting renowned taiko drummer Kenny Endo to add taiko drumming to much of the action, casting sumo wrestler Ace Yonamine as the Lord High Executioner's sword bearer, and bringing in Masatoshi Muto, then Hawaii's consul general of Japan, as an extra. At the beginning of the second act, Muto walked onto the stage in a business suit and declared in a somber, deadpan tone, "On behalf of the Hawaii Opera Theatre and the government of Japan, I assure you that what takes place in this opera has nothing, absolutely nothing, to do with the country I represent."[17]

In an interview with Mari Yoshihara, Akina explained his directorial choices: "I wanted to make this silly opera into something that is relevant to us today.... In trying to make it less offensive and more fun for everybody, the idea was to include lots of Japanese elements that we like and bring in characters like the sumo wrestler."[18] Because of Hawaii's large Japanese American population, the familiarity of Japanese American elements and the incongruity of the faux-Japanese elements had special relevance; as Akina commented, this is "an audience who would appreciate the absurdity of the theatrical staging of such elements for what it is—deliberately absurd staging—rather than to take it literally and be offended by it, as audiences in other locations might do."[19] He suggests that preserving the original script is not inconsistent with this revision:

There are traditional areas of updating (the script) and there are other areas where people are very religious about not changing. I've tried to make the human comedy clearer rather than look at it as something ethnic or cultural or whatever, and we're rather unabashed about (sticking to the original story)—but we do have the joy of taiko, too!

It seemed a way to include the Japanese community in maybe enjoying "The Mikado" and being inclusive rather than exclusive (by going) either in the British or the Japanese direction. I think there'll be a rich theatrical event that people can enjoy and, hopefully, on many levels.[20]

That Japanese American audience members did enjoy the production was confirmed by its being advertised in the newsletter for the Japan-American Society of Hawaii, which praised the production's "hilarious antics and innuendos highlighting Japanese customs" and noted:

Artistic Director, Henry Akina, revised some of the character lines to bring this classic 1885 "light opera" up to modern times. The result was a presentation that the audience could easily relate to, despite Japanese Consul General Masatoshi Muto's humour[ous] claim (made in his cameo appearance) that "this is a different Japan than the one I know and represent." Add to this, the distinctive sounds of the taiko (Kenny Endo), beautifully-designed costumes (Anne Namba), and an authentic sumo wrestler (Ace Yonamine) and you have a show that was thoroughly enjoyed by all who attended.[21]

In opera productions in Hawaii throughout the twentieth century, Gilbert and Sullivan works were immensely popular. In 1890 *The Mikado* drew full houses in the Hawaii Opera House for its four performances, and in 1935 *The Mikado* marked the very first production of the Honolulu Community Theater.[22] These earlier productions are in marked contrast to the Akina production, which had a multiracial cast and played up its connections to Japanese and Japanese American audience members. Janos Gereben comments that the 1890 production, for instance, though advertised as "set in Japanese style—presented by local talent," did not reflect the racial diversity of Hawaii at the time; instead it "once again underlined the all-haole [all-white] nature of the opera world in the Islands of this period."

In 1890, the population of the Hawaiian Kingdom was 89,990, with native Hawaiians (and part-Hawaiians) still in the majority (34,000 and about 20,000), followed by Chinese and Japanese (15,300 and 12,300), and Portuguese (8,600)—and a rather small white minority, including 1,900 Americans and 1,300 Britishers.

Two-thirds of the population lived outside Honolulu, but almost all the Caucasians were residents of the city and they formed the influential minority which acted as both producers and consumers of such European-type entertainment as opera.

Gereben notes that "although there were more Japanese in the Islands by this time than English and Americans and the 1890 *Mikado* production had a Japanese setting," the cast for this production "excluded any non-haoles," with names such as "Monteagle, Hoogs, Bishop, Lewers, Widemann, Nolte, Bowler, Lishman, Dimond, Monsarrat, Brown."[23]

If the frequent production and immense popularity of these earlier productions suggest the dominance of "haole" taste, the refurbishing of Akina's 2004 production for Japanese American audience members is a significant departure from the past. At the same time, it brings up questions about how the opera is used to celebrate contemporary Japanese culture and Japanese American heritage in Hawaii and why it earned so much praise from reviews, such as in the *Honolulu Star-Bulletin* for its "encouraging precedent" of "a light and entertaining spectacle designed specifically for local tastes and conditions."[24]

The Akina production is set off from earlier *Mikado* productions in its turn toward the local, highlighting a sense of community and fellowship, in-jokes and insider knowledge. Touches of real Japanese flavor or allusions to local politics produced a comic dislocation with the opera's fantastical vision. The production neutralizes the ways that the opera might be insulting to the Japanese or Japanese Americans by celebrating the visible stature of Japanese Americans and the influence of Japanese presence and culture in today's Hawaii, and Akina's clever reframing targets those who might be entertained by the contrast between Gilbert and Sullivan's Titipu and a local culture. Although Gilbert's Titipu is set up against what is supposedly a real vision of both Japanese influence and Japanese American culture, this representation is itself highly selective. This particular use of the term "local" suggests that the opera has once again been used to put forward a carefully managed racial image defined by the pleasing use of colorful costumes, kabuki makeup, and humorous references to sumo and taiko. This celebratory vision of Japanese American success and cultural ties with Japan does not give much away about the complex background for this visibility: how Japanese Americans rose to contemporary economic and political influence in Hawaii.

The first Japanese immigrants in Hawaii arrived as contract laborers for the sugarcane and pineapple plantations. Japanese and other Asian immigrant coolies were systematically exploited and victimized by racist laws, prejudice, and economic constraints. However, in the years following World War II, the status of Japanese Americans, as well as Chinese Americans and Korean Americans, has changed to the extent that "in the minds of many in the local community, Asians are more central than marginal."[25] In particular, Japanese American success, as measured in terms such as income, home ownership, education, and political visibility and as evidenced by the election of those such as Senator Daniel K. Inouye and three-term Governor George Ariyoshi, has clearly risen. Any celebrations of their prominence, however, tends to obscure how, as Jonathan Okamura has suggested, social inequality in contemporary Hawaii is still very much defined along ethnic and racial lines, with whites, Japanese Americans, and Chinese Americans in economic and social positions of power and the "lower levels of the ethnic/racial stratification order" still "occupied by Filipinos, Native Hawaiians, and Samoans, a situation that appears unlikely to change in the next generation."[26] Any awareness of social and economic disparities, racial tensions, and native Hawaiian sovereignty becomes obscured by familiar images of Hawaii as an idealized multiracial paradise, with Japanese American success prominently featured.

What capacity does a production of *The Mikado* have to show this history or this contemporary reality? Not much, and perhaps that is the point. As we have seen, the opera disclaims any responsibility for racial representations even while visions of racial difference are at its very heart. *The Mikado*, after all, promises an escape from the sometimes ugly realities of commerce and exchange, particularly from reminders of laboring coolies, once so closely associated with the Japanese in Hawaii. Thus even while the Akina production purports to correct the opera's lightness with a glimpse of Japanese and Japanese Americans, these local references themselves are lightened, turned into easily consumed spectacles that are mobilized to ease the enjoyment of such guilty pleasures.

We want to leave the theater humming, not thinking. But is there a way to produce *The Mikado* that allows us to do both? To contemplate this possibility, we turn to Lodestone Theatre's 2007 adaptation, *The Mikado Project*,[27] which restages the opera as a commentary on Asian American theater. Esther Kim Lee has pointed out that Asian American theater is not a unified entity but rather "a huge web of links that are profoundly personal, professional, chronological, geographical, spatial, racial, ethnic, gendered, generational, and multicultural."[28] What seems common to many in this vast web are concerns with racial representation and the long history of orientalist discourse. Thus to look at *The Mikado Project* is to turn some of the fundamental aspects of the opera (such as its distinctively light racial impersonation and its fascination with oriental commodities) more directly toward commentary on Asian American racial representation.

Lodestone Theatre, *The Mikado Project* (2007)

Written by Doris Baizley and Ken Narasaki, *The Mikado Project* takes a subject that has become emblematic in Asian American theater: the difficulties faced by Asian American actors as they attempt to find meaningful roles. Plays and films such as Philip Kan Gotanda's *Yankee Dawg You Die* (1986), Eric Michael Zee's *Exit the Dragon* (1993), Justin Lin's *Finishing the Game* (2007), and Sun Mee Chomet's *Asianamnesia* (2008) highlight these actors' professional woes in order to criticize the continuing racism of mainstream theater and Hollywood film and to bring attention to the larger problems of representing Asian American identity as it exists apart from racial stereotypes and orientalist fantasies.

The plot echoes a host of movies and plays for which "let's put on a show" has become a mantra. A small theater company, short on resources but full of ambition, stages a classic. Performers muddle through rehearsals, worry about funding, cobble together scenery and costumes, and challenge one another's concepts for the production. The rehearsal process is full of backstage squabbles, flirtations, rivalries, and moments of artistic crisis, but in the end gumption, true love, and an addiction to the stage triumph as the company finally comes together to put on their show. These histrionics also comment on and challenge *The Mikado*'s status as a classic. Violent criticism of the opera's racial and gender representations is voiced from the beginning, when director Lance reveals to his Asian American theater company that they will be performing *The Mikado*. Cheryl, slated to play Yum-Yum, argues to the others that by performing *The Mikado* "we'll be putting our stamp of approval on an Imperialist-Colonial,

White-Male-centric, dick-waggling... racist piece of crap." She calls the Three Little Maids "submissive whimpering Asian morons" and points out that "the only name that's actually Japanese is "Ko-Ko... and it means 'radish'!... They consider us so 'other,' we don't deserve human names!" Other characters defend *The Mikado*; Ben (Ko-Ko) and Viola (Katisha) comment, "It was the most popular piece of musical theater... until *Cats*," whereupon Cheryl retorts, "And instead of furry costumes, you get *yellow-face and gibberish*!" Lance insists on his choice by arguing that the opera is a perfect forum for contemporary political commentary and experimentation. When Cheryl attacks the opera's racist nostalgia and outdated gender taboos ("And don't forget Ko-Ko's engaged to marry Yum-Yum, his own adopted daughter"), Lance sees potential for contemporary commentary ("You see? Woody Allen–style incest! It's totally *edgy*!") One suspects, however, that Lance's choice of *The Mikado* comes not only from his deconstructionist aims but also from a childhood attachment to the music ("I have to confess, I loved the music when I saw it as a boy, before I came to understand the political baggage").

Characters in the play closely connect with the opera either as a misrepresentation of their identities or as a familiar and even nostalgic cultural marker. Ultimately, however, Lance reveals that his true motives for staging the opera come from its name recognition and marketability, since the grant underwriting his envisioned production of *The Mikado* is the only thing keeping their small company afloat. Thus the play illustrates how a limited repertoire and racial stereotypes continue to dictate the opportunities of Asian American actors, singers, and other performing artists. The predicament of having to perform in *The Mikado* or face financial ruin becomes a metaphor for the performers themselves, who cannot find adequate work in mainstream television or film. This is stated overtly as Ben and other cast members revise Ko-Ko's "list" to enumerate instances of media racism such as "the pestilential talk show hosts / Who say "ching chong" on "The View" / And angry white male radio jocks / Who really make me spew" and to detail the casting problems faced by Asian American performers.

> BEN: There's the trendy TV casting guy
>   Who says he's color blind,
> CHERYL: If he says race don't exist,
>   You can put him on the list!

BEN: Then he casts you as the take-out boy
   And doesn't think you'll mind!
CHERYL: I don't think he'll be missed
   I'm sure he won't be missed.
TEDDY: Now he wants you Filipino
   But that won't last very long,
   Next he'll only want Koreans
   Or Chinese from Hong Kong
TERRI: If you're female
   You're a prostitute,
   A math whiz or a geek.
   "Hey soldier wanna boom-boom"
   Is the first line
   That you'll speak.
VIOLA: But it really doesn't matter—
   In New York or in L.A.—
ALL: You won't work any way
   You won't work an-y way

Playing in *The Mikado* as an Asian American performer highlights the overall predicament of the Asian American artist: how careers are sustained through playing stereotypes predicated on yellowface. Yet *The Mikado Project* shows these characters making use of the opera as well as struggling against its terms. The company rallies around the idea of doing a thoroughly revisionist production, with the first difference being the casting of Asian American rather than white performers; as Lance tries to reassure Cheryl, "You're angry about the Yellow-face, but if *we* do it, it won't be Yellow-face." Other members of the cast, including Teddy (Nanki-Poo), chime in enthusiastically, reiterating both the possibilities for deconstructing the opera and for the continued enjoyment of its music:

LANCE: We make it in our own image. Overthrow the Mikado.
   Free it from its past. *(Handing out scripts.)*
   Liberate the text.
TEDDY: And that way, we get to sing the songs!

The play thus provides several opportunities not only for critique but also for imagining how the opera might be liberated in order to comment on the politics of race, gender, and sexuality. What emerges is a running series of alternative characterizations of *The Mikado* that transform the characterizations of the opera. Nanki-Poo becomes a cool masculine rebel as Teddy performs "A Wandering Minstrel" as a rap song. The combination of coy, yet flagrant sexuality is brought out as Cheryl, Viola, and Terri perform "Three Little Maids" with drug-crazed "wild Tokyo schoolgirl looks" and vogue, break, and "strike porn poses" as they sing. The Gentlemen of Japan are proposed as a "sexy" version of corporate clones; the first act is reset in "the courtyard of an office building in Tokyo" with "Japanese executives discovered standing and sitting in attitudes suggested by Money Magazine."

This move to revise the opera in contemporary terms seems at first to suggest only the possibility of further typecasting. Even doing what Lance calls a "deconstructed, post-modernist" revision cannot fully redeem the opera for them. When at the end of the first act Viola appears, dressed for her entrance as Katisha as "an over-made-up society matron" complete with "a big blonde bouffant wig, gaudy handbag, fake Chanel suit loaded with strands of giant pearls," Cheryl resumes her opposition to doing the opera: "Look at us! Vi's dressed up like a hag, and we're all doing ching-chong Japanese! Even if it ain't yellowface, its still a Minstrel Show!" Each of the new concepts for the production becomes a reiteration, however hyperbolic, of an old stereotype, with the performers exuberantly performing "Miya sama" in a fabulously exaggerated array of fans and oriental "Super Chinky Japanese" poses. However, pushing the limits of the opera does allow alternative forms of expression to emerge. Their rehearsals provide ample opportunities for in-jokes about identities and representation ("If you want to know who we are / We are Asians who eat spam"). They also provide space for critique of a different kind. As three different couples—Cheryl and Terri, Lance and Teddy, and Ben and Viola—rehearse the song "Were You Not to Ko-Ko Plighted," Yum-Yum and Nanki-Poo's forbidden expressions of affection include displays of same-sex attraction. The Mikado's prohibition against heterosexual flirting translates into contemporary sexual repression, as Cheryl declares triumphantly, "We bust taboos, we stand up for every Nanki-Poo and Yum-Yum who was ever forbidden to love the person they loved by some uptight, right-wing Mikado-Court." An extravagant and hilarious reworking of "Braid the Raven Hair" is sung to a Yum-Yum played in drag by Teddy, and gender roles are even further dismantled when Viola, wearing a suit, finally steps in to play the Mikado.

Ultimately, the characters do find room in their rendition of the opera for a much more satisfying expression of politics and emotion. The radical revisions that they propose finally give way to a much more straightforward rendering of the opera's songs. Ben and Viola sing "Tit-Willow" as a romantic duet, and Terri and Cheryl sing "The Sun Whose Rays" as a quiet affirmation of their self-worth. In these songs the performers, without elaborate makeup or costume or gesture, use Gilbert's words and Sullivan's music to express simple and honest feelings for one another and about themselves. In the end, the company agrees to stage a play that is about a struggling Asian American theater company that is forced to do *The Mikado*.

Ultimately, the charm of this revision is not so much in its spirited redoing of Gilbert and Sullivan but in its appeal to an audience that is familiar with Asian American politics and theater. The play pokes fun at its own vision of real and fake Asian American experience, as the character of Jace proposes how *The Mikado* might be restaged as serious representational drama, set in a World War II internment camp:

> JACE *(pitching)*: Manzanar, 1943 ... no, Manzanar's over-used ... Minidoka! 1943: A high school drama teacher, well-intentioned, cares for the people who have been wrongly interned, decides to put together a production of an operetta that he's always loved: Gilbert and Sullivan's THE MIKADO. THE MINIDOKA MIKADO! He thinks that this will uplift his students and make them proud of their heritage, instead of ashamed. But, of course, his Nisei students are into Tommy Dorsey— ... Nor do they know anything about the Japanese emperor or any of the nonsensical customs and laws portrayed in the play. So, he has to, in a way, teach them how to be Japanese. But he—that is, I—
>
> LANCE: YOU???
>
> JACE: In white-face, of course.

When Jace, the prodigal cast member, returns to the company in order to propose a "Minidoka Mikado," complete with a starring role for himself as the white teacher who inspires ethnic pride, he mocks both *The Mikado* and the internment camp plays that are the staple of Asian American theater. This moment in the play skewers painfully earnest depictions of Asian Americans as victims of internment and the subjects of racial oppression.

In its proposed revision into a camp play, this revised *Mikado* points to other kinds of racial clichés. That the rest of the cast unequivocally rejects Jace's idea, declaring emphatically, "No More Camp Plays Ever Again," also suggests that Asian Americans themselves are ready for new kinds of racial theater.

Though in so many ways *The Mikado Project* wholeheartedly discards Gilbert and Sullivan's initial conception, its own satirical edge redirects rather than replaces the opera's irreverent attractions. *The Mikado Project* thus becomes an opportunity for revising the opera so that it speaks to the possibilities of new meanings even within these old and well-worn roles. The continued life of the opera does not mean simply the reproduction of yellowface in the old style but instead promises to crack it wide open. Thus *The Mikado Project* both critiques and celebrates the power of its namesake, and in so doing proposes an alternative direction for *The Mikado*'s future resurrections.

Chapter 8

The Mikado in Japan

By now, the stories around the Savoy's employment of the inhabitants of the Knightsbridge Japanese Native Village to coach its *Mikado* performers is well known. François Cellier described the "Geisha, or Tea-girl," as "a charming and very able instructress, although she knew only two words of English—'Sixpence, please,' that being the price of a cup of tea as served by her at Knightsbridge," and outlined her role in the racial transformation of the Savoy players:

> To her was committed the task of teaching our ladies Japanese deportment, how to walk or run or dance in tiny steps with toes turned in, as gracefully as possible; how to spread and snap the fan either in wrath, delight, or homage, and how to giggle behind it. The Geisha also taught them the art of "make-up," touching the features, the eyes, and the hair. Thus to the minutest detail the Savoyards were made to look like "the real thing."

Momentarily, Cellier lingers over the possibility of a reversal as he relates, "our Japanese friends often expressed the wish that they could become as English in appearance as their pupils had become Japanesey."

> Somebody suggested they should try a course of training under Richard Barker, who could work wonders. Had not he succeeded in making little children assume the attitude and bearing of adults? If anybody could transform a "celestial" into an "occidental," Dick Barker was the man. But I don't think the experiment was ever tried.[1]

The prospect of Japanese performers assuming occidental roles, considered to be as formidable a challenge as the training of children in adult parts, is never acted on. The Japanese never appear onstage, although their presence is necessarily evoked to sustain the illusion of the Savoyards as "the real thing."

In the 1920s, a brochure for the Milton Aborn Operatic Companies made available for the Chautauqua and Lyceum circuit of traveling performers in the United States, included, as part of its array of featured artists, a photograph of "Shimozumi as Yum Yum."[2] The singer's Japanese identity emerges without comment alongside the more typical yellowface performances of others, such as "Sisson as Nanki Poo" or "Welsh as Butterfly." Not much else can be found about her. Perhaps a visiting artist, or even a Japanese American student at the school associated with the Milton Aborn Operatic School of New York company, Shimozumi doesn't appear in any other pictures.

Perhaps her casting testified to the growing ability of Japanese and other Asian performers to use Western opera as a forum for personal and professional development and to foster national pride. Such was the case for Japanese soprano Miura Tamaki, whose career in the West was defined by her successful portrayal of Cio-Cio-San in Puccini's *Madame Butterfly* and who toured the role extensively to major cities around the world after her debut in London in 1915. As Mari Yoshihara has illustrated, Miura's success enabled other Japanese singers, such as Koike Hisako (aka Hizi Koyke), Miyagawa Yoshiko, and Tanaka Michiko, who similarly made their careers through performing this role.[3] Cio-Cio-San, like Yum-Yum, is a role defined primarily by white performers in yellowface, and thus the success of Miura and others suggests that audiences responded to the novelty of this casting, perhaps seeing it as lending the opera a racial authenticity even more compelling than that of scenery or costume.

And yet a kind of incongruity exists between the predictable yellowface tradition and the visibly racialized body of the performer. When acclaimed Japanese actress Sada Yakko performed in London in 1901, one critic complained that music from *The Mikado* and *The Geisha* was played during the intermission. "With real Japan before us, the last thing we wish to be reminded of is the sham Japan of cockney invention."[4] Japanese bodies cannot simply be added in the same way as fans, screens, and bridges to provide authenticity or color to the production; this casting calls into question fundamental aspects of the opera's reliance on yellowface. Instead of a light racial impersonation in which the performer can easily dispense with the disguise of Japaneseness, the racial identity of the performer seems indelible.

COMMUNITY OR HOME TALENT PRODUCTIONS

ARRANGEMENTS may be made with this office for the production of opera in cities where it is desired to use local talent. The production may be made under the auspices of choral societies or any body of people organized for the promotion of opera and musical affairs. These community or home talent operatic performances may be given entirely, cast and chorus, by the local singers or a cast may be sent and the local singers would form the chorus. In either case a dramatic director to stage the production would be sent on after the music of the opera has been thoroughly rehearsed by the local director. This method of producing opera has proved very successful and has been the means of creating an unusual amount of interest in local musical affairs.

Figure 21. Photographs of Shimozumi as Yum-Yum and Sisson as Nanki Poo, from a brochure for the Milton Aborn Operatic Companies, circa 1922. Records of the Redpath Chautauqua Collection, Special Collections Department, University of Iowa Libraries, Iowa City, Iowa.

However little else we know of her or her performance, Shimozumi's presence draws attention to both the hopeful possibilities and the dead ends facing performers of Asian descent in the West. Can we read Shimozumi's long-buried performances of Yum-Yum—a singular instance of Asian casting in early *Mikado* production—not only as an instance of personal success but also as an inspiration to other performers of Asian descent whose opportunities, like those of African American performers, were tightly restricted by race? It is a stretch to imagine that Shimozumi might have been offered more parts with Milton Aborn or elsewhere in the United States than the limited role of Yum-Yum. It is hard to imagine that, if she indeed had been a student at the Milton Aborn Operatic School, she would have been able to fulfill their stated goals to "educate singers who desire to make a serious study of opera and to give to the singers of this country the same opportunity for such preparation here as formerly made a European trip necessary" and to offer a course of instruction "systematized so that the student may become proficient in any number of roles."[5] But can we at least take her casting as a sign, however small, of the ability to challenge the veracity of orientalist representation, to trouble rather than simply to authenticate the sham Japan by her mere presence?

As we have seen, *The Mikado* relies on a particular kind of yellowface performance that despite strategic touches of realism relies on its own lack of seriousness. Part of the charm of *The Mikado* is in watching the temporary racial transformation of non-Asian bodies into these familiar decorative versions of japonaiserie. This is consistent with the opera's commodity racism, whereby playing Japanese becomes a matter of associating oneself with objects that can be quickly disposed of. Yellowface is performed as a flirtation rather than as a more lasting bodily transformation. Performers thus easily transform themselves into Japanese through formulaic racial gestures and iconic objects and just as easily retreat from these racial incarnations.

The tightly controlled performances of the 1885 D'Oyly Carte *Mikado*s produced a spectacular fantasy of race that has its own corporeal and material tangibility. Its strategic use of Japanese details of costume, scenery, and gesture, as well as its reliance on Japanese objects, reinforced the authority of its depictions as to what was Japanese. Despite this, however, these racial impersonations remain temporary rather than sustained enterprises. Audiences of repertory companies such as D'Oyly Carte were thoroughly familiar with the performers and delighted in seeing them act in varied roles. None of these performers ever made a career out of yellowface, unlike the best-known blackface minstrels; these racial impersonators would leave off being Japanese immediately after the curtain fell. The pleasure of *The Mikado*'s yellowface is in a racial transformation unencumbered by the real, a version of playacting that could be easily adopted and just as easily dispensed with.

Contemporary versions of the opera that reference the D'Oyly Carte tradition adhere to this version of yellowface just as dearly. Their versions of Japanese are abstracted from selected examples of Japanese dress, movement, and music into distinctive modes of choreography and spectacle, using iconographic objects and costumes to undergird these racial impersonations. Because of this quality of abstraction, of escape from reality, *The Mikado* can accommodate a number of images of what is Japanese. As we have seen, this is precisely what allows more contemporary stereotypes of the yellow peril or the barbed racial insult to hide itself in the gaps between innocent merriment and more serious representation. Though *The Mikado* harbors political sentiments of all kinds, it consistently escapes the charge that it means any of them. This shifty quality is ingrained in the nature of its yellowface: seemingly light, it can easily disavow any mean intention. Thus contemporary productions that move away from the D'Oyly Carte style toward a presumably de-Japanned interpretation nonetheless still throw out truncated yet obvious reminders of the opera's Japanese status. The white-on-white production of Jonathan Miller, for instance, still uses some scenic and stylistic reminders of japonaiserie, such as kimonos or the glimpse of Mount Fuji through the window, as well as casually racist gestures. The very flippancy of these gestures further intensifies their effect, reminding us simultaneously how easy it is to demean nonwhite bodies and denying that such careless actions might impact real people.

As a form of racial mimicry, the yellowface of *The Mikado* demonstrates a pointed lack of commitment to representation. What happens to this nonchalance when *The Mikado* is played not in yellowface but by Japanese performers? As we have already seen with Asian American performers, Asian bodies inhabit *The Mikado* much differently than do their white counterparts, drawing attention to more serious aspects of the opera's racial representation. Shimozumi, or the Knightsbridge Japanese Village inhabitants brought into coach the Savoy performers, or the actors playing them for Mike Leigh's *Topsy-Turvy*, all might be used to authenticate the opera; however, their presence also raises a certain uneasiness about the comparison between playing Japanese and being Japanese. Dissonance ensues when racial mimicry is taken over by racial performers in the flesh.

This chapter examines Japanese productions of *The Mikado*, which define a much more modest yet significant aspect of the opera's racial history. Having Japanese performers in *The Mikado* challenges the logic of its racial impersonation. These examples belie the claim that the opera is only about England and insist on its power as a representation of Japan. In turn, they present versions of a Titipu that show the complexity of claims to a distinctively Japanese history for the opera.

These productions are framed not only by their rarity within a world overwhelmingly populated by yellowface versions of *The Mikado*, but also by the long history of resistance to the opera on the part of Japan. As chapter 7 suggested, the official response by the Japanese government to the 1885 productions of *The Mikado* was negative. According to Naoki Inose and Sumiko Enbutsu, Japanese travelers who viewed productions in London and Munich pointed out inaccuracies in the opera's names and characterizations and fired off scathing reviews to Tokyo.[6] Early productions were heavily censored within Japan. In November 1885, the Emelie Melville Opera and Comedy Company attempted to stage *The Mikado* in foreign settlements in Kobe. The British consul persuaded them to eliminate the piece even for a foreign audience. The Gaiety Theatre in Yokohama, built primarily for foreign residents, booked Salinger's Opera Bouffe Company for *The Mikado* in 1887, which caused a great worry to Acting Consul J. Carey Hall and Minister Francis R. Plunkett. Threatened with severe penalties, the company changed the name of the opera to "Three Little Maids from School" and excised references to the emperor. The Stanley Opera Company followed this precedent when it performed *The Mikado* at the Gaiety in 1890.[7]

As chapter 7 illustrated, the censorship of the opera was interpreted by Gilbert and others as an unreasonable concession to diplomatic politesse, a deference due to the touchiness of Japanese politicians, who in their rush to promote the image of Japan as a modern nation took this comic opera far too seriously. But the initial ban of *The Mikado* in Japan shows that the response to the opera might actually have stemmed from a more complicated policing of foreign settlements in Japan where British businessmen and other foreigners resided. The censorship of *The Mikado* in Japan was in response to foreign opera companies who presented the opera largely for the benefit of non-Japanese audiences. The perceived danger of *The Mikado* was thus not so much about the possible offense of Japanese spectators at the characterization of their emperor but about preserving the government's ability to control productions directed mainly at foreigners living in Japan, who bore an ambivalent, if not hostile, relationship to their host country.

However, even in the wake of the disestablishment of foreign settlements in 1899, the Japanese authorities were determined to prohibit *Mikado* performances no matter what changes were made.[8] This ban against productions in Japan continued through March and April 1923, with the denial of permission for a Savoy Theatre touring troupe under the direction of C. Herbert Workman to present *The Mikado* in Tokyo, Yokohama, and Kobe even with a changed title and script changes. Masahiko Masumoto suspects, however, that *The Mikado* was performed surreptitiously for an audience in Kobe on April 25 under the title "Gilbert and Sullivan: Vaudeville Entertainment," without the character of the Mikado.[9] Still, official censorship was sustained, which registered growing sensitivity within Japan to orientalist representations. *Madame Butterfly*, for instance, also came under strong criticism by Japanese observers from the time of its New York premiere in 1907.[10]

Thus it is perhaps not surprising that the first twentieth-century production of *The Mikado* in Japan was staged less as musical exchange and more as a military exercise by the U.S. occupation forces. A series of three productions was performed by Army personnel with a unit of civilian actresses from the United States in the Takarazuko Gekijō, renamed the Ernie Pyle Theater, beginning July 22, 1946.[11] The *New York Times* reported that this production used a "cast of sixty-five singers with a sixty-piece theatre symphony orchestra augmented by a Japanese girls ensemble" and was "the most lavish show yet attempted by the Ernie Pyle production unit."[12] Joseph Raben, who served as a military translator during the U.S. occupation, recalled,

> The leads were all American, Canadian and British, but the male singing chorus and the female dancing chorus were Japanese. The costumes for the leads were, with one exception, those rented by the royal court for coronations; even after half a century, I recall their splendor. The exception was the Mikado, a tall man, who had to have his own trousers of gold and blue diamond panels. The set

was equally magnificent, with overhanging cherry blossoms and an elaborate bridge from the rear. The reason for this extravagance was the Allied policy of demanding huge reparations for the war, but not taking any of that money out of the country. These so-called blocked yen were available in prodigious quantities to be fed back into the economy, so that the producers apparently had an unlimited budget.[13]

The *Chicago Tribune* noted that Sgt. Donald G. Mitchell, aged 19, who played the Mikado despite "an attack of malaria," was costumed in a "kimono that was Japan's original inauguration robe first worn 2,000 years ago."[14]

The production, which ran for three nights,[15] was meant for U.S. military personnel and not Japanese audiences, although the cast included forty-two Japanese girls in the chorus and ballet and fifteen Japanese male chorus members. The audience, as recalled by Raben, "was entirely GI" and, aside from him, not altogether appreciative: "I suspect that the majority of those watching it would have preferred a recent movie." Raben also noted that he "saw a Russian general in a box one night, but did not recognize MacArthur or any other U.S. brass at any performance,"[16] although a later article in the *Chicago Daily Tribune* noted that General MacArthur, Mrs. MacArthur, and their son were among the guests at one of the productions.[17] The *Chicago Daily Tribune* reported, "Only a few Japanese have seen the famous operetta. None will be allowed to attend the current performances" although "[a] few Japanese, guests of members of the cast, attended a dress rehearsal yesterday."[18] But *Life* reported that the production "was also seen by several hundred curious Japanese, including Prince Kuni, a brother-in-law of the present Mikado, who was invited to a sneak preview"; moreover, the report took care to add that "they seemed to enjoy the spoofing immensely."[19]

Japanese audiences did attend a 1948 production of *The Mikado* in Tokyo, performed by the Nagato Miho Opera Company and the Tokyo Philharmonic with a Japanese cast. This production was directed by noted Japanese American dancer and choreographer Michio Ito,[20] who had already won acclaim for his earlier choreography for 1927 and 1928 productions of *The Mikado, Cherry Blossoms,* and *Madame Butterfly* in Los Angeles.[21] *Time* magazine reported, "The producers had gambled a whopping 1,800,000 yen ($36,000) on the production. Reserved seats went for

80 yen, the highest theater prices in Japanese history."[22] The initial performances of this costly production, planned initially for summer 1947, were at first suspended due to the lack of copyright permission. After British officials relayed a request to the D'Oyly Carte Opera Company, permission was eventually granted, and the opera was performed at the end of January 1948. At the first performance was Emperor Hirohito's brother Prince Nobuhito Takamatsu, accompanied by his wife and the brother of the Empress Nagato, Prince Kumi.[23]

Among Gilbert and Sullivan aficionados, these two productions were the comeuppance of the 1907 ban on the Savoy's production. For Leslie Baily, Gilbert finally exacts revenge for the previous ban on his opera:

> Puck put a girdle around the world in Shakespeare's imagination. Gilbert and Sullivan have beaten all imagination by doing so in reality, and by holding the globe girdled in their bond of fun through all these changing years. A truly Gilbertian example of this happy bondage came when American occupation troops landed in Japan—and one of the first entertainments they staged was *The Mikado;* and this was followed (1948) by a production of the opera in Tokio by an all-Japanese cast, before an audience including Prince Nobuhito Takamatsu, the Emperor's brother. Events had turned full circle since the British government's ban in fear of offending the Japanese in 1907.[24]

However, the "happy bondage" imagined by Baily's account hides a more uncertain assessment of the meaning of these two productions, one that Joseph Raben foregrounds in his description of the Ernie Pyle production:

> Apparently there had been some private performances [of *The Mikado*], but with emperor worship still the rule in the country, only the army of occupation could undertake such a gross action of lese majeste.... What impact this production might have had on the native Japanese is hard to calculate. I did meet a professor of English literature who seemed (to a young recent graduate) knowledgeable about his subject. But the performance of *Swan Lake* that I saw around the corner at a Japanese theater was pitifully crude, as if directed by someone who had heard of the ballet but never seen it performed. It would be interesting to see whether

any native-language newspapers of that time had any knowledge of this impudent but magnificent gesture, a tribute to their culture in a sense, but also an assertion of the Americans' right to do as they pleased in a conquered country.[25]

John Dower has characterized the U.S. occupation of Japan as "the last immodest exercise in the colonial conceit known as 'the white man's burden,'"[26] and as an ideological as well as military enterprise.

> Their [American] reformist agenda rested on the assumption that, virtually without exception, Western culture and its values were superior to those of "the Orient." At the same time, almost every interaction between victor and vanquished was infused with intimations of white supremacism. For all its uniqueness of time, place, and circumstance—all its peculiarly "American" iconoclasm—the occupation was in this sense but a new manifestation of the old racial paternalism that historically accompanied the global expansion of the Western powers. Like their colonialist predecessors, the victors were imbued with a sense of manifest destiny. They spoke of being engaged in the mission of civilizing their subjects. They bore the burden (in their own eyes) of their race, creed, and culture. They swaggered, and were enviously free of self-doubt.[27]

These productions of *The Mikado*, then, were not so much a heady sign of Western victory staged to audiences longing for Gilbert and Sullivan as they were more subtle reminders of the superiority of American democracy over an imagined backward Japan. In fact, *The Mikado* was suggested as the alternative to performances of traditional Japanese theater such as Kabuki. In mid-November 1945, the Civil Information and Education Section of General MacArthur's command banned all performances of Japanese theater, film, and other entertainment companies that dealt with the following themes or subjects:

1. Vendettas, revenge
2. Nationalism, warlike behavior, or exclusivity
3. Distortion of historical facts
4. Segregation or religious discrimination
5. Feudal loyalty
6. Praise of militarism in the past, present, and future

7. Approval of suicide in any form
8. Women's submission to men
9. Death, cruelty, or the triumph of evil
10. Antidemocracy
11. Approval of the illegal or unreasonable treatment of children
12. Praising personal devotion to a state, nation, race, the emperor, or the Imperial Household
13. Anything against the Potsdam declaration or the orders of GHQ [General Headquarters] authorities.[28]

While performances in such forms as Kabuki supposedly celebrated totalitarian and feudal values associated with old Japan and needed to be censored, a production of *The Mikado*, which lampooned so many of these themes, was actively promoted. According to Naoki Inose, the Nagato Miho company had requested permission from General Headquarters to perform the classic revenge drama *Chūshingura* at the Tōkyō Gekijō (Tokyo Theater). Matsuji Yoshida, interpreter for the renowned Kabuki company Shochiku, remembered that second lieutenant and chief censor Earle Ernest of the Civil Censorship Detachment instructed them that it would be easier to perform *Chūshingura* if *The Mikado* were performed first, telling Yoshida that the performance at the Ernie Pyle was "very popular and you can borrow the stage set from them."[29] With *The Mikado* production held up due to British copyright restrictions, the Nagato Miho production was temporarily canceled despite a considerable investment of time and money. After Major Faubion Bowers, a Kabuki enthusiast, replaced Earle Ernest as censor, a nearly full-length production of *Chūshingura*, with an all-star cast, was performed at Tokyo Theater beginning on November 5, 1947, a few months before *The Mikado* was performed.

With both *Mikado* productions in occupied Japan, there was considerable curiosity as to how Japanese audience members might receive the opera. The few attendees of the 1946 production had their opinions actively solicited. According to the *Chicago Tribune*, several of these Japanese spectators seemed wary of the production. One commented rather obliquely, "If we had won the war we never would have been able to see this."[30] Others were more direct:

"We don't think the way we used to about the emperor, but even so we think the operetta ridicules him and we don't like that very well," said one woman spectator. Another more sophisticated

Japanese said he thought the emperor himself would not be offended because "Americans in the cast portray their Japanese roles so convincingly. But we Japanese can't find anything in it to laugh about."[31]

In contrast, the *New York Times* reported that "Japanese spectators laughed heartily today" and of the "fifty or more Japanese who saw the operetta for the first time said very little of it was objectionable and they thought the performance was 'thoroughly enjoyable.'"[32] Later *New York Times* reports, however, stated that the Japanese who saw the 1946 production "said they enjoyed its humor but were 'surprised and slightly embarrassed' by its satire of the Emperor."[33] The royal party's reaction to the 1948 production was under special scrutiny.

> Prince Nobuhito Takamatsu sat in a first row balcony seat of the Hiniya [Hibiya Kokaido, or Hibiya Public Hall] Theatre, together with his wife and Prince Kuni, the Empress Nagato's brother. The party smiled throughout, but did not applaud.
> Leaving a few minutes before the end of the performance, Takamatsu said he thought the program "very interesting. I enjoyed it very much."[34]

The close attention to the Japanese responses to *The Mikado* indicate the desire to understand the production, like other aspects of the military occupation, as not just a clear exercise of power, but a more benevolent enterprise. "Progress" thus was measured by the ability of the Japanese to enjoy *The Mikado*, and productions of *The Mikado* during occupation could be taken as hopeful signs that the Japanese would benefit from their new topsy-turvy situation. *Time* magazine announced of the Nagato Miho production, "Now that neither the Emperor nor his people felt so strongly about the sacredness of His Majesty, the first all-Japanese performance of The Mikado was all set to be played last week in Tokyo."[35] One unsigned editorial to the *New York Times* stated this hope even more directly:

> Prince Nobuhito Takamatsu, brother of Emperor Hirohito of Japan, accompanied by his wife and by Prince Kumi, brother of the Empress, it is reported from Tokyo, attended there a few days

ago the first performance in Japanese of Gilbert and Sullivan's "The Mikado." Prince Nobuhito, we are told, said that it was "very interesting" and that he had "enjoyed it very much." Other Japanese in the audience, however, called it "unreal" and "fantastic," and perhaps the Emperor's brother, despite his laudatory comment, also decided that the Japan portrayed in that miniature masterpiece of the two inimitable Savoyards was, in comparison with the real Japan, a thing of utter unreality and unbridled fantasy.

Yet, why should they? From their point of view, can anything in Gilbert and Sullivan be more remote from reality as they used to know it than the Japan into which Hirohito and his family have been violently projected? Which, one is impelled to ask, is to them the more incredible—the impossible country in which Ko-Ko and Pooh-Bah, Yum-Yum and Nanki-Poo disport themselves in irresponsible gaiety, in which common sense is stood on its head and all that is upside down becomes sober normality—or the realm of "reality" into which the Emperor and his kin have been flung, in which that Oriental "Son of Heaven" is in daily contact with Occidental democracy, in which American soldiers saunter where armored Samurai once trod, and power commensurate with that of Hirohito's ancestors in [their] heyday is wielded by an American general backed by American regiments and American warships? Where, in all Gilbert and Sullivan, can one find a situation as fantastic?

May the radiant absurdity of Gilbert and Sullivan help to banish the tragic absurdity of Tojo and Yamashita forever from post-war Japan—and thus add still more laurels to the bounteous crop already harvested from the Savoy operas by their effervescent and irrepressible creators![36]

However mixed its reception, the 1948 Nagato Miho production inaugurated a series of Japanese *Mikado*s in the following decades. This company in particular made the most of this opportunity; by 1970, it had staged the opera more than one thousand times, as well as broadcasting it on NHK television.[37] Other professional companies such as the Fujiwara Opera Company, as we shall see in the next section, not only played in Japan but also toured their productions abroad. There were also some nonprofessional productions of *The Mikado* in Japan, for instance, by music students at Nagoya University of Arts in 1996. Few of these later productions, aside from the 2001 Chichibu production, have attracted much fanfare or controversy. Still, their playing of Gilbert and Sullivan draws from an alternative history for the performance of Western opera in Japan and illustrates a different trajectory for *The Mikado*'s racial history.

Fujiwara Opera U.S. Tour (1956)

Reviewers of productions of *The Mikado* in occupied Japan desired to see performances of *The Mikado* not just as the triumph of Gilbert and Sullivan over Japanese enemies, but also as the willing concession of Japanese to a Western alliance that would benefit them. Such sentiments continued into the cold war. The United States, emerging as a new superpower, was under pressure to show itself as a liberal nation, deserving of its prominence as a world power and morally superior to its World War II enemies, Germany and Japan. As Christina Klein notes, U.S. global influence came at a time when antinationalist and anticolonialist movements were also gaining ground, particularly in Asia, thus causing a kind of paradox: "How can we define our nation as a non-imperial world power in the age of decolonization?"[38] U.S. expansion into Asia was thus "predicated on the principle of international integration rather than on territorial imperialism," and relied on "an ideology of global interdependence rather than one of racial difference."[39]

For the American public, a larger shift in the image of Japan from war enemy to occupied dependant meant a return of the older images of Japan as "elf-land." Naoko Shibusawa has noted that during the American occupation of Japan there was a resurgence of the nineteenth-century image of Japan as an exotic tourist locale, and for American military personnel during the occupation, buying Japanese souvenirs, particularly those that suggested the familiar icons of japonaiserie, was an especially popular pastime. For instance, Lucy Herndon Crockett, an American Red Cross worker during the occupation, noted that military and diplomatic missions became "hectic shopping tours" for "cheap white silk kimonos embroidered with flamboyant dragons and flowers ... white silk scarves, handkerchiefs, pajamas, and doilies similarly embroidered or brightly painted with pictures of Fuji-yama, geisha girls, cherry blossoms, and torii gates" as well as other products made for "foreign consumption."[40] Attempts to refigure Japan from enemy to postwar ally also figured in post–World War II Hollywood films, which featured "vision after vision of cherry-blossom Japan, receptive Japanese women, and grateful, smiling Japanese children."[41]

Such a spirit of benevolent patronage and a renewed interest in the queer and quaint register in the reception of the Fujiwara Opera Company productions of *The Mikado* that toured the United States eighteen years later. Traveling to cities such as San Francisco; Los Angeles; Denver; Washington, D.C.; Hartford, Connecticut; Asbury Park, New Jersey; and Boston,[42] this 1956 *Mikado* production was performed in tandem with a production of *Madame Butterfly* in which the Japanese cast members sang in Japanese and the Americans in English. In the years ensuing, the company returned to the United States on tour and took these two productions to Europe.[43]

Their *Madame Butterfly* in particular was praised by American reviewers for its "uncommon realism":

> Up to a point the nationalistic realism is rather charming. The young women are pretty and graceful and their mannerisms are real, not acquired. The men, too, seem to be recognizable types and their naturalism is to be preferred to the caricatures one is accustomed to in Italianized opera. There is no very strong acting ability anywhere around, but they all do what comes naturally with a reasonable amount of conviction.[44]

Unlike the Fujiwara Opera's *Butterfly,* their productions of *The Mikado* seem to be troubled rather than benefited by their Japanese performers. For U.S. reviewers, one consistent complaint was that the cast was unable to measure up to the standard set by D'Oyly Carte. For the reviewer from the *Los Angeles Times,* "everything but the style of Gilbert and Sullivan's 'The Mikado'" was authentic when the Fujiwara Opera Company, an import from Tokyo, performed this popular operetta at Philharmonic Auditorium Saturday night:

> But as it is precisely style and tradition that matter most in Gilbert and Sullivan the production did little or nothing to warm the cockles of a true Savoyard's heart.
>
> The cast, of course, looked perfect in their parts, the costumes

and even shoes were absolutely correct, and if the sets were disappointing they had an atmosphere reminiscent of what was seen when the Kabuki troupe visited here.

The performance, however, was another matter. It was constantly on the slow side musically, never really polished let alone precise, and the small orchestra, conducted by Allen Jensen, was little comfort to those who missed the sonorous voices that can lift Gilbert and Sullivan work to the level of a first-rate event.[45]

The *L.A. Times* complained that some of the words were "simply unintelligible," observing that "there was plenty of good-natured amusement in the audience as Gilbert's idiomatic dialogue emerged in what sounded like the Mikado's rather than the King's English."[46] The *Hartford Courant* concluded:

> Actually, it was not a very wise course, in many ways, for the Fujiwara Opera Company to undertake "The Mikado." True, the work has a Japanese setting, and bits of Rising Sun stage business here and there. But the sprit of the fooling is indelibly English, and above all, its successful presentation depends of matchless clarity of English diction. The humor is almost totally in the lines, and if the witty turns of Gilbert's libretto do not come over the footlights, you lose half the pleasure of the evening. Last night at the Bushnell, the visitors from overseas were completely floored by our tongue, with a single exception. What they sang sounded like a foreign language. As a matter of fact, it was very like Italian, the language of "Madama Butterfly" which I believe they do sing in the original [according to the review of *Madame Butterfly* in the *Los Angeles Times*, the company sang in English and Japanese]. They made a gallant try at being understood, but English phonetics and English sense were too much for them.[47]

Uniformly, reviewers focused on the linguistic problems of the Japanese cast, of which the *Washington Post* notes:

> The trouble is, of course, that Gilbert was writing in English, hilariously in English. Our visitors are not at home in English, indeed have evidently learned their roles phonetically. The result is that

they can't begin to get at the hidden glints of humor, painfully misrhyme the lyrics and, indeed, can scarcely be heard across the big amphitheater.⁴⁸

Even when praising the production, reviewers emphasized the inability of the cast to capture the true nuances of Gilbert's lyrics, relying on repetitive and mechanical pronunciation rather than expression and parodying their distinctively Japanese pronunciation. *Time* magazine joked, "There may merely be something piquant in what sounds like 'Three little meds from skoo are we' or 'The fathers that bloom in the spring, twa-la,'" though it found "a certain toylike appeal" in the production.⁴⁹ The *Hartford Courant* noted,

> On the other hand, of course, there is always Sullivan's beguiling music, and having downgraded the Fujiwara people for their English, let us hasten to extol their singing and musicianship. For this is a company of fine, lyric voices, expressive and communicative in any language as far as music goes. The soloists were first-rate, the ensemble work was excellent.⁵⁰

A number of the reviews observed that the audience seemed amused rather than critical of these mistakes, with the *Hartford Courant* remarking, "Nevertheless, there was a great deal that was charming in its Japanese way about this 'Mikado,' and though the audience was at times audibly amused by the company's battle with language, its sympathy was warmly with the players. It was an oddly enjoyable event."⁵¹ Even the disgruntled *Washington Post* reviewer who disparaged the production as "the Molto Andante Mikado" commented, "One regrets writing this [negative criticism] for our visitors are so charmingly anxious to please."⁵²

Of the 1948 Nagato Miho production in Tokyo, *Time* magazine remarked on the painstaking efforts of the performers in preparation for their *Mikado* debut: "Nervous, white-haired Michio Ito, who had spent 20 years in the U.S. directing dance productions, had rehearsed the cast for two months. The 49-man Tokyo Philharmonic had been drilled on the tricky rhythms of Sullivan's music. Kiyoshi Takagi, as Ko-Ko, had learned how to sing 'teet wiro, teet wiro.'"⁵³ This review seemed to emphasize the amount of effort that it would take for Japanese performers to learn the English lyrics of the opera. But as the comments on Takagi's mispronunciation indicate, these eager efforts only resulted in an inevitable gap between the classic *Mikado* and the Japanese performers aspiring to become these faux-Japanese characters. The reviews of the touring production of the Fujiwara Opera echoes these sentiments. Yet the Fujiwara *Mikado* cannot be understood simply as an inevitably inferior imitation of D'Oyly Carte, nor can it be seen as Japanese mimicry of orientalist tropes in a gesture of cold war subservience. The U.S. reviewers' criticism of the Fujiwara *Mikado,* though focused on the flaws of the performers, also confirmed the limitations of *The Mikado*'s version of yellowface. The aspects of the production that did not fit neatly into either the "toylike" fantasy of Japan or the recognizable style of D'Oyly Carte were dismissed. These reviews remind us that unlike the role of Cio-Cio-San, on which Japanese sopranos made international reputations, the characterizations of *The Mikado* stood to lose rather than gain in credibility with Japanese performers in the flesh.

We can also read into the production more subtle yet willful attempts to revise the opera. The Fujiwara's touring production of *Madame Butterfly,* in which Japanese cast members sang in Japanese and the Americans in English, seems to have followed the precedent set by earlier productions of it in Japan, which sought to correct the cultural inaccuracies inherent in Puccini's opera. Mari Yoshihara describes a four-day performance of the opera in 1930 at the Kabuki-za Theater in Tokyo, featuring Kōsaku Yamada, the foremost Japanese composer of the period, as director and conductor, and the libretto translated by Keizō Horiuchi. They cast Japanese singers in Japanese roles and white performers in American roles. Dialogues among the American characters were in English, as well as Pinkerton's songs. Details of characterization such as Cio-Cio-San's age and Count Yamadori's occupation were changed to be more plausible, and Yamada changed some of Puccini's faux-Japanese melodies to make them more "natural."[54] Interviews and reviews commented on the producer's struggle to eliminate inaccuracies of dress and manner; translator Horiuchi commented, "Even Westerners must find it absurd that these characters with *chonmage* [top-knot] appear onstage—one cannot tell whether the setting is supposed to look like Japan or China—in shuffling steps, put their hands on the ground, and bow up and down."[55] One newspaper article praised the producers in trying "to eliminate the national humiliation generated by the quasi-Nippon performances of this opera traditionally done by the Westerners,"[56] but another questioned whether such changes were warranted:

There are two questionable points about this production. One is that Butterfly and other Japanese characters were so realistic both in their costume and in their acting that the exotic flavor of the original is almost entirely eliminated. Of course, it is understood that in the case of this particular opera, what is exotic in the West is not at all exotic in Japan. Nonetheless, since one of the strengths of this opera is in its exoticism, is it appropriate to direct the piece in ways that lose that element?[57]

As Mari Yoshihara has stated, opera and other kinds of Western classical music were embraced in East Asia as part of a larger project of modernization, whereby "association with modernity, Westernization, and hence national progress was at the heart of the eagerness with which Asian nations adopted the music into their own educational and cultural institutions." However,

the later history of Asian engagement with classical music has been far from a simple continuation or variation of this opening theme. Although the association with modernity has remained an important factor in Asians' interest in classical music, as Asians gained more agency in defining the meanings of the music for themselves and using it for their own goals, they translated the original motive into many different forms. Interestingly, in the nation- and empire-building period in East Asia, Asian intellectuals and governments used Western music as a tool for promoting Asian, rather than simply Western, cultural values and political objectives. Especially during war and revolution, Asians invested distinct political meanings into classical music, and musicians practicing classical music were treated as arbiters of imperialism, or nationalism, or sometimes both.[58]

Founded by tenor Yoshie Fujiwara in 1934, Fujiwara Opera Company was the first opera company in Japan. Fujiwara's tour of *The Mikado* built another dimension to its productions of *Madame Butterfly,* which had already toured the United States in 1952 and 1953, with a staging "designed to represent authentic Japanese culture and correct prejudices against Japan in Western production."[59] Thus the Fujiwara's *Mikado* did make subtle changes in presentation and interpretation. Reviewers noted that "such sacred songs as 'I've got a little list' have been brutally cut, and such profanities as 'teenagers' and 'Hollywood' have been barbarously added."[60] The production added what the *Washington Post* described as a "quaint seriousness," attributed by the reviewer to "what also boils down to the Stanislavsky method's Tokyo vogue. We have a Ko-Ko who suggests Sal Mineo in his more restrained moments and a Pooh-Bah who considers every one of his multisyllabled words. We brood instead of caper."[61] This probably contributed to how certain roles became more believable; for instance, the reviewer for the *Hartford Courant* remarked, "Komino Saegusa raised the unsympathetic role of Katisha to dramatic proportions,"[62] changing this characterization to the point that another reviewer remarked, "The Katisha positively has charm."[63] These revisions seem understated yet are significant departures from the dictates of D'Oyly Carte, whose rigid hold on British productions was still in effect at the time.

Super Ichiza (1992)

The Fujiwara Opera is acknowledged as the first opera company in Japan. It first specialized in Italian operas; its debut performance, for instance, was Puccini's *La Bohème* on June 6 and 7, 1934, in the Hibiya Public Hall. Its founder tenor Yoshie Fujiwara had studied opera in Italy and made his debut there in 1921 before returning to Japan in 1923. However, the performance of opera in Japan preceded the formation of this company, and Fujiwara's own considerable accomplishments as a principal singer and director might well be traced to an earlier and less hallowed precedent, the Asakusa Opera.[64] The Asakusa Opera began with singers trained by G. V. Rossi, an Italian director of operettas working in England, who came to Tokyo in 1912 to start a Japanese company at the prestigious Imperial Theater. Though Rossi was ultimately unsuccessful and departed in 1918, his singers migrated to Asakusa and created a popular entertainment that incorporated operatic numbers along with Western musical comedy and vaudeville. As Ken Ito writes, in the Taisho period (1912–1926), Asakusa became a center for mass entertainment of many kinds:

> In an era suspended between the Meiji emergence of an urban industrialized Tokyo and the migration of entertainments of transit hubs during the Showa period (1926–89), Asakusa captured the public imagination and glowed with the assurance of being the biggest and the latest. For a moment, Asakusa caught the pulse of the

mass consumer society arising on the shadow of the industrializing economy.[65]

Asakusa Opera was not for opera connoisseurs; it served as a form of popular entertainment. Acclaimed novelist Jun'ichirō Tanizaki writes:

> Thus, Rossini's *The Barber of Seville* and Eichberg's comic opera *The Doctor of Alcantra* were introduced, and Suppé's *Boccacio,* Offenbach's *Orpheus in the Underworld,* and Mascagni's *Cavalleria Rusticana* came to be performed before an audience of nursemaids and riffraff, children bored with moving pictures, and good men and women on their way home from praying to the Kannon. The skills of the performers and the orchestra had been crude and infantile to begin with, something on the order of calisthenic exercises. The moment they fell to performing in Asakusa, they became coarser still; but the innocent and ignorant masses applauded without knowing a single thing. There is no need to go into shock hearing that the operas *Faust, La Traviata,* and *Carmen* were present in Asakusa. For what were performed were not Gounod's *Faust,* but Asakusa's, not Verdi's or Bizet's *Traviata* and *Carmen,* but the Asakusa versions. As I have said before, everything that entered Asakusa became a distinct creature of that environment.[66]

The attraction of Asakusa Opera was its gaudy and attractively foreign vision of European culture, giving its Japanese audiences "a West that was at once exotic and peculiarly Japanese,"[67] as Tanizaki describes:

> The audience welcomed an opera, even if there was no coherent plot to speak of, as long as men and women in Western dress frolicked noisily about the stage, carrying on in a way that was cheerful and gay. Among the productions there were some that could hardly be distinguished from what goes on at a school playground. No, "among" isn't accurate: there could finally be no objection to saying that the essence of these operettas was that of a playground, with a bit of decadence and exoticism thrown in.[68]

This view of Asakusa Opera as a site of riotous energy and cultural hybridity helped to inspire a 1992 rock Kabuki *Mikado* by Super Ichiza in 1992. Founded in 1979 by Shinichi Iwata, Super Ichiza (Super company) in Nagoya is one of three major Japanese theater companies known for innovative new versions of kabuki.[69] Super Ichiza has created innovative modern adaptations of Western dramas and parodies of Kabuki, pioneering a style of rock Kabuki that, as Natsuko Inoue describes, "comically dramatizes *kabuki* themes using the same stylized acting forms and period costumes as traditional *kabuki*, but accompanies them with live rock music rather than the traditional instruments."[70] In addition to a rock Kabuki *Macbeth* in 1984 and *King Lear* in 1987, Super Ichiza has performed a number of works by Gilbert and Sullivan including *The Pirates of Penzance*, *H.M.S. Pinafore*, *Utopia Limited*, *The Gondoliers*, as well as, post-*Mikado*, a version of Sidney Jones's *The Geisha*.[71]

Super Ichiza's founder, Shinichi Iwata, has evoked the influence of the Asakusa Opera on its rock Kabuki version of *The Mikado*. Super Ichiza's *Mikado* directly responded to the decorative stereotypes of Japan in the West, but chose to revisit rather than to replace them. Their *Mikado*, Super Ichiza's first foray into Western opera, is reimagined in the spirit of Asakusa's popular entertainment, which set a precedent for its innovative and irreverent approach. In a letter to Professor Yuko Matsukawa of Seijo University, Iwata says, "Our theater company is deeply interested in Japanese culture and we perform kabuki plays"; however, their choice of *The Mikado* resisted how "Japanese culture has come to be defined":

> Now, though we have been interested in Japanese culture, we have been also very dissatisfied with how Japanese culture in general is understood today. That is, since we believed that Zen, wabi, sabi, simplicity, spirituality, are not the only things that stand for Japan, a more flamboyant Japan—that is, the Japan of Nikko, Yoshiwara, kabuki, and so on—seemed much more contemporary to us. So we found that the Japan seen by foreigners, which is usually described as superficial and exotic, to be more refreshing than the culturally conventional image of Japan has been forced upon us. So we decided to perform *The Mikado* as an example of this. Words that have been thought to be prejudicial, such as "Fujiyama" and "geisha" are now fresh and new to us.[72]

Super Ichiza's promotion of its version of *The Mikado* evokes the Japan craze of late nineteenth-century Europe but projects it through a very different lens. Iwata's letter recounts the history of *The Mikado* and its initial popularity. He analyzes the reasons for the opera's lack of popularity in Japan, which for him hinge both on the opera's inaccuracies and in "Japanese cultural conventions that elevate grand opera and show disdain for enjoyable operettas." He praises the "delightful and beautiful songs" of *The Mikado,* but for him, an even more compelling reason to produce it is the chance to reappropriate and rework Gilbert's exotic depictions of Japan. For Iwata, "one of the reasons why this work is so fascinating is that it is set in Japan."

> At the end of the nineteenth century, Japonisme swept the western world. One of the reasons was that it provided a new perspective, as we can see from the works of artists like Van Gogh. Another reason was simply exoticism. *The Mikado* was a great hit because of its exotic depictions, but if we think about the larger popularity of such images, it is because they dream of a paradise impossible in real life, and transpose it upon a foreign country. Exoticism means dreaming about paradise. And the place most suitable for paradise to be transposed was Japan. Japan, admired by Morse [the collector Samuel Morse, the benefactor of the Peabody of Museum in Salem, Massachusetts], loved by Yakumo [Koizumi Yakumo, or Lafcadio Hearn]. That Japan no longer exists today.
> What is there in Japan today that would allow paradise to be transposed here? Now, all we can do is reconfirm the paradisiacal qualities of Japan by re-experiencing the Japanese paradise that the West once dreamt about.

The vision of Super Ichiza's *Mikado* is nostalgic, not for the Victorian England of Gilbert's day and not for the queer and quaint yellowface images of the Savoy, but for the late nineteenth-century Japan that so transformed the world as well as its popular image.

According to Iwata, Super Ichiza wished to perform Kabuki as an art for the masses and so premiered *The Mikado* for its broad appeal and comic nature. *The Mikado* is played not because it reiterates the queer and quaint image of Japan, but because it reflects the spirit and energy of popular entertainments such as the Asakusa Opera. Super Ichiza's promotional materials for the production clearly referenced the working-class audience, decadent exoticism, and cultural hybridity characteristic of Asakusa. One flyer blithely announces the "Comic Opera *The Mikado*" and that "seventy years after Asakusa Opera, transcending time and space, it is revived with the birth of 'Osu Opera.'" The flyer recalls, "Seventy years ago, Asakusa Opera was all the rage and swept everyone—students and apprentices and craftsmen and people of all classes—into its hot maelstrom, only to disappear like a dream after the great Kanto Earthquake," and "its incredible cheer and broad appeal is revived here and now." It extends a hearty invitation to audiences: "To hell with haughty and high-priced opera! Come enjoy the cool evening breeze, have a beer, and watch Osu Opera, a local specialty."[73]

Iwata reported that his audiences were receptive: "Our audience is comprised not of general opera fans, but rather kabuki fans, both young and old and male and female (other theater companies do not have this broad appeal). All sorts of people enjoyed Sullivan's *The Mikado*. With the success of our *The Mikado* run, we were able to get what is now our opera series on track." He recalls that "we did not change the script at all; it was a straightforward performance," but there was "no criticism of how the Mikado or Emperor was depicted nor of an exoticized Japan."

Iwata attributes the success of Super Ichiza's *Mikado* production to three things: "the comic nature of the piece, the gorgeous costumes that derive from this opera's being set in Japan, and the likeable melodies." His comment brings to mind one of the appeals of the Asakusa Opera: its staging of female bodies in Western dress, which, according to Tanizaki, introduced "the masses of Tokyo" to the fact that "beauty resided not only [in] the face, but in the bosom, the legs, the arms, the wrists, the heels, the ankles, the back [of] the teeth, and the gums."[74] What was attractive was not the direct import of models of Western femininity, but the construction, through the enactment of these roles by Japanese women, of a new ideal of beauty:

> At the Asakusa Opera one could see not only caricatures of Charlie Chaplin, but living reproductions of such stars as Pearl White, Ruth Roland, Doris Kenyon, Billie Burke, and Dustin Farnum. The reproductions were, of course, crude knock-offs, hardly comparable to the originals, but paradoxically they charmed the audience precisely because they were crude. They appealed to us because their eyes were black like ours, because they showed us rose-colored cheeks not discernible in the movies, because they sang at the top of their lungs, and because they catered to us in our own language. Their allure was that they constructed of Japanese

flesh and blood a certain new ideal of feminine beauty, a beauty of features, expression, and physique that had heretofore not been in evidence among us. Perhaps it is going too far to say they "constructed" this new ideal; what they did was attempt to construct, and in this effort affirmed the possibility of eventually constructing, the new beauty. In any case, they turned our eyes away from the old and toward a new feminine ideal.[75]

Asakusa opera suggests multiple racial transformations and their attendant desires; the 1992 Super Ichiza *Mikado* evokes these as well. On the cover of the pamphlet advertising the 1992 Super Ichiza *Mikado* is a female figure based on the familiar piece of japonaiserie, Monet's "La Japonaise."

Figure 22. Flyer, Super Ichiza's The Mikado *(1992).*

Instead of just referencing a familiar instance of yellowface, this production associates the image with both the transformation of the white performer into Japanese and its complement, the Japanese enactment of whiteness. Clearly Super Ichiza did not simply reproduce orientalist tropes through its *Mikado,* nor was theirs a politely intercultural production that simply applied Kabuki techniques to a Western classic. Instead of using *The Mikado*'s japonaiserie to represent Japan, it built on the erotic energies of multiple racial impersonations and commented on the operatic history of the Asakusa, in which both orientalism and its Japanese counterpart, occidentalism, collided.

Chichibu (2001)

The hybrid sensibility, mass appeal, and bright restlessness of the Super Ichiza production contrasts with the earnestness of a much more publicized production of *The Mikado* in 2001. The performances held in Chichibu, a town in Saitama Prefecture, some fifty miles northwest of Tokyo, drew international attention. The Chichibu productions were inspired by Rokusuke Ei, an essayist, songwriter, and radio host, who believed that the town of Chichibu served as a real-life inspiration for Gilbert's Titipu.[76] Ei drew his ideas from historical events in Chichibu's history. From October 31 to November 10, 1884, thousands of silk farmers protested the government's deflationary policy that kept them in poverty. The imperial army was called to suppress the uprising. Both on his regular radio program and in a lecture in Chichibu in 1984, Ei explained his theory that Gilbert got wind of the uprising and then used it as his inspiration for the opera.

The theory that Chichibu was the inspiration for Titipu evolved into different versions, none of them consistent with Gilbert's own accounts. Ei's theory that the opera was inspired by a local rebellion against authority gave way to another version of the story, used to promote the productions: that Chichibu's raw silk, used for women's kimonos, might have been featured at the Knightsbridge Japanese Native Village. Shinichi Miyazawa, a professor of English literature at Saitama Women's Junior College, also suggested that Ernest Satow's *Handbook for Travelers in Central and Northern Japan* (1881), which mentions Chichibu, might have also influenced Gilbert.

In 1991, print shop owner Takashi Inoue heard Ei tell his version of the opera's origins on the radio and told his friend Yasuichi Tsukagoshi, proprietor of a coffee shop. The two watched the 1982 Stratford performance on laser disc, and joined with others, including mayor Zenichi Uchida, to investigate the possibility of organizing an exhibition or lecture. This ultimately led to plans for a performance in conjunction with the 2001 celebration of the fiftieth anniversary of the incorporation of Chichibu as a city. The first performances took place on March 10 and 11, 2001. The successful production was remounted in Chichibu and Ikebukuro, Tokyo, in March 2003, and also played at the International Gilbert and Sullivan Festival in Buxton, England, in 2006.

This production was very much about civic pride and the interests of local community. The production opened with a scene from the annual Chichibu Yomatsuri (evening fair); Yasuichi Tsukagoshi, who headed the organizing committee, said, "We in Chichibu have many festivals all year round—they're a kind of communication tool for us living in a basin land (that isolates us from other towns), and thus I think of our production of *The Mikado* as yet another festival."[77] The production drew together an appreciative audience to watch the singers and dancers; many with local connections performed key roles. One newspaper article remembered a deceased music teacher, Masao Takanami, who worked at Chichibu High School for more than twenty years and taught twelve of *The Mikado* performers.[78] Local associations and schools supplied volunteers as performers and stagehands. Costumes were created by Fumio Ino, a local Kabuki actor and costume designer. Translated into Japanese, and with Japanese cast members, the lyrics and references became much more accessible to audience members. One account suggested that the audience appreciated the allusions to the Mikado that put them in mind of another national figure:

> Watching a full house enjoying the comic opera, Uchida Zen'ichi, the mayor, and Tsukagoshi Yasuichi, a local businessman, savored a great sense of achievement. They were especially relieved by the audience's response to the Mikado, played by baritone Shimada Keisuke, as he mimicked the Shōwa emperor, Hirohito. Every time Shimada said "ah so" with a nod of the head, a chorus of laughter arose as the audience recalled their late monarch's endearing verbal tic.

Reviewer Minoru Okamoto noted the enthusiam of the audience and the introduction of the local dialect and topical references.[79] The production signaled pride and recognition of local and national identity that became a way of taking back *The Mikado* for Japanese audiences, just as having performers return to Chichibu to perform enacted a literal homecoming. In this light, the claims of the opera's origins become even more interesting. As we have seen, several stories of how the opera originated appear in accounts of *The Mikado*, from an imagined trip to the Knightsbridge Japanese Village to a sword falling from Gilbert's wall. What is particularly interesting is not so much the degree of plausibility as the different meanings these origination stories have. Each story revises the opera's meaning; seeing *The Mikado* as inspired by a peasant uprising against unjust authority makes the opera more about challenging official injustice. The *New York Times* described how at the time of the production, Chichibu was a "down on its luck mountain city": "Silk farming was down, going the way of kimono sales. Closed shops lined Bamba Dori, the main street. Rising above the town, sacred Mount Buko had been permanently disfigured by abandoned limestone quarries."[80]

Thus performing *The Mikado* was less important as deference to a foreign work of art and more significant as a way "to boost municipal spirits."[81] Stories about the origins of *The Mikado* become references to a past moment of historical pride that was even more important to recall in light of contemporary economic hardship. Tsukagoshi declared, "Chichibu silk was shipped all over the world, and its name reached England,"[82] and he and others strongly urged the production of the opera as a means of civic pride. These stories of the origin of Gilbert's Titipu revise the basic terms of *The Mikado*'s commodity racism. Touting the opera means furthering Chichibu's own claim to fame through a history of exporting; the Japanese object turns back into a local product made by actual workers who become the proud forbears of the current community.

Reviews of these productions from Western sources cited the theories of Chichibu-as-Titipu more out of curiosity than credibility. But however tentative their belief in the theories of Ei or other Japanese on the connection between Chichibu and Gilbert's Titipu, the production generated was warmly received by non-Japanese fans of Gilbert and Sullivan. When the Chichibu production played at the Buxton Gilbert and Sullivan festival in 2006, one longtime fan commented:

> This was an experience which I will never forget—it has been one of the highlights of the Festivals over the last thirteen years. The costumes were magnificent—and of course, being a Japanese com-

pany they would be very accurate! All the actors were excellent and how they enjoyed the performance. It is not often we have a standing ovation at the Festival but we had one tonight. Demand for seats was so great that they had to put a large screen in the Paxton Theatre and pipe the live show into there.[83]

The production itself, with its beautiful costumes and scenery, confident singing, and broadly comic characterizations, confirmed the charming fantasy of the opera as an uncomplicated instance of cultural exchange between Japan and England. The inconvenient historical conflicts over *The Mikado* as racial representation seem to be smoothed over. In so doing, the production erases the long history of *Mikado* protest, the uneasy circumstances of the military production during the U.S. occupation, and any subsequent qualms about yellowface production. The Chichibu production could be hailed as proof that Gilbert and Sullivan fans no longer need be embarrassed by their adulation of this yellowface opera.

The story behind the Chichibu *Mikado*—that the town of Chichibu deserves recognition as the inspiration for Titipu—revised accounts of how Gilbert's opera was created and tips the emphasis back onto the real Chichibu. As this production moved away from Chichibu, however, it lost some of this hometown resonance. By the time it was presented at the International Gilbert and Sullivan Festival in Buxton, where it was featured alongside other groups also performing *The Mikado,* the local stars, inside jokes, and specific appeal to a community were long gone. Instead, the humor was directed at making the dialogue and lyrics, now translated into Japanese, accessible to an English-speaking audience, and the production was received in many ways as a quaint novelty. The illustrations for the program—so strikingly different from other *Mikado* images—had been altered, reset against a much more Japanese background of ornate cranes and with faces made more yellow in tone.

The praise for the Chichibu/Tokyo production was most definitely occasioned by the larger circumstances of its production, not just for its artistic merits. These productions represented an idealized version of collaboration between East and West in which the encounter of cultures takes place as a generous exchange of culture, without coercion, hostility, or suspicion. In this light, the Chichibu productions are imagined as the antidote to a difficult racial history. Yet even this apparent anodyne has other sides, reminding us that *The Mikado* does not carry the same meanings for

Figure 23. Programs for Chichibu Mikado *in Chichibu (2001) and at the International Gilbert and Sullivan Festival, Buxton, England (2006).*

its Japanese audiences as it does for Gilbert and Sullivan fans in the West. Productions such as the Chichibu *Mikado,* despite their humor and spectacle, defy the overwhelmingly light spirit of the original by bringing the fantasy back down to earth.

In closing this chapter, it is wise to keep in mind that there is no one Japanese response to the opera. Nonetheless, these productions and various responses to them indicate a critical awareness of the power of the opera to misrepresent Japan. Even early in the history of Japanese *Mikados*, there are reminders that not all participated in the adulation of the opera; their guarded judgment undercuts the fantasies of the opera and its yellowface practices and provides a fitting conclusion to our study.

In 1887, under pressure from legal proceedings instigated by complaints from the Japanese Government to the British Consulate, Mr. N. Salinger finally agreed to cut offending representations of the Mikado out of his company's production of Gilbert and Sullivan's opera. Salinger's English Opera Bouffe Company performed the expurgated version *The Little Maids from School* at the Gaiety Theatre in Yokohama on April 29 and 30, the Gymnasium Theatre in Kobe on May 3, and the Public Hall in Nagasaki on May 5. The changes made to the opera affected more than just the role of the Mikado; commentary in the *Japan Weekly Mail* on the Yokohama performance noted that the opera opened with a truncated version of "If You Want to Know Who We Are" in which the men's chorus declared, "We are Gentlemen of *Siam*." Pish-Tush's "Young Man, Despair" was omitted, and "So Please You, Sir, We Much Regret" was sung by the men's chorus.[84] Perhaps hearing Sullivan's melodies as sounding more Chinese than Japanese, this commentator also described several "Chinese" airs in the overture and at the beginning of act 2. Audiences packed the theater in Yokohama, but the *Rising Sun and Nagasaki Express* reported that in Nagasaki "there was but a meager audience, which included a fair proportion of Japanese."[85] The reception was enthusiastic—according to the *Japan Weekly Mail,* the laughter at the Yokohama performances "never ceased from beginning to end"; and the *Hiogo News* found the Kobe performance to be "most heartily enjoyed by everyone present,"[86] despite the apparent lack of a ladies' chorus. Still, in closing, the commentator on the first performance in Yokohama concluded, "We question if the opera will ever again draw so good a house," complaining, "the actors and actresses have a great deal to learn in the matter of gesture, bearing, and attitude," even if "the parts ... were fairly well filled according to the lights [sights?] of Westerns who were supposed to be acting Eastern characters."

> The dresses were good as a spectacle, but that is about all that can be said in their favour. If Gilbert and Sullivan had spent a couple of months on the spot, the work would certainly have been very different in every respect, for the music entirely lacks local colour, if a few bars of a Chinese air be excepted, and the plot and incidents would do for any country. The libretto is funny in a few places, but is applicable to no particular country or people, and the names of the characters are nonsensical.[87]

Acknowledgments

I WOULD LIKE TO ACKNOWLEDGE the generosity of so many who helped turn an unwieldy research project into a book, including Richard Morrison, Adam Brunner, and Doug Armato of the University of Minnesota Press. Karen Shimakawa and Mari Yoshihara provided valuable advice on the manuscript in its first incarnation. Thanks to Sara Cohen and Tomoko Hoogenboom for their hard work with library research and translation; I am also overwhelmingly grateful to Yukiko Terawaza for her excellent assistance in researching productions of *The Mikado* in Japan. I am honored by the trust of so many artists, and I would like especially to acknowledge the generosity of Shinichi Iwata for sharing his thoughts on the 1992 Super Ichiza production, and Yasuichi Tsukagoshi and Toru Sakakibara for allowing me access to materials and videorecordings of the Chichibu *Mikado*. My deep thanks to Ken Narasaki, Doris Baizley, Chil Kong, and Lodestone Theatre Ensemble for inviting me to see *The Mikado Project* and for sharing their script with me. Duncan Taylor-Jones and Mary Glen Chitty kindly allowed me the use of their original poster designs and family pictures, and I express my gratitude to them as well as to William Becker, Anne Covell, Erin Schleigh, and Wilfrid de Freitas for illustrations for this book.

My research was supported by a sabbatical and funding from the College of Liberal Arts, University of Minnesota, as well as by research support from the Department of English, the Humanities Institute, and the Institute for Advanced Study. I am grateful not only for this financial support from my university but also for the intellectual exchange, professional wisdom, and moral support of students, colleagues, and friends too numerous to list here. My special appreciation goes to Paula Rabinowitz, Michael Hancher, Lois Cucullu, Maria Fitzgerald, Sarah Pradt, Maki Isaka, Jigna Desai, and Margaret Werry. I have had the great pleasure of sharing many of these ideas at much earlier stages with colleagues in Asian American studies and Asian American performance; Imogene Lim, Bob Lee, Kent Ono, SanSan

Kwan, Dan Bacalzo, Esther Kim Lee, Sean Metzger, Lucy San Pablo Burns, Priya Srinivasan, Jack Tchen, and Krystyn Moon all contributed wonderful ideas to this project. A warm thank-you to Cathy Choy and Tamara Ho, who shared their recollections of Pomona College with me.

I count myself extremely lucky to have such a rich and vital community of colleagues, friends, and family in which to grow this project. I could not have survived this research project without the constant encouragement of my dear friend and colleague Erika Lee, whose graceful command not only of history but also of common sense constantly amazes me. I also thank Mark Buccella, Joe Gerteis, Teresa Swartz, Doug Hartmann, Karen Ho, Jeff Chen, Leyla Ezdinli, Ranu Samantrai, De Witt Kilgore, Nicole Chaisson, Laura Gurak, Nancy Bayer, Ruth Dill-Macky, and the many others whose polite interest in *The Mikado* never seemed to flag, even though mine certainly did. I have been supported in work and at play by my loving family: my mother, sisters, and the rest of the Lee, Kinneavy, Tsou, Robinson, Wait, Battista, Porter, Munro, and Chapman clans. My father died before I could show him this book in print, but I know he would have been proud of my latest work of scholarship. My husband Kevin and sons Julian and Dylan deserve the most credit for seeing this book through to its logical end. Finally, *The Japan of Pure Invention* really would not have been possible without Yuko Matsukawa, whose expert knowledge, creative powers, and passionate intellectual life have long inspired me. Anyone who knows her will recognize her generosity of mind and spirit at work here.

During one of the first summers after Kevin and I moved to Minnesota, we spent a beautiful summer evening bicycling by Lake Harriet. As we paused to admire the view—the blue lake, people picnicking, children and dogs frolicking in the grass—the orchestra in the bandshell struck up strains of a familiar overture, followed by singers performing a selection of the most famous songs from *The Mikado*. Full makeup and scenery were not necessary for this concert version; only kimonos and fans indicated that these white performers were meant to be Japanese. As a trio pertly trilled "Three Little Maids," coquettishly parading with fans in hand, I tried to explain to my husband what the lasting attraction of this opera and its quaint racial mimicry might be. "Do you think," he asked, "that they really understand what they're doing?" I couldn't, at the time, answer this question, but I am grateful to my dear husband and so many others for asking it then and repeatedly, in so many words, over the following years until it became my own.

Notes

Introduction

1. This and all subsequent quotations from the operas of Gilbert and Sullivan are taken from Ian Bradley, *The Complete Annotated Gilbert and Sullivan* (Oxford: Oxford University Press, 1996).

2. Roland Barthes, *The Empire of Signs* (New York: Hill and Wang, 1970), 99–100.

3. For an excellent study of American racial stereotypes of Asians, see Robert Lee's *Orientals: Asian Americans in Popular Culture* (Philadelphia: Temple University Press, 2000).

4. At the Nazi prison camp Stalag 383 in Hohenfels, Bavaria, hundreds of male prisoners staged four of Gilbert and Sullivan's operas. Trevor Hills, a retired D'Oyly Carte singer, has recounted these events at the International Gilbert and Sullivan Festival, excerpts of which appear on the DVD *Oh Mad Delight!* (49-North Productions, 2005).

5. Asian American Drama Listserv, posting titled "yellowface in NYC," January 22, 2004.

6. The 1991 protests were directed at the New York productions of *Miss Saigon*, in which Pryce had been promised the leading role of the Engineer. Actor's Equity eventually conceded its demands that Cameron Mackintosh cast an Asian American actor in the role after Mackintosh threatened to cancel the production.

7. Thomas C. Holt, *The Problem of Race in the Twenty-first Century* (Cambridge: Harvard University Press, 2000), 20.

8. Anne McClintock, *Imperial Leather: Race, Gender and Sexuality in the Colonial Context* (New York: Routledge, 1995), 209.

9. Claire Jean Kim, "The Racial Triangulation of Asian Americans," *Politics and Society* 27, no. 1 (1999): 105–38, 107.

10. Matthew Calbraith Perry, *Narrative of the Expedition of an American Squadron to the China Seas and Japan: Performed in the years 1852, 1853, and 1854, under the command of Commodore M. C. Perry* (New York: D. Appleton, 1856), 488.

11. Eric Lott, *Love and Theft: Blackface Minstrelsy and the American Working Class* (Oxford: Oxford University Press, 1993), 18.

12. Ibid.

13. Commentary on *The Cool Mikado* at "A Gilbert and Sullivan Discography," http://www.cris.com/~oakapple/gasdisc/mikcool.htm (accessed August 20, 2008).
14. Ian Bradley, *Oh Joy! Oh Rapture! The Enduring Phenomenon of Gilbert and Sullivan* (Oxford: Oxford University Press, 2005), 95.
15. Ibid., 23.
16. "Gilbert & Sullivan Very Light Opera Company," http://www.gsvloc.org/general2/aboutus.htm (accessed May 14, 2007).

1. My Objects All Sublime

1. John Ayers, Oliver Impey, and J. V. G. Mallet, *Porcelain for Palaces: The Fashion for Japan in Europe, 1650–1750* (London: Oriental Ceramic Society, 1990); Anna Jackson, "Imagining Japan: The Victorian Perception and Acquisition of Japanese Culture," *Journal of Design History* 5, no. 4 (1992): 245–56, 245.
2. François Cellier and Cunningham Bridgeman, *Gilbert and Sullivan and Their Operas, with Recollections and Anecdotes of D'Oyly Carte and Other Famous Savoyards* (New York: Benjamin Blom, 1914), 189.
3. W. S. Gilbert, "The Story of a Stage Play: Mr. Gilbert Relates the History of the Evolution of *The Mikado*," *New York Daily Tribune*, August 9, 1885, 9.
4. Interview with Gilbert published in the *Daily News* "Workers and their Work" series, reprinted in *Musical World*, March 14, 1885, and quoted in Audrey Williamson, *Gilbert and Sullivan Opera: An Assessment* (New York: Macmillan, 1953), 141.
5. Bradley, *Complete Annotated Gilbert and Sullivan*, 576.
6. Jackson, "Imagining Japan," 247.
7. Ibid., 249.
8. Bradley, *Complete Annotated Gilbert and Sullivan*, 642.
9. Dawn Jacobson, *Chinoiserie* (London: Phaidon Press, 1999), 198–99.
10. T. J. Jackson Lears, *Fables of Abundance: A Cultural History of Advertising in America* (New York: Basic Books, 1995), 65; Lears, "Beyond Veblen: Rethinking American Consumer Culture," in *Consuming Visions: The Accumulation and Display of Goods in America, 1880–1920*, ed. Simon Bronner (New York: W. W. Norton, 1989), 78.
11. Lee, *Orientals*, ix.
12. "Editor's Easy Chair," *Harper's New Monthly Magazine*, February 1886, 476–78.
13. For instance, only a lone caricature of an oversized Sir Joseph on a boat crowns a set of songs from *H.M.S. Pinafore* published by White, Smith, and Company (Boston, 1878); "La Tonkinoise" march by Leopold de Wenzel and "La Tonkinoise" quadrille by C. A. White, both published by White, Smith, and Company (Boston) in 1884, feature a pagoda and a Chinese junk with a mountain in

the background, all framed by a banner prominently displaying the title. A scene on the cover of the earlier instrumental "Chao kanc, galop chinois" (1841), by Gustave Blessner, depicts an elderly mandarin with a pipe, a man holding a scroll, a woman with a stringed instrument, and in the foreground an elegant woman with a fan, who may be dancing to the music.

14. Toshio Yokoyama, *Japan in the Victorian Mind: A Study of Stereotyped Images of a Nation, 1850–80* (London: Macmillan, 1987), 175.

15. Ibid., 150.

16. Bill Brown, *A Sense of Things: The Object Matter of American Literature* (Chicago: University of Chicago Press, 2003), 31–32.

17. Rotem Kowner, "Lighter than Yellow, But Not Enough: Western Discourse on the Japanese 'Race,' 1854–1904," *Historical Journal* 43, no. 1 (2000): 103–31, 125, 104, 112.

18. Jackson, "Imagining Japan," 248.

19. Rutherford Alcock, *Art and Art Industries in Japan* (London: Virtue and Company, 1878), 17.

20. Jackson, "Imagining Japan," 248.

21. Alcock, *Art and Art Industries in Japan*, 262.

22. Rutherford Alcock, *The Capital of the Tycoon: A Narrative of a Three Years' Residence in Japan*, 2 vols. (New York: Harper and Brothers, 1863), 1:179.

23. Ibid.

24. Ibid., 180.

25. Ibid.

26. Williamson, *Gilbert and Sullivan Opera*, 141.

27. Cellier and Bridgeman, *Gilbert and Sullivan and Their Operas*, 188–89.

28. *Illustrated Sporting and Dramatic News*, March 28, 1885, 45; quoted in Jane Stedman, "Gilbert's Stagecraft: Little Blocks of Wood," in *Gilbert and Sullivan: Papers Presented at the International Conference Held at the University of Kansas in May 1970*, ed. James Helyar (Lawrence, Kansas: University of Kansas Libraries, 1971), 195–212, 201.

29. William Beatty-Kingston, *Theatre*, April 1, 1885; quoted in Leslie Baily, *The Gilbert & Sullivan Book* (London: Cassell and Co., 1952), 248.

30. Rebecca A. T. Stevens and Yoshiko Iwamoto Wada, *The Kimono Inspiration: Art and Art-to-Wear in America* (Washington, D.C.: Textile Museum; San Francisco: Pomegranate Artbooks, 1996), 24–25.

31. See, for instance, Yashima Gakutei, "Design for Critique of Yoshiwara Figures in the Four Seasons" (Yoshiwaragata Shiki Saiken), in Linda Gertner Zatlin, *Beardsley, Japonisme, and the Perversion of the Victorian Ideal* (Cambridge: Cambridge University Press, 1997), 109.

32. See Zatlin, *Beardsley, Japonisme, and the Perversion of the Victorian Ideal*.

33. Sally Ledger, "The New Woman and the Crisis of Victorianism," in *Cultural*

Politics at the "Fin de Siècle," ed. Ledger and Scott McCracken (Cambridge: Cambridge University Press 1995), 22–44, 27.

34. Edmond de Goncourt, December 29, 1883, quoted in Lionel Lambourne, *Japonisme: Cultural Crossings Between Japan and the West* (London: Phaidon, 2005), 131.

35. George du Maurier's drawing in *Punch,* October 30, 1880. For an account of Wilde's remark, see Richard Ellman, *Oscar Wilde* (New York: Alfred A. Knopf, 1988), 45.

36. Bradley, *The Complete Annotated Gilbert and Sullivan,* 269.

37. Mari Yoshihara, *Embracing the East: White Women and American Orientalism* (New York: Oxford University Press, 2003), 18.

38. Bradley, *Oh Joy!,* 33.

39. Ricketts based his costume design on highly stylized versions of 1720 Japanese dress; his designs remained the standard until the closure of the D'Oyly Carte Opera Company in 1982.

40. Letter from Gilbert to Richard D'Oyly Carte on April 30, 1890; quoted in Jane Stedman, "Gilbert's Stagecraft: Little Blocks of Wood," 198.

41. Cellier and Bridgeman, *Gilbert and Sullivan and Their Operas,* 196.

42. Stedman, "Gilbert's Stagecraft," 207.

43. Cellier and Bridgeman, *Gilbert and Sullivan and Their Operas,* 196.

44. The attention Bond receives has lasting benefits; according to her autobiography, she eventual married Lewis Ransome, the admirer who tells her that he attended *The Mikado* with his sister, "and when we were talking it over afterwards I said I liked the one with the big sash best. So next day when she saw a photograph of you in a shop window she went in and bought it. She gave it to me and I have it now." Jessie Bond, *The Life and Reminiscences of Jessie Bond, the Old Savoyard* (London: Bodley Head, 1930), 120–21.

45. Thomas Richards, *The Commodity Culture of Victorian English: Advertising and Spectacle, 1851–1914* (Stanford, Calif.: Stanford University Press, 1990); and Richard Wightman Fox and T .J. Jackson Lears, eds., *The Culture of Consumption: Critical Essays in American History, 1880–1980* (New York: Pantheon, 1983).

46. "In the 'Mikado' Rooms: The Latest Fashionable Craze in New York Homes," *New York World,* September 27, 1885, supplement no. 2, 18.

47. Ibid.

48. "The Land of Titipu," *Chicago Daily Tribune,* October 11, 1885, 26.

49. Ibid.

50. Estelle Stoughton Smith, *The Mikado Room and How to Furnish It* (self-published, Baltimore, 1886), Library of Congress.

51. John Kuo Wei Tchen, *New York before Chinatown* (Baltimore, Md.: Johns Hopkins University Press, 2001), 101–6.

52. Ibid., 99.

53. "In the 'Mikado' Rooms," 18.
54. Edmond de Goncourt, October 29 1868, quoted in Lambourne, *Japonisme*, 131.
55. H. L. Mencken, *Baltimore Sun*, November 29, 1910.
56. "Stage History of 'The Mikado,'" *New York Times*, May 29, 1910, X7.
57. "Notes of the Stage," *New York Times*, July 1, 1885, 4.
58. Baily, *The Gilbert & Sullivan Book*, 256.
59. Colin Prestige, "D'Oyly Carte and the Pirates: The Original New York Productions of Gilbert and Sullivan," in Helyar, *Gilbert and Sullivan*, 113–48, 137.
60. Advertisements, *Chicago Daily Tribune*, October 25, 1885, 6.
61. "Gossip of the Theatres," *New York Times*, July 12, 1885, 3.
62. *New York World*, September 27, 1885, 3.
63. "Sir Arthur Very Wroth," *New York Times*, July 14, 1885, 1.
64. "John Duff's Mikado Suffers by Comparison with the Fifth Avenue Production," *Boston Globe*, August 25, 1885, 2.
65. In a letter to Algernon Mitford, former attaché in Japan, Gilbert is flattered to be complimented on "the fidelity with which the local characteristics are reproduced." Gilbert to Algernon Mitford, 17 March 1885; quoted in Jane W. Stedman, *W. S. Gilbert: A Classic Victorian and His Theatre* (Oxford: Oxford University Press, 1996), 225; Michael Ainger, *Gilbert and Sullivan: A Dual Biography* (Oxford: Oxford University Press, 2002), 245.
66. Yuko Matsukawa, "Onoto Watanna's Japanese Collaborators and Commentators," *Japanese Journal of American Studies* 16 (2005): 31–53, 42.
67. T. J. Jackson Lears, *No Place of Grace: Antimodernism and the Transformation of American Culture, 1880–1920* (New York: Pantheon, 1981); and Christopher Benfrey, *The Great Wave: Gilded Age Misfits, Japanese Eccentrics, and the Opening of Old Japan* (New York: Random House, 2003).
68. Jeff Nunokawa, *Tame Passions of Wilde: The Styles of Manageable Desire* (Princeton, N.J.: Princeton University Press, 2003), 48.
69. Edison and international photographic film catalogue, April 1897, p. 10 [MI]; Edison films catalog, no. 105, July 1901, p. 53 [MI]. Library of Congress Motion Picture, Broadcasting and Recorded Sound Division.
70. G. Waldo Browne, *The New America and the Far East: A Picturesque and Historic Description of these Lands and Peoples*, vol. 2 (Boston: Marshall Jones, 1907), 316.
71. Oscar Wilde, "The Decay of Lying," in *The Complete Works of Oscar Wilde* (New York: Harper and Row, 1989), 988.
72. Karl Marx, *Capital: A Critique of Political Economy* (1867), trans. Ben Fowkes (Harmondsworth, Middlesex: Penguin, 1990), 1:163.
73. Estelle Stoughton Smith, *The Mikado Room and How to Furnish It*.

2. "My Artless Japanese Way"

1. Bradley, *Complete Annotated Gilbert and Sullivan*, 555.
2. For a history of this tune, see Paul Seeley, "The Japanese March in *The Mikado*," *Musical Times* 126, no. 1710 (August 1985): 454–56, 455.
3. Most commonly, "Miya sama" and the utterance of "O ni! bikkur shakkuri to! Oya! Oya!" (the first a warlike tune describing the waving of the imperial banner, the second a hodgepodge of Japanese insults loosely translated by Michael Beckerman as "You devil! With fright! with hiccups! hey! Hey!"). Raymond Knapp, *The American Musical and the Formation of National Identity* (Princeton, N.J.: Princeton University Press, 2005), 249–60; Michael Beckerman, "The Sword on the Wall: Japanese Elements and their Significance in *The Mikado*," *Musical Quarterly* 73, no. 3 (1989): 303–19. Also see Robert Fink, "Rhythm and Text Setting in *The Mikado*," *19th-Century Music* 14, no. 1 (Summer 1990): 31–47.
4. Alcock, *Capital of the Tycoon*, 2:124. The illustration of the "wandering minstrel" is from 125.
5. Ibid., 124.
6. S. Takeda, "A Japanese Criticism of the *The Mikado*," *Chicago Daily Tribune*, November 29, 1885, 27.
7. "A Japanese Village in London," *London Times*, January 10, 1885, 6D.
8. "The Japanese Village," *Illustrated London News*, February 21, 1885, 203.
9. "A Japanese Village in London," *London Times*, January 10, 1885.
10. Ibid.
11. "The Japanese Village," *Illustrated London News*, February 21, 1885.
12. Ibid.
13. "Sir R. Alcock on Japanese Work," *London Times*, January 12, 1885, 10E.
14. O. Buhicrosan, *Japan: Past and Present; The Manners and Customs of the Japanese and a Description of the Japanese Native Village*, ed. R. Reinagle Barnett, published by the Proprietors of the Japanese Native Village (1885), 3; microfilm, Harvard Library.
15. Ibid., 161.
16. Ibid., 79–80.
17. Kurata Yoshihira, *1885 nen London Nihonjin mura* (1885 London Japanese Village) (Tokyo: Asahi Shimbunsha, 1983), 96; quoted in Ayako Kano, *Acting Like a Woman in Modern Japan: Theater, Gender, and Nationalism* (New York: Palgrave, 2001), 92–93.
18. "A Japanese Village in London," *London Times*, January 10, 1885.
19. "The Japanese Village," *Illustrated London News*, February 21, 1885.
20. "Sir R. Alcock on Japanese Work," *London Times*, January 12, 1885.
21. Bill Brown, *A Sense of Things: The Object Matter of American Literature* (Chicago: University of Chicago Press, 2003), 94.

22. Ibid., 92.
23. "A Japanese Village in London," *London Times*, December 20, 1884, 10E.
24. "News," *Illustrated London News*, April 18, 1885, 3.
25. "The Fire at the Japanese Village," *London Times*, May 6, 1885, 9f.
26. Kano, *Acting Like a Woman in Modern Japan*, 252n19.
27. "The Japanese Village," *London Times*, December 2, 1885, 6D.
28. Kano, *Acting Like a Woman in Modern Japan*, 252n19.
29. The souvenir booklet *A Veritable Japanese Village* at Madison Square Garden is dated December 4, 1885; the guide for the "Japanese Village Company" at Boston's Horticultural Hall in 1886 is titled *A Veritable Japanese Village: Under the Sanction of the Imperial Japanese Government: A Colony of Japanese Men, Women and Children in Native Costume Who Daily Illustrate the Art Industries of Japan*; the Philadelphia exhibition had an associated pamphlet titled *Domestic Drama of Japanese Life*, by Ella Sterling Cummins (New York: J. B. Rose, 1886).
30. "The Japanese Village: Where One Sees Cloisonné Made and Falls in Love with a Japanese Girl," *New York Times*, December 3, 1885, 4, col. 7.
31. Ibid.
32. "The Ladies of the Tea House," in *A Veritable Japanese Village* (Madison Square Garden, New York, December 4, 1885), 8, 9. All subsequent references to the guides come from this version.
33. "The Tailor," in *A Veritable Japanese Village*, 7.
34. "Japanese Art Workers," *Boston Evening Transcript*, January 1, 1886, 6; quoted in Cynthia A. Brandimarte, "Japanese Novelty Stores," *Winterthur Portfolio* 26, no. 1 (Spring 1991): 1–25, 10.
35. "The Japanese Village," *Art Interchange* 16, no. 5 (February 27, 1886): 66; quoted in Brandimarte, "Japanese Novelty Stores," 10.
36. "The Tailor," in *A Veritable Japanese Village*, 7.
37. "The Cabinet-Maker," in *A Veritable Japanese Village*, 2.
38. "Silk Weaving," in *A Veritable Japanese Village*, 6.
39. "Silk Twisting," in *A Veritable Japanese Village*, 6.
40. "Ota Pottery," in *A Veritable Japanese Village*, 3.
41. "Satsuma Decoration," in *A Veritable Japanese Village*, 4.
42. "Silk Embroidery Department," in *A Veritable Japanese Village*, 4.
43. "The Shippo Designer," in *A Veritable Japanese Village*, 5.
44. *A Veritable Japanese Village*, 1.
45. Ibid., 13.
46. Gilbert writes, "The market people were subsequently discarded, as it was thought advisable not to 'discover' our ladies, but to reserve their entrance for a special effect later on." "The Story of a Stage Play," *New-York Daily Tribune*, August 9, 1885, 9.

47. Vijay Prashad, *Everybody Was Kung Fu Fighting: Afro-Asian Connections and the Myth of Cultural Purity* (Boston: Beacon Press, 2002), 72.

48. Ibid., 71–72.

49. David Porter, *Ideographia: The Chinese Cipher in Early Modern Europe* (Stanford, Calif.: Stanford University Press, 2001), 135, 134.

50. Jacobson, *Chinoiserie*, 183.

51. Ibid., 199.

52. Alcock, *The Capital of the Tycoon*, 1:62.

53. Neil Harris, "All the World a Melting Pot? Japan at American Fairs, 1876–1904," in *Mutual Images: Essays in American-Japanese Relations*, ed. Akira Iriye (Cambridge, Mass.: Harvard University Press, 1975), 24–54, 28, 46.

54. James Dabney McCabe, *The Illustrated History of the Centennial Exhibition, Held in Commemoration of the One Hundredth Anniversary of American Independence* (Cincinnati: Jones Brothers, 1876), 414–17.

55. Ibid.

56. Kowner, "Lighter than Yellow, But Not Enough," 114.

57. Lee, *Orientals*, 60–61, 82.

58. Sheet music for Septimus "Sep" Winner, "The Coolie Chinee" (Philadelphia: Lee & Walker, 1871) Library of Congress, Music Division.

59. Oscar Wilde, "House Decoration," May 11, 1882, in Oscar Wilde, *Essays and Lectures* (London: Methuen, 1908; rprt., Whitefish, Mont.: Kessinger, 2004), 79.

60. "American Barbarism: The Apostle of Estheticism Exposes Our Sins," *San Francisco Daily Chronicle*, March 30, 1882, 2.

61. Christopher Bush, "The Ethnicity of Things in America's Lacquered Age," *Representations* 99 (Summer 2007): 74–98, 87–88.

62. McCabe, *The Illustrated History of the Centennial Exhibition*, 418–19.

63. Ibid., 417.

64. Marietta Holley, *Josiah Allen's Wife as a P.A. and P.I.: Samantha at the Centennial* (Hartford, Conn., 1878), 444–45, quoted in Harris, "All the World a Melting Pot?" 35.

65. Edward C. Bruce, *The Century: Its Fruits and Its Festival* (Philadelphia, 1877), 244; quoted in Harris, "All the World a Melting Pot?" 35.

66. In a scrapbook of Centennial clippings, Historical Society of Pennsylvania, 92; quoted in Harris, "All the World a Melting Pot?" 35.

67. Julian Hawthorne, *Humors of the Fair* (Chicago, n.d.), 93; quoted in Harris, "All the World a Melting Pot?" 43.

68. D. C. Taylor, *Halcyon Days in the Dream City* (n.p., n.d.), 35, 42; quoted in Harris, "All the World a Melting Pot?" 43.

69. H. G. Cutler, *The World's Fair: Its Meaning and Scope* (Chicago, 1892), 286; quoted in Harris, "All the World a Melting Pot?" 43.

70. "The Centennial Grounds: Progress of the Work," *New York Times,* February 4, 1876, 1; quoted in Harris, "All the World a Melting Pot?" 29.

71. Ronald Takaki, *Strangers from a Different Shore: A History of Asian Americans* (New York: Penguin Books, 1989), 180.

3. Magical Objects and Therapeutic Yellowface

1. "Gorgeous Receptions: Mrs. Marshall Field's Mikado Ball in Honor of Her Son's Birthday," *Chicago Daily Tribune,* January 2, 1886, 6.

2. According to their Web site, PEERS, based in Alameda, California, is an organization "dedicated to remembering, researching, and re-creating the performing arts of the past" that organizes regular costume events such as the Pride and Prejudice Picnic on August 4, 2007, and a Chicago Speakeasy Ball on May 3, 2008, http://www.peers.org/ (accessed July 19, 2007).

3. Bradley, *Oh Joy!,* 29.

4. Kenneth Sandford in conversation with Ian Smith, Buxton, August 2, 2001; quoted in Bradley, *Oh Joy!,* 34.

5. William Littler, "The Mikado," *Toronto Star,* January 12, 1986, G1.

6. Chris Pasles, "Staging Turns 'The Mikado' on Its Ear; Christopher Renshaw Takes Populist Approach as Stage Director for Opera Pacific's Gilbert and Sullivan Offering," *Los Angeles Times,* November 10, 1997, F2.

7. Noel Goodwin, "London Reports," *Opera News,* April 9, 1983, 52–53, 53.

8. Pasles, "Staging Turns 'The Mikado' on Its Ear," F2.

9. Cora Kaplan, *Victoriana: Histories, Fictions, Criticism* (Edinburgh: Edinburgh University Press, 2007), 3.

10. The film was nominated for several Academy Awards and won for Best Costumes and Best Makeup. It also won New York Film Critics awards for Best Picture and Best Director.

11. Scott Tobias, "Interview with Mike Leigh," *Onion A.V. Club* 36, no. 3, February 2, 2000, http://www.avclub.com/content/node/22903 (accessed April 26, 2006).

12. Jason Anderson, "Smooth Operetta: Mike Leigh Re-creates the World of Gilbert and Sullivan," *Eye Weekly,* January 20, 2000, http://www.eye.net/eye/issue/issue_01.20.00/film/topsy.html (viewed April 28, 2006).

13. Lears, *No Place of Grace,* 190.

14. See, for example, Lambourne's *Japonisme* or Christopher Benfrey's *The Great Wave: Gilded Age Misfits, Japanese Eccentrics, and the Opening of Old Japan* (New York: Random House, 2004).

15. Leigh describes, "The Savoy Theater was, as you may know, the first public building in the world to be lit by electricity. And at the time of the film it was to

be in existence four or five years. There is no reference to that because there is no logical reason for anyone to mention it. Bt we looked at that, and we got some demonstrations of old equipment. In fact, a company made us a thousand period bulbs for nothing as a gift. So there are a lot of shots where you actually see those lighting buttons with those authentic 1880s lighting bulbs." Adam M. Goldstein, "The Method to His Madness," *MovieMaker*, no. 37, http://www.moviemaker .com/magazine/issues/37/37_madness.html (accessed April 28, 2006).

16. Ainger, *Gilbert and Sullivan*, 233.

17. Ibid., 237–38.

18. Goldstein, "The Method to His Madness."

19. Cellier, *Gilbert and Sullivan and Their Operas*, 192.

20. Ibid.

21. Anderson, "Smooth Operetta."

22. Tobias, "Interview with Mike Leigh."

23. Ibid., 192–93.

24. Eric Layton, "A Topsy-Turvy Science," *Ent-today.com*, November 2003, http://www.ent-today.com/1-14/leigh-feature.htm (accessed November 10, 2003).

25. Tobias, "Interview with Mike Leigh."

26. Yoshihara, *Embracing the East*, 43.

4. "And Others of His Race"

1. Hallie Flanagan, *Arena* (New York: Duell, Sloan and Pearce, 1940), 144.

2. Bernard Simon, "He Had a Lot of Negroes Handy, So He Heated Up Sullivan Music," *New York Herald Tribune*, March 26, 1939, sec. 6, 5.

3. Ibid.

4. Interview with Duncan Whiteside, technical director for the Great Northern Theater, 1938–39, by Karen Wickre for the Research Center for the Federal Theatre Project, George Mason University, Fairfax, Virginia, August 13, 1978; quoted in Stephanie Leigh Batiste, "Darkening Mirrors: Imperial Representation, Otherness and Subjectivity in African American Performance during the Depression Era" (Ph.D. dissertation, George Washington University, 2003), 231–32.

5. *The Mikado*. Production Title File, Federal Theatre Collection, Library of Congress; quoted in Batiste, "Darkening Mirrors," 233.

6. Batiste, "Darkening Mirrors," 232.

7. "Swing Mikado's Songs Hailed by Lovers of Gilbert and Sullian: Swing Copies and Orchestrations Now Available for Harry Minturn's Successful Swing Production," *Music World Almanac* 10, no. 9 (Radio City, New York, 1938); quoted in Batiste, "Darkening Mirrors," 232.

8. Rena Fraden, *Blueprints for a Black Federal Theatre, 1935–1939* (Cambridge: Cambridge University Press 1996), 187.

9. Dorothy Day writes, for example, that the concept "to give the famous Gilbert and Sullivan opera as seen through the eye of the Negro" was lacking because in particular "the clipped diction, so necessary to the lyrics and lines of the books, and so foreign to the Negro tongue, is beyond the scope of the actors, and the production falls into the doldrums after the novelty has worn off." "This 'Mikado' Unconvincing," *Chicago Herald and Examiner,* September 27, 1938, 20.

10. John Anderson finds, "When they really swing it the show goes crazy with the heat and works up an outlandish and sometimes hilarious fascination. When it follows Sullivan's music exactly, which is most of the time, it is merely an indifferent blackface 'Mikado' with bizarre costumes and sets. It ought to swing from end to end; it ought to get into the groove and stay there and knock the cats into the alley. Its fun is gaudy, but intermittent." "Swing Mikado Stomps in, Running High and Wide," *New York Journal American,* March 2, 1939, 14.1.

11. Brooks Atkinson, "Chicago Unit of the Federal Theatre Comes in Swinging the Gilbert and Sullivan 'Mikado,'" *New York Times,* March 2, 1938, 18.

12. Michael Pickering, "John Bull in Blackface," *Popular Music* 16, no. 2 (May 1997): 181–201, 181.

13. Jane Stedman writes, "Gilbert amused himself on 6 March [1877] by attending the annual benefit of G. W. Moore (Moore and Burgess Minstrels), followed by a supper party and ball." Stedman, *W. S. Gilbert: A Classic Victorian and This Theatre,* 146.

14. Minstrelsy apparently proved popular enough that a young Sullivan participated in the creation of a small performance with his friends for a Leipzig audience in or around December 1860 while in Germany on the Mendelssohn scholarship that would eventually lead to his fame. Two documents support this claim. One, a letter to his brother, Fred [at Christmas of 1860], states the matter in a fairly explicit manner: "We were wishing for you to come over and give us your valuable assistance here a short time ago. We had a grand nigger performance at Mrs. Barnett's and all the English and Americans in the Conservatorium invited to witness it. The performers were four in number. Taylor [Professor Franklin Taylor], banjo (played upon my *tenor*); Barnett [John Francis Barnett], bones, deficiency supplied by castagnets; Wheat, violin, and myself, tambourine. We composed the whole entertainment amongst us, and a very good one it was too; most of the audience had never seen anything of the kind before, and the consequence was they were most of them ill with laughing. In the same sort of case, in fact, that father and I were in after we had seen Christy's. In our rehearsals, when we were at a standstill or in a difficulty, the general exclamation was, 'Now, if Sullivan's brother were here he'd be the fellow. Yes, write to Fred Sullivan and tell him to give us a few hints,' so you see your reputation is firmly established in Leipzig." In Arthur Lawrence, *Sir Arthur Sullivan: Life Story, Letters, and Reminiscences* (Chicago: H. S. Stone, 1900), 42–43. Sullivan's obituary in the December 1900 publication of

the *Musical Times* noted that he had been a member of a minstrel group and that he "had such a shock of curly red hair that a nigger wig was quite in the nature of superfluity." In "Arthur Sullivan," unsigned obituary, *Musical Times*, December 1, 1900, 786.

15. Bradley, *Complete Annotated Gilbert and Sullivan*, 1049–51.

16. Prestige, "D'Oyly Carte and the Pirates," 113–48, 119.

17. Gerald Bordman, *American Musical Theatre: A Chronicle* (Oxford: Oxford University Press, 1991), 92; Robert Toll, *Blacking Up: The Minstrel Show in Nineteenth-Century America* (Oxford: Oxford University Press, 1974), 172.

18. Toll, *Blacking Up*, 172.

19. See ibid., chap. 6.

20. This is clearly a name designed to satirize Hamaikari Nagakichi, one of the few child acrobats to come to the United States, who was known as little "All Right," a phrase that he had first used during performances in San Francisco that evolved into a nickname. He was a sensation in San Francisco and New York, where theatergoers were impressed by his agility in a perch act with his adopted father Hamaikari Sadakichi (the lead performer of the troupe) and in an aerial routine on the slack wire. Krystyn Moon, "Paper Butterflies: Japanese Acrobats in Mid-Nineteenth-Century New England," in *Asian Americans in New England: Culture and Community*, ed. Monica Chin (Durham: University of New Hampshire, 2009), 66–90.

21. Toll, *Blacking Up*, 170.

22. Ibid., 173.

23. Harry Reynolds, *Minstrel Memories: The Story of Burnt Cork Minstrelsy in Great Britain from 1836 to 1927* (London: Alston Rivers, 1928), 137–38.

24. James Weldon Johnson, *Black Manhattan* (New York: Knopf, 1930; reprint, New York: Da Capo Press, 1991), 93.

25. Moon, "Paper Butterflies," 133.

26. Ibid., 141.

27. Henry T. Sampson, *The Ghost Walks: A Chronological History of Blacks in Show Business, 1865–1910* (Metuchen, N.J.: Scarecrow Press, 1988), 483.

28. Ibid., 442, 440.

29. Ibid., 438.

30. David Krasner, *Resistance, Parody, and Double Consciousness in African American Theatre, 1895–1910* (New York: St. Martin's Press, 1997), 142.

31. Ibid., 148.

32. According to Errol Hill and James Hatch, "Having a very fair complexion, Isham was often assumed to be white, which gave him a decided advantage in gaining responsible employment, booking shows, or dealing with agents and managers. Errol G. Hill and James V. Hatch, *A History of African American Theatre* (Cambridge: Cambridge University Press, 2003), 146.

33. Thomas L. Riis, "The Experience and Impact of Black Entertainers in England, 1895–1920,"*American Music* 4, no. 1 (Spring 1986): 50–58, 52.

34. *Washington (DC) Morning Times,* November 9, 1896; quoted in Henry T. Sampson, *Blacks in Blackface* (Metuchen, N.J.: Scarecrow Press, 1980), 65.

35. James Weldon Johnson writes that in 1896, Mr. John W. Isham, the advance agent of the all–African American burlesque show *The Creole Show* (1890), and *The Octoroons* (1895), produced *Oriental America*. "This was a more ambitious production than *The Octoroons;* for although it was built on the minstrel model, the afterpiece, instead of being made up of burlesque and specialties, cake-walk, 'hoe-down,' and walk-around finale, was a medley of operatic selections. Mr. Isham, in addition to having in the company clever performers and pretty girls, had some of the best-trained Negro singers available. He signed Sidney Woodward, who has quite a reputation in Boston as a tenor; J. Rosemond Johnson, then a student of music in the same city; William C. Elkins, Miss Maggie Scott, and several others who had made a study of singing. Miss Inez Clough, who, more recently, has achieved success in Negro dramatic plays, was also a member of the company. The final of the show consisted of solos and choruses from *Faust, Martha, Rigoletto, Carmen,* and *Il Trovatore. Oriental America* broke all precedents by being the first coloured show to play Broadway proper; it opened at Wallack's Theatre, at that time called Palmer's. *Oriental American* broke further away from the minstrel pattern than did [Isham's earlier productions] the *Creole Show* and *The Octoroons,* and it was the first coloured show to make a definite break from the burlesque houses" (*Black Manhattan,* 96–97). David Krasner records somewhat differently that *In Dahomey* was the first all-black show to perform in a Broadway theater, opening February 13, 1903 (*Resistance, Parody, and Double Consciousness,* 67), and Gerald Bordman confirms that *In Dahomey* is "the first full-length musical written and played by blacks to be performed at a major Broadway house (*American Musical Theatre,* 219). Neither Krasner nor Bordman ever mentions *Oriental America* as playing in a Broadway theater.

36. Toll, *Blacking Up,* 197–98.

37. Eileen Southern, "The Georgia Minstrels: The Early Years," in *Inside the Minstrel Mask: Readings in Nineteenth-Century Blackface Minstrelsy,* ed. Annemarie Bean, James V. Hatch, and Brooks McNamara (Hanover, N.H.: Wesleyan University Press and University Press of America, 1996), 163–78, 166.

38. Richard Waterhouse, "The Minstrel Show and Australian Culture," *Journal of Popular Culture* 24, no. 3 (March 2004): 147–66, 158.

39. Toll, *Blacking Up,* 197–98; "Variety," *New York Clipper,* January 5, 1884, 713; Frank Dumont, "The Golden Days of Minstrelsy," *New York Clipper,* December 19, 1914, 2–3.

40. Poster for Sam Hague "The Great American Slave Troupe and Japanese Tommy" at the Grand Circus Pavilion, 1869; Women in Jazz archives, Cambrian

Indexing Project, Swansea Reference Library, Swansea, Wales, http://www.womeninjazzswansea.org.uk/history/1869.asp (accessed November 21, 2008).

41. "'Japanese Tommy's' Funeral," *New York Times*, July 13, 1887, 8.

42. Ibid.

43. Moon, "Paper Butterflies," 134.

44. Reynolds, *Minstrel Memories*, 169; Dale Cockrell, *Demons of Disorder: Early Blackface Minstrels and Their World* (Cambridge: Cambridge University Press, 1997), "Blackface in the Streets," 30–61.

45. "Things Theatrical," *Wilkes Spirit of the Times*, March 16, 1861, 32.

46. Masao Miyoshi, *As We Saw Them: The First Japanese Embassy to the United States (1860)* (Berkeley: University of California Press, 1979), chaps. 2 and 3.

47. *Philadelphia Inquirer*, June 15, 1860, and *New York Herald*, June 17, 1860; quoted in Miyoshi, *As We Saw Them*, 43.

48. *Harper's Weekly*, May 26, 1860; *Washington Evening Star*, May 14, 1860; *Philadelphia Press*, June 11, 1860; quoted in Miyoshi, *As We Saw Them*, 67.

49. "Natural Mistakes," *Harper's Weekly*, June 30, 1860, 416.

50. See Cockrell on Henry Washington Dixon, in *Demons of Disorder*, chap. 4; or Michael Rogin on Al Jolson, in *Blackface, White Noise: Jewish Immigrants in the Hollywood Melting Pot* (Berkeley: University of California Press, 1996), chaps. 4 and 5.

51. *Chicago Broad Ax*, December 9, 1905; quoted in Reginald Kearney, *African American Views of the Japanese: Solidarity of Sedition* (Albany, N.Y.: State University of New York Press, 1998), 15.

52. Bill V. Mullen, *Afro-Orientalism* (Minneapolis: University of Minnesota Press, 2004), xx; Prashad, *Everybody Was Kung Fu Fighting*.

53. Mullen, *Afro-Orientalism*, xx.

54. L. P. Williams, *New York Age*, June 4, 1914, 6.

55. R. G. Doggett, "'The Mikado' A Success," *New York Age*, March 13, 1913, 6.

56. Ibid.

57. Lester A. Walton, "The Critic Criticised," *New York Age*, March 27, 1913, 6.

58. "Cooper Okays WPA Theater," *New York Amsterdam News*, March 18, 1939, 20.

59. Nahum Daniel Brasher, "The Mikado Rates Season's Best, Reviewer Pleased with Singing and Acting of Cast," *Chicago Defender*, October 1, 1938, 18.

60. Atkinson, "Chicago Unit of the Federal Theatre,'" *New York Times*, March 2, 1938, 18.

61. C. J. Bulliet, "Negro 'Mikado' is Season's Major Hit, Tom-Tom Mikado Frenzied Theater," *Chicago Daily News*, January 19, 1939, 22.

62. Ronald Radano, "Hot Fantasies: American Modernism and the Idea of Black Rhythm," in *Music and the Racial Imagination*, ed. Ronald Radano and Philip V. Bohlman, 459–80 (Chicago: University of Chicago Press, 2000), 459.

63. Ibid., 471.
64. Lloyd Lewis, "Mikado Malayed," *Chicago Daily News*, September 26, 1938, 14.
65. Rosamond Gilder, "Portraits and Backgrounds: Broadway in Review," *Theatre Arts Monthly*, May 23, 1939, 318–29, 326.
66. Langston Hughes, from *Autobiography: The Big Sea*, in *The Collected Works of Langston Hughes*, ed. Joseph McLaren (Columbia: University of Missouri Press, 2002), 13:176.
67. Hughes, from *The Poems: 1941–50*, in *The Collected Works of Langston Hughes*, ed. Arnold Rampersad (Columbia: University of Missouri Press, 2001), 2:197.
68. Stephen M. Vallillo, "The Battle of the Black Mikados," *Black Literature Forum* 16, no. 4 (Winter 1982): 153–57, 155.
69. Fraction, a native of Texas of Mexican and American parentage, played in Harvey's Greater Minstrels for two years as well as with the Lafayette Players for ten years; he had been recruited by his friend Adolph Gertner, impresario of Yiddish plays in the Midwest, to play in some productions in Yiddish theaters ("Swing Mikado Negro Actor Once Played in Yiddish," *New York Post*, 13 May 1939, 8).
70. John Mason Brown, writing for the *New York Post*, praises "Sammy Dyer's superbly rhythmic dance numbers with their African overtones" and "Herman Greene's droll-faced Ko-Ko and Edward Fractions's cake-walking Mikado" ("The Swing Mikado Comes to Broadway," *New York Post*, March 2, 1939, 18).
71. Rogin, *Blackface, White Noise*, 197.
72. Atkinson, "Chicago Unit of the Federal Theatre."
73. Kowner, "Lighter Than Yellow," 113.
74. George Bigot, *Japanese Album of Etchings, Japanese Life and Character, Yokohama* (1893), in T. Haga, I. Shimizu, T. Sakai, and K. Kawamoto, *Bigot sobyo korekushon 1, 2, 3* (Tokyo: Iwanami Shoten, 1989).
75. The Widow Twankay, still a popular tradition, was first popularized in the 1861 burlesque by Henry Byron, *Aladdin or The Wonderful Scamp*, with Twankay named after a Chinese port famous for the tea trade.
76. Anonymous, "Ebony Rose," in *Christy's Nigga Songster, as Sung by Christy's, Pierce's, White's, and Dumbleton's Minstrels* (New York: T. W. Strong, 1850); electronic edition published by Stephen Railton, Institute for Advanced Technology in the Humanities, Electronic Text Center Pubplace, Charlottesville, Virginia, 2000, at http://www.iath.virginia.edu/utc/minstrel/gallchrsf.html.
77. John Mason Brown, "Bill Robinson Appears in *The Hot Mikado*," *New York Post*, March 24, 1939.
78. Brooks Atkinson, "Bill Robinson Tapping Out the Title Role in 'The Hot Mikado' at the Broadhurst Theatre," *New York Times*, March 24, 1939, 26.
79. "New Play in Manhattan," *Time* magazine, April 3, 1939, 23.

80. "Hot Mikado," *Variety*, March 29, 1939, 42.

81. Richard Watts Jr., "The Theater: Swing and Hot in Tipitu," *New York Herald Tribune*, April 2, 1939, sec. 6, p. 1.

82. Geoffrey Parsons Jr., "Six Times Eyewitness of Swing Mikado," *New York Herald Tribune*, February 26, 1939, sec. 6, p. 1. Greene was recognized by reviewer Dorothy Day for his previous role in *Little Black Sambo*, a children's play by Charlotte Chorpenning, running concurrently with Swing Mikado at Great Northern Theatre from August 29, 1938, through June 30, 1939: "Herman Greene, who did such a good job as the father of 'Little Black Sambo,' gives a vaudeville impression of Ko-Ko but continues to be a likable and genial gent." Day, "This 'Mikado' Unconvincing."

83. Atkinson, "Bill Robinson Tapping Out the Title Role."

84. Williamson, *Gilbert and Sullivan Opera*, 166.

85. Lott, *Love and Theft*, 118–19.

86. Marshall Stearns and Jean Stearns, *Jazz Dance: The Story of American Vernacular Dance* (New York: Da Capo Press, 1994), 332.

87. Yoshihara, *Embracing the East*, 100.

88. Karen Sánchez-Eppler, *Touching Liberty: Abolition, Feminism, and the Politics of the Body* (Berkeley: University of California Press, 1993), 133, 134.

89. "Tropical Pinafore," *Time*, April 22, 1940.

90. Derek Jewell, "The Key to a Musical," *London Sunday Times*, May 4, 1975.

91. Harold Hobson, "Blithe Spirit," *London Sunday Times*, May 11, 1975, 39.

92. Clive Barnes, "'A Little Night Music' Goes Cockney to London's Delight," *New York Times*, September 17, 1975, 41.

93. Alain Locke, "The Negro's Contribution to American Culture," *Journal of Negro Education* 8, no. 3 (July 1939): 521–29, 529.

94. Ibid., 527.

95. Susan Gubar, *Racechanges: White Skin, Black Face in American Culture* (Oxford: Oxford University Press 1997), 31.

96. Fraden, *Blueprints for a Black Federal Theatre*, 195.

97. *The Hot Mikado*, souvenir program at the New York World's Fair, p. 10, number 11 in file MWEZ and n.c. 15,400. Billy Rose Theatre Collection, Performing Arts Research Center at Lincoln Center.

98. Cholly Atkins and Jacqui Malone, *Class Act: The Jazz Life of Choreographer Cholly Atkins* (New York: Columbia University Press, 2001), 43.

99. Ibid., 44.

100. Ibid., 45.

5. Titipu Comes to America

1. Toll, *Blacking Up*, 172.

2. Advertisement, *Chicago Tribune*, October 25, 1885, 6.

3. William J. Mahar notes the frequency of the appearance of Italian and English songs in blackface and suggests that this points to both "a shared concern about whether the United States had or could have a national culture" and "a nativist critique of foreign cultural imports that were the markers of the growing consciousness of class distinctions based on wealth and taste similar to those common to England." *Behind the Burnt Cork Mask: Early Blackface Minstrelsy and Antebellum American Popular Culture* (Champaign: University of Illinois Press, 1998), 151, 156.

4. Bordman, *American Musical Theatre*, 188.

5. Baily, *The Gilbert & Sullivan Book*, 414–15.

6. Gilder, "Portraits and Backgrounds: Broadway in Review," 327.

7. Batiste, "Darkening Mirrors," 248.

8. Christina Klein, *Cold War Orientalism: Asian in the Middlebrow Imagination, 1945–1961* (Berkeley: University of California Press, 2003), 183.

9. Will B. Johnstone, "Swing Explodes *Mikado* Myth," *New York World Telegram*, April 8, 1939, 6.

10. Hedy Weiss, "Multicultural 'Mikado' Heats Up the Stage" *Chicago Sun-Times*, April 24, 2003, 41.

11. Lyn Gardner on the 2006 Watermill Theatre (Newbury, U.K.) production of *The Hot Mikado*, *The Guardian*, July 19, 2006, 34.

12. Rhoda Koenig, "Theatre: They should Ko-Ko," *Independent*, June 2, 1995, 25.

13. Alastair Macaulay, "Gilbert and Sullivan Syncopated," *London Financial Times*, May 26, 1995, Arts, p. 15.

14. Steven Winn, "Gilbert and Sullivan in Dancing Shoes: 'Hot Mikado' a Jazzy Update in San Jose," *San Francisco Chronicle*, October 27, 1998, D6.

15. Richard Christiansen, "'Hot Mikado': Gilbert and Sullivan Meet the Energizer," review of Chicago Marriott's Lincolnshire Theatre, *Chicago Tribune*, June 25, 1993, 28.

16. Macaulay, "Gilbert and Sullivan Syncopated."

17. Koenig, "Theatre: They should Ko-Ko."

18. Lott, *Love and Theft*, 27, 25.

19. Weiss, "Multicultural 'Mikado' Heats Up the Stage."

20. Koenig, "Theatre: They should Ko-Ko."

21. Jeremy Kingston, "Mighty Troupers of Titipu," *London Times*, 27 May 1995, 1.

22. Later in the production, the Mikado himself pulls the same stunt, according to J. Wynn Rousuck, "'Hot Mikado' Offers Cuteness but Its Sizzle Is Spotty," *Baltimore Sun*, June 3, 1994, 24.

23. Louise Sweeney, "New 'Hot Mikado' passes up operetta's charm," *Christian Science Monitor*, April 4, 1986, Arts and Leisure, 23.

24. Dan Hulbert, "Hot Mikado," *Atlanta Constitution*, August 28, 1997, D1.

25. "Q. H." comments that the film is "hardly a serious contribution to the

lengthening history of Savoy Opera." Review of *The Cool Mikado, Gilbert and Sullivan Journal* 8, no. 11 (May 1963): 170.

26. Melani McAlister, *Epic Encounters: Culture, Media, and U.S. Interests in the Middle East, 1945–2000* (Berkeley: University of California Press, 2001), 30, 40.

27. Lee, *Orientals*, 167, 85.

6. "The Threatened Cloud"

1. Antony Best, "A Royal Alliance: Court Diplomacy and Anglo-Japanese Relations, 1900–41," symposium paper presented at the Suntory and Toyota International Centres for Economics and Related Disciplines, London School of Economics and Political Science," February 23, 2006, p. 23, available at http://sticerd.lse.ac.uk/dps/is/is512.pdf (accessed January 22, 2007).

2. Sidney Dark and Rowland Grey, *W. S. Gilbert: His Life and Letters* (1923; repr., New York: Benjamin Blom, 1972), 100–101.

3. Editorial, *Pall Mall Gazette*, May 1, 1907; quoted in Andrew Goodman, "The Fushimi Incident: Theatre Censorship and *The Mikado*," *Journal of Legal History* 1. no. 3 (December 1980): 297–302, 301–2.

4. Baily, *The Gilbert & Sullivan Book*, 393.

5. Ibid.

6. Ibid.

7. Ibid.

8. This was written in 1908, but not published until 1921. Gilbert Sullivan, *The Story of The Mikado*, illus. Alice B. Woodward (London: Daniel O'Connor, 1921), 1–2.

9. Ibid., 92.

10. See Kowner, "Lighter Than Yellow."

11. William Elliot Griffis, *The Mikado: Institution and Person; A Study of the Internal Political Forces of Japan* (London: Humphrey Milford Oxford University Press, 1915), 16.

12. Gina Marchetti, *Romance and the "Yellow Peril"* (Berkeley: University of California Press, 1993), 2.

13. Colleen Lye, *America's Asia: Racial Form and American Literature, 1893–1945* (Princeton, N.J.: Princeton University Press, 2005), 19.

14. Jack London, "The Yellow Peril," in *Revolution and Other Essays* (New York: Macmillan 1910), 261–89, 281.

15. *New York Times*, April 25, 1943.

16. *Baltimore Sun*, July 27, 1945.

17. Beatty-Kingston, *Theatre*, April 1, 1885; quoted in Baily, *The Gilbert & Sullivan Book*, 248.

18. Philipp Franz von Siebold, *Manners and Customs of the Japanese: Japan and

the Japanese in the Nineteenth Century; From Recent Dutch Travels, Especially the Narrative of Von Siebold (London: John Murray, 1852), 198–99.

19. Peter G. Davis, "'Penzance' As You Like It," *New York Times*, May 17, 1981, A37.

20. Frederik L. Schodt, *America and the Four Japans* (Berkeley, Calif.: Stone Bridge Press, 1994), 65.

21. Alvin Klein, "Mikado, Inc.," *New York Times*, June 17, 1990, A15.

22. Mark Mobley, "The 'Not Mikado' Plugs in Gilbert and Sullivan Operetta," *Virginian Pilot*, January 17, 1993, G7.

23. Andrew Porter, "Musical Events, Too-looral-lay!" *New Yorker*, May 30, 1983, 92–97, 97.

24. Dorothy Samachson, "Report from Chicago," in "Our Critics Abroad," *Opera* 34, no. 9 (September 1983): 979–80, 979.

25. John von Rhein, "'Mikado' Makes Wicked Mockery of Modern Manners," *Chicago Tribune*, May 13, 1983, sec. 3, p. 1.

26. John von Rhein, "Improved 'Mikado" a Sojourn of Outrageous Fun," *Chicago Tribune*, May 16, 1983, sec. 2, p. 7.

27. Samachson, "Report from Chicago," 979.

28. Von Rhein, "Improved 'Mikado.'"

29. Donal Henahan, "Music View; Just What Are the Motives for This Irreverent 'Mikado'?" *New York Times*, May 22, 1983, A23.

30. Robert Jacobson, "Report from Chicago," *Opera News* 48, no. 2 (August 1983): 35–36, 36.

31. Porter, "Musical Events, Too-looral-lay!" 95.

32. Quoted in Kowner, "Lighter Than Yellow," 7–8.

33. Susan McClary, foreword to *Opera, or The Undoing of Women*, by Catherine Clément, trans. Betsy Wing (Minneapolis: University of Minnesota Press, 1988), xvii.

34. The Gilbert and Sullivan discography Web site reports that "the film was by Swank Telefilms (supported by Australian Film Development Corporation). It was distributed by Wonderland Video, and sold by Paragon Video Productions (1982)"; at http://www.cris.com/~oakapple/gasdisc/mdtitipu.htm (accessed July 22, 2008).

35. Cast list for 1998 Catchment Players (Victoria, Australia) *Hot Mikado*.

36. Rebecca J. Ritzel, "Gilbert and Sullivan Swing in Pulton's 'Hot Mikado,'" *Lancester (PA) Intelligencer Journal*, March 5, 2004, 1.

37. Review of Musical Theatre West (Long Beach, California) 2004 *Hot Mikado*; David C. Nichols, "Hepcats Spin a 'Hot Mikado,'" *Los Angeles Times*, February 27, 2004, E30.

38. Henahan, "Music View."

39. George Grossmith did his pratfalls in "The Flowers That Bloom in the

Spring," while Henry Lytton used the same song for his famous "toe business"; see Harold Orel, ed., *Gilbert and Sullivan: Interviews and Recollections* (Iowa City: University of Iowa Press, 1994), 172, 190.

40. Williamson, *Gilbert and Sullivan Opera*, 164.

41. Ibid., 166.

42. Letter from Rupert D'Oyly Carte, *London Times*, May 28, 1948; quoted in Bradley, *Complete Annotated Gilbert and Sullivan*, 572.

43. J. M. Balkin and Sanford Levinson, "Interpreting Law and Music: Performance Notes on 'The Banjo Serenader' and 'The Lying Crowd of Jews,'" (1999), 1–56, 12; electronic version of essay at http://www.yale.edu/lawweb/jbalkin/articles/interp1.pdf (accessed December 8, 2007).

44. G. K. Chesterton, "Gilbert and Sullivan," in *The Eighteen Eighties*, ed. Walter de la Mare, 136–58 (Cambridge: Cambridge University Press 1930), 152.

45. Ibid., 152–53.

46. "Wigs Are the Key," electronic discussion from "The Gilbert and Sullivan Archive," at http://math.boisestate.edu/gas/Mikado/discussion/6_1.html#6.2.5 (accessed May 20, 2003). The archive was a compilation of thoughts of subscribers to Savoynet Maillist between April 17 and May 17, 1997. Many of the subscribers were clearly experienced performers or directors of Gilbert and Sullivan, as well as fans.

47. Interview with Michael Romain, "Work in Progress: A Dialogue with Jonathan Miller," in Michael Romain, *A Profile of Jonathan Miller* (Cambridge: Cambridge University Press 1992), 66.

48. Ibid., 157.

49. Kondo, *About Face: Performing Race in Fashion and Theater* (New York: Routledge, 1997), 251.

50. Ibid., 253.

51. Ibid.

52. "Cheap Pickets," *Mikado* discussion from "The Gilbert and Sullivan Archive," at http://math.boisestate.edu/gas/Mikado/discussion/6_2.html#6.4 (accessed May 20, 2003).

7. Asian American *Mikados*

1. Susan Bennett, *Performing Nostalgia: Shifting Shakespeare and the Contemporary Past* (London: Routledge, 1996), 12.

2. Interview with Catherine Ceniza Choy, Minneapolis, March 29, 2007.

3. *If You Want to Know What We Are: A Carlos Bulosan Reader*, ed. E. San Juan Jr. (Minneapolis: West End Press, 1983), 78–79.

4. Harriet Brown, "Authentic 'Mikado' Gorgeous, Exciting," *Madison Capital Times*, February 22, 2003; online version at http://www.madison.com (accessed May 20, 2003).

5. Michael Penn, "Mixed Media," *On Wisconsin,* Wisconsin Alumni Association; http://www.uwalumni.com/onwisconsin/winter02/arts.html (accessed November 10, 2003).

6. Ibid.

7. Michael Penn, "Kabuki Director Reclaims *Mikado* for Japan," *Japan Journal,* Japan Information Center, Consulate General of Japan at Chicago (December 2002/January 2003), 2.

8. Michael Billington review of 2002 Savoy production, directed by Ian Judge, *Guardian Unlimited,* July 2, 2002, at http://www.guardian.co.uk/arts/critics-review/0,1169,747824,00.html (accessed May 20, 2003).

9. Julie Holledge and Joanne Tompkins, *Women's Intercultural Performance* (London: Routledge, 1995), 12.

10. Una Chaudhuri, "The Future of the Hyphen: Interculturalism, Textuality, and the Difference Within," in *Interculturalism and Performance: Writings From PAJ,* ed. Bonnie Marranca and G. Dasgupta (New York: Performing Arts Journal, 1991), 196.

11. Robert Young, *Colonial Desire: Hybridity in Theory, Culture, and Race* (London: Routledge, 1995).

12. Holledge and Tompkins, *Women's Intercultural Performance,* 114.

13. Rhustom Bharucha, *The Theater and The World: Performance and the Politics of Culture* (London: Routledge, 1993), 2.

14. Jacob Stockinger, "UW Director Strives for Authenticity," *Capital Times,* February 21, 2003; at http://www.madison.com (accessed May 5, 2003).

15. John Berger, "'Mikado' Revels as Un-PC," *Honolulu Star Bulletin,* August 6, 2004, at http://archives.starbulletin.com/2004/08/06/features/story1.html (accessed January 9, 2007).

16. Ibid.

17. Mari Yoshihara, *Musicians from a Different Shore: Asians and Asian Americans in Classical Music* (Philadelphia: Temple University Press, 2007), 213.

18. Ibid.

19. Ibid.

20. John Berger, "'Mikado' Revels as Un-PC."

21. "Hawaii Opera Theatre's 'The Mikado,'" newsletter of the Japan-America Society of Hawaii, *Japan-America Journal* 22, no. 3 (Fall 2004), at http://www.jashawaii.org/nl200403.asp#18 (accessed January 9, 2007).

22. Janos Gereben, "Ho'okani hana keaka: A History of Opera in Hawaii" (1973; appendix, 1999): 1–23, 20; electronic version at http://home.earthlink.net/~janos451/hot1223.htm (accessed September 3, 2007).

23. Ibid., 8.

24. E. Douglas Bomberger, "Taiko Drums and Gag Lines Add Local Flavor to Operetta," *Honolulu Star-Bulletin,* August 9, 2004, at http://archives.starbulletin.com/2004/08/09/features/story2.html (accessed January 9, 2007).

25. Rodney Morales, "Literature," in *Multicultural Hawai'i: The Fabric of a Multiethnic Society*, ed. Michael Haas (New York: Garland, 1998), 116.

26. Jonathan Okamura, "Social Stratification," in Haas, *Multicultural Hawai'i*, 200–201.

27. Doris Baizley and Ken Narasaki, *The Mikado Project*, Lodestone Theatre, Los Angeles, 2007.

28. Esther Kim Lee, *A History of Asian American Theatre* (Cambridge: Cambridge University Press, 2006), 3.

8. The Mikado in Japan

1. François Cellier and Cunningham Bridgeman, *Gilbert and Sullivan and Their Operas*, 191.

2. *The Milton Aborn Operatic Companies*, brochure, circa 1922, from the University of Iowa Special Collections digital collection, Traveling Culture: Circuit Chautauqua in the Twentieth Century, records of the Redpath Chautauqua Collection, at http://sdrcdata.lib.uiowa.edu/libsdrc/details.jsp?id=/miltona/1.

3. For Miura, for instance, "the Japanese Butterfly, the opera provided an international stage on which she could demonstrate her nation's rise to power and also allowed her to live a life that was quite atypical of Japanese women of the time." Mari Yoshihara, "The Flight of the Japanese Butterfly: Orientalism, Nationalism, and Performances of Japanese Womanhood," *American Quarterly* 56, no. 4 (Dec 2004): 975–1001, 997.

4. "Criterion Theatre," *London Times*, July 8, 1901, 3; quoted in Lesley Downer, *Madame Sadayakko: The Geisha Who Bewitched the West* (New York: Gotham Books, 2003), 185.

5. *The Milton Aborn Operatic Companies* brochure.

6. Naoki Inose, *Mikado no Shōzō* (A Portrait of the Mikado) (Tokyo: Shinchosha, 1992), chap. 9; Sumiko Enbutsu, "*The Mikado* in the Town of Chichibu," *East* 38, no. 6 (March/April 2003): 6–11, 7.

7. James E. Hoare, *Japan's Treaty Ports and Foreign Settlements: The Uninvited Guests, 1858–1899*, Meiji Japan Series, 1 (Folkestone, Kent: Japan Library, 1994), 42–43.

8. Enbutsu, "*The Mikado* in the Town of Chichibu," 7.

9. Masahiko Masumoto, "Foreign Theatres and *The Mikado*: Japonism Produced in Japan," in *Ibunka e no shisen: Atarashii hiraku bungaku no tame ni*, ed. Hideaki Sasaki (Nagoya, Japan: University of Nagoya Press, 1996), 59–76.

10. See Arthur Groos, "Return of the Native: Japan in 'Madama Butterfly/Madama Butterfly' in Japan," *Cambridge Opera Journal* 1, no. 2 (July 1989): 167–94.

11. The *Chicago Tribune* reports the opening as August 12 ("'The Mikado' Opens in Tokyo for Allies; Japs Can't Attend," *Chicago Daily Tribune*, August 13,

1946, 14), while the *New York Times* describes a performance on July 22 ("Army Group to Present 'The Mikado' in Tokyo," *New York Times*, July 11, 1946, 25).

12. "Army Group to Present 'The Mikado' in Tokyo."

13. Joseph Raben, "The Mikado in Japan as Recalled in 1998," Gilbert and Sullivan Archive, at http://math.boisestate.edu/gas/mikado/html/mikado_japan.html (accessed December 7, 2006).

14. "Role of Mikado Taken in Tokyo by Suburban GI," *Chicago Daily Tribune*, September 8, 1946, W3.

15. Though scheduled to tour other military sites, the production ran into technical difficulties in part because of its elaborate design. Raben reported: "Later that year, awaiting discharge in Fort Ord, California, I met the sergeant of the squad that was in charge of the Japanese staff that ran the Ernie Pyle. He told me that the production had been scheduled to tour all the major US Army establishments in Japan (and probably those of the other occupying powers), but that the sets had been designed to fit into American-style freight cars, and the Japanese railroads at that time all were the narrow-gauge type, much too small to accommodate the scenery. So the entire run was limited to those three nights in Tokyo. According to the sergeant, the lieutenant in charge of the theater was court-martialed." These claims are disputed, though, by Robert S. Telford, the administrative officer for the Ernie Pyle (1st Lt, Infantry, World War II) who calls them "entirely baseless" (Robert S. Telford, Gilbert Sullivan Archive).

16. Raben, "The Mikado in Japan as Recalled in 1998."

17. "Role of Mikado Taken in Tokyo by Suburban GI."

18. "'The Mikado' Opens in Tokyo for Allies," *Chicago Daily Tribune*, August 13, 1946, 14.

19. "GIs play 'Mikado' in Tokyo: Opera, banned for 61 years in Nippon, is put on with Japanese help," *Life* magazine, September 9, 1946, 42–43.

20. The *New York Times* noted Ito as a "former Hollywood dance director, whose son served in the American Navy during the recent war." "'Mikado' Seen in Tokyo," *New York Times*, January 30, 1948, 21.

21. For example, John Mason Brown praised Ito's choreography for L.A. versions of *The Mikado*: "They flow easily from one enchanting composition into another, without ever having a self-conscious or stiff pictorial quality." "The Dull Devil of Melodrama: Broadway in Review," *Theatre Arts Monthly*, October 1927, 826.

22. "No Mikado, Much Regret," *Time* magazine, June 16, 1947, 40.

23. "'Mikado' Seen in Tokyo."

24. Baily, *The Gilbert & Sullivan Book*, 426.

25. Raben, "The Mikado in Japan."

26. John W. Dower, *Embracing Defeat: Japan in the Wake of World War II* (New York : WW. Norton and Company, 1999), 23.

27. Ibid., 211–12.

28. Katawake Shigetoshi, "Kabuki Tsuihō no Kiroku" (Record of *Kabuki*'s banishment), *Engekikai* 1 (January 1961): 35–36; quoted in Shiro Okamoto, *The Man Who Saved Kabuki: Faubion Bowers and Theatre Censorship in Occupied Japan*, trans. and adapted by Samuel L. Leiter (Honolulu: University of Hawai'i Press, 2001), 59.

29. Inose, *Mikado no Shōzō*, 395–96.

30. "Role of Mikado Taken in Tokyo by Suburban GI."

31. "'The Mikado' Opens in Tokyo for Allies; Japs Can't Attend."

32. "Japanese Laugh Heartily as 'The Mikado' is Shown," *New York Times*, August 12, 1946, 9.

33. "Japan May See 'Mikado,'" *New York Times*, June 16, 1947, 25.

34. "'Mikado' Seen in Tokyo," *New York Times*, January 30, 1948, 21.

35. "No Mikado, Much Regret," *Time* magazine, June 16, 1947, 40.

36. Unsigned editorial, "Double Unreality," *New York Times*, February 3, 1948, 24.

37. "*The Mikado* at the National Theatre: Performed by the Nagato Miho Opera Company," *Asahi Shimbun*, January 5, 1970, 9.

38. Klein, *Cold War Orientalism*, 9.

39. Ibid., 16.

40. Lucy Herndon Crockett, *Popcorn on the Ginza: An Informal Portrait of Postwar Japan* (New York: William Sloane Associates, 1949), 112; quoted in Naoko Shibusawa, *America's Geisha Ally: Reimagining the Japanese Enemy* (Cambridge, Mass.: Harvard University Press, 2006), 16.

41. Ibid., 259.

42. "Fujiwara Opera Company," *Christian Science Monitor*, August 28, 1956, 5.

43. "Fujiwara Opera Company Performs in Europe," *Yomiuri Shimbun*, August 31, 1960, 5.

44. Albert Goldberg, "The Sounding Board: Realism Marked in 'Madame Butterfly,'" *Los Angeles Times*, November 17, 1956, B2.

45. "'Mikado' Sent Over by Japan," *Los Angeles Times*, November 19, 1956, C11.

46. Ibid.

47. "Fujiwara Opera Seen in 'Mikado,'" *Hartford Courant*, October 25, 1956, 14A.

48. "Gilbert's Lyrics Elude Park's Tokyo Visitors," *Washington Post*, August 30, 1956, 41.

49. "Old Operetta on Tour," *Time*, October 29, 1956, 100.

50. "Fujiwara Opera Seen in 'Mikado,'" *Hartford Courant*, October 25, 1956, 14A.

51. Ibid.

52. "Gilbert's Lyrics Elude Park's Tokyo Visitors."

53. "No Mikado, Much Regret."

54. Mari Yoshihara, *Musicians from a Different Shore*, 31–32.

55. Keizō Horiuchi, "Kageki 'Madamu Batafurai' Jōen ni tsuki," n.t., [1930],

76. Aymada Kōsaku Collection, Microfilm 90, Scrapbook 16, frame 290. Nihon Kindai Ongakukan, quoted and translated in Yoshihara, *Musicians from a Different Shore*, 31.

56. "Katakoto majiri de Kokujoku Kaifuku no Iki" [With Smattering of English, Actress Determined to Rectify National Humiliation], n.t., [1930], n.p. Yamada Kōsaku Collection, Microfilm 90, Scrapbook 16, frame 285; quoted and translated in Yoshihara, *Musicians from a Different Shore*, 31.

57. "'Ochō Fujin' wo Miru," n.t., [1930], n.p. Yamada Kōsaku Collection, Microfilm 90, Scrapbook 16, frame 288; quoted and translated in Yoshihara, *Musicians from a Different Shore*, 31.

58. Yoshihara, *Musicians from a Different Shore*, 47.

59. Groos, "Return of the Native," 186.

60. "Old Operetta on Tour," *Time* magazine, October 29, 1956, 100.

61. "Gilbert's Lyrics Elude Park's Tokyo Visitors," *Washington Post*, August 30, 1956, 41.

62. "Fujiwara Opera Seen in 'Mikado,'" *Hartford Courant*, October 25, 1956, 14A.

63. "Old Operetta on Tour," *Time* magazine.

64. According to Alison J. Ewbank and Fouli Papageorgiou, Yoshie Fujiwara was first trained in the Asakusa Opera. Alison J. Ewbank and Fouli Papageorgiou, *Whose Master's Voice? The Development of Popular Music in Thirteen Cultures* (Greenwood, Conn.: Greenwood Press, 1997), 159.

65. Ken K. Ito, *Visions of Desire: Tanizaki's Fictional Worlds* (Stanford, Calif.: Stanford University Press, 1991), 67.

66. Tanizaki Jun'ichirō, *Tanizaki Jun'ichirō zenshū*, 28 vols. (Tokyo: Chūō Kōronsha, 1966–70) 7:86; quoted in Ito, *Visions of Desire*, 72.

67. Ito, *Visions of Desire*, 72.

68. Ibid., 71–72.

69. According to Natsuko Inoue, the other two are Hanagumi Shibai (Flower Group Theater), founded by Yukikazu Kanō in 1987, and Gekidan Chōjū Giga (Caricature of Birds and Beasts Company) founded by Masabumi Chinen in 1975. Natsuko Inoue, "New (Neo) *Kabuki* and the Work of Hanagumi Shibai," in *A Kabuki Reader: History and Performance*, ed. Samuel Leiter, 186–207 (New York: M. E. Sharpe, 2002), 187.

70. Ibid.

71. This and other information on Super Ichiza is from a letter of August 23, 2007, from Shinichi Iwata to Yuko Matsukawa, translated by Yuko Matsukawa.

72. Ibid.

73. Promotional flyer for Super Ichiza's production of *The Mikado*, 1992, translated by Yuko Matsukawa.

74. Tanizaki, *Tanizaki Jun'ichirō zenshū*, 7:89; quoted in Ito, *Visions of Desire*, 73.

75. Ibid., 73.

76. Enbutsu, "*The Mikado* in the Town of Chichibu," 7–8.

77. Quoted in Yukiko Kisinami, "'Mikado' Returns Home to Chichibu," *Daily Yomiuri*, March 13, 2003, 15.

78. "To the Deceased Teacher: The Operetta Performance Last Month in Chichibu," *Asahi Shimbun* (Saitama), April 1, 2001, 1.

79. Minoru Okamoto, "The Mikado in Commemoration of the 50th Anniversary of the City's Incorporation," *Nihon Keizai Shimbun*, March 15, 2001, 8.

80. James Brooke, "Japanese Hail 'The Mikado,' Long-banned Imperial Spoof," *New York Times*, April 3, 2003, A8.

81. Ibid.

82. "The Homemade Operetta by Citizens of 'Titipu' in Chichibu," *Asahi Shimbun* (Saitama), February 8, 2001, 2.

83. Comments on the production at the International Gilbert and Sullivan Festival in Buxton, England, from David Sandham's Gilbert and Sullivan Web site, at http://myweb.tiscali.co.uk/sandham/buxton_200631.htm (accessed December 12, 2006).

84. *Japan Weekly Mail*, April 30, 1887; in Masahiko Masumoto, "A Production History of *The Mikado* in Japan, 1885–1946," *Kan Taiheiyou Mondai Kenkyu*, March 1988, 177–207, quote on 197–98.

85. *The Rising Sun and Nagasaki Express*, May 11, 1887; quoted in Masumoto, "A Production History of *The Mikado* in Japan," 202.

86. *Japan Daily Herald Mail Summary*, May 4, 1887; and *Hiogo News*, May 4, 1887; quoted in Masumoto, "A Production History of *The Mikado* in Japan," 199, 201.

87. *Japan Weekly Mail*, April 30, 1887; quoted in Masumoto, "A Production History of *The Mikado* in Japan," 198.

Index

Akina, Henry, 175–80
Alcock, Rutherford, 11–12, 30, 39, 40, 41, 47–48, 58
Asakusa Opera, 206–12
Atkins, Cholly, 119–20

Barthes, Roland, viii
Beatty-Kingston, William, 14–15, 149
Bigot, Georges, 108–9, 153
Black Mikado (1975), 115–17
Bond, Jessie, 21–22, 113, 224
Bradley, Ian, xx–xxi, 39
Brown, Bill, 8, 11, 48–49
By the Sad Sea Waves (1899), 122

Cellier, François, vii, 4, 13, 20–21, 74–75, 77, 187
censorship (1907), 142–45, 164; in Japan (1885–1923), 192–93, 216–17
Chesterton, G. K., 161
Chichibu (2001), 212–17
Chūshingura, 197
Cool Mikado (1963 film), 126, 133–37
Cooper, Maurice, 101

Dilward, Thomas (Japanese Tommy), xviii, 94–98
Duff, James C., 27–30

Ernie Pyle Theater, 193–94

Fujiwara Opera, 199, 201–6
Furumoto, David, 171–75

Gallaher, Simon, 156–57
Gentlemen of Titipu (1972), 154–55
Goncourt, Edmond de, 16, 25
Goodchild, Tim, 67–71
Gould, David, 157
Grossmith, George, 21, 158

Hawaii Opera Theatre (2004), 175–80
H.M.S. Pinafore, 88, 115
Hughes, Langston, 103–4

Idle, Eric, 162–63
Interculturalism, 173–74
Ito, Michio, 194, 203
Iwata, Shinichi, 207–12

Japanese Tommy. *See* Dilward, Thomas

Kabuki Mikado (University of Hawaii–Manoa 1996), 175–76
Kondo, Dorinne, 165–66

Lee, Esther Kim, 181
Lee, Robert, 7, 60, 137
Leigh, Mike. *See Topsy-Turvy*
Lodestone Theatre: *The Mikado Project* (2007), 181–86

Madame Butterfly, xi, xiv, 153, 188, 193, 201, 205
Marx, Groucho, x
Matsukawa, Yuko, 31–32, 208–12
Mencken, H. L., 26
Miller, Jonathan, 162–64, 191
Milton Aborn Operatic Companies, 188–90
Minneapolis, xxi
Minturn, Harry, 83–84
Mitford, Algernon, 30
Moon, Krystyn, 91, 232

Nagato Miho Opera Company, 194–99
Nagoya University of Arts (1996), 200
Noriyuki, Tateishi Onojirō, 96–97

Oberlin College, 162
Oriental America, 93, 233

Patience, 18–19
Perry, Matthew, Commodore, xvii
Philadelphia Centennial 1876, 58–59, 62–63
Pirates of Penzance, 156–57
Pomona College, 164–66, 169, 171
Prashad, Vijay, 55–56, 99
Princess Ida, 108

Raben, Joseph, 193–96
Red Moon, The, 92–93
Renshaw, Christopher, 67–71
Robinson, Bill, 85, 118

Rosenfeld, Sydney, 28–30
Russell, Anna, 154

Sada Yakko, 188
Sampson, Henry T., 90
Sánchez-Eppler, Karen, 114
Schertzinger, Victor, x
Sellars, Peter, 152–54, 158
sheet music, 8, 9, 10, 61, 222–23
Shimozumi, 188–91
Smith, Estelle Stoughton (*Mikado Room*), 37–38
Stetson, John, 27–30
Story of The Mikado (1908), 142, 145–46
Stratford Festival (1982), 155–56
Super Ichiza (1992), 207–12

Tanizaki, Jun'ichirō, 207, 210–11
Tchen, John Kuo Wei, 24
Todd, Michael, 85
Topsy-Turvy, xvi, 67, 72–80

U.S. occupation of Japan, 193–201
Utopia Unlimited, 87–88

Von Siebold, Philipp Franz, 150

Whiteside, Duncan, 84
Wilde, Oscar, 18–19, 36–37, 61–62
willow pattern china, 6

Yoshihara, Mari, 19, 72, 113, 177, 188, 204–5

JOSEPHINE LEE is associate professor of English and Asian American studies at the University of Minnesota. She is author of *Performing Asian America: Race and Ethnicity on the Contemporary Stage* and coeditor (with Imogene Lim and Yuko Matsukawa) of *Re/Collecting Early Asian America: Essays in Culture History.*

www.ingramcontent.com/pod-product-compliance
Lightning Source LLC
Chambersburg PA
CBHW031804220426
43662CB00007B/524